Duchamp and the painting

D1649588

Samuel Beckett and the primacy of love

JOHN ROBERT KELLER

Manchester University Press

Manchester and New York

distributed exclusively in the USA by Palgrave

Published by Manchester University Press
Oxford Road, Manchester M13 9NR, UK
and Room 400, 175 Fifth Avenue, New York, NY 10010, USA
www.manchesteruniversitypress.co.uk

Distributed exclusively in the USA by
Palgrave, 175 Fifth Avenue, New York, NY 10010, USA

Distributed exclusively in Canada by
UBC Press, University of British Columbia, 2029 West Mall,
Vancouver, BC, Canada V6T 1Z2

British Library Cataloguing-in-Publication Data
A catalogue record for this book is available from the British Library

Library of Congress Cataloging-in-Publication Data applied for

ISBN 0 7190 6312 4 *hardback*
0 7190 6313 2 *paperback*

First published 2002

10 09 08 07 06 05 04 03 02   10 9 8 7 6 5 4 3 2 1

Typeset in Dante with Tiffany display
by Koinonia Ltd, Manchester
Printed in Great Britain
by Bell & Bain Ltd, Glasgow

For Liwah, beautiful flower

Contents

Acknowledgements—*page* viii

Foreword by Lance St John Butler—ix

Introduction—1

1	Preliminaries and *Proust*	9
2	No Endon sight: Murphy's misrecognition of love	49
3	This emptied heart: Watt's unwelcome home	90
4	A strange situation: self-entrapment in *Waiting for Godot*	133
5	The dispeopled kingdom: the hidden self in Beckett's short fiction	172

Epilogue—217

References—219

Index—225

Acknowledgements

I am grateful to many individuals for their support and guidance. My primary reader (and listener) was Ian Alexander, who until recently taught Beckett at the University of Aberdeen. Shane Murphy, who currently teaches Beckett at Aberdeen, also read the manuscript and provided sage commentary. Lance St John Butler advised me in many ways and wrote a most generous foreword. In Toronto, both Don Carveth and Otto Weininger discussed my work with me on many occasions. Ron Ruskin kindly invited me to present my work on *Waiting for Godot* at the Day in Applied Psychoanalysis. Norman Holland, at the University of Florida, published sections of this study in the online journal *Psyart* and made helpful comments on the Introduction. The team at Manchester University Press – in particular Matthew Frost and Kate Fox – and freelance editor Susan Williams, are consummate professionals, and managed to do the impossible in making the publication process an enjoyable one. I must also thank my patients, from whom I learn continually.

On a personal note, I am grateful to Victor Likwornik, Charles Hanly, Joshua Levy and to Doug Frayn, all of whom have been central to my development as a psychoanalyst, writer and person. My friends and colleagues Fadi Abou-Rihan, Keith Haartman, Mimi Ismi and Jane Baldock have always been patient, helpful listeners for me. For obvious reasons, writers always acknowledge their partners, whose patience and support is crucial to their work. My wife Betty's encouragement allowed the original conception of this study, and her unfailing sacrifice made its completion possible. Our three daughters, Liwah, and the twins, Annika and Katrina, were born during the course of this project. They have inspired it more than they can ever know.

Foreword

Beckett once remarked that he was interested in 'fundamental sounds' and the challenge for Beckett critics has been to find a metalanguage in which they can adequately comment on the profound noises of his drama and prose. A number of studies have considered Beckett's work alongside analogies from philosophy and, more recently, there has been an interest in Beckett as a sort of 'dud mystic' and espouser of what in theology is called the *Via Negativa*. Aesthetically he has been seen as a minimalist minimalist.

But what is 'fundamental' can also include the psychological, and there have been several attempts at trying out the mind (rather than the nature of things, or the soul) as the locus of the Beckettian anguish. John Keller, a practising psychoanalyst, has plunged into these bottomless waters with great energy and insight and has written a book that throws more light onto the Beckettian murk, at least for this long-term reader of his work, than has been available before. I came away from reading the manuscript of this book with a sense of clarity and simplicity: whatever else Beckett is about, it now seems to me certain that his work is also a response to childhood trauma and an extended exploration of the effects on human beings of the primal loss.

Keller has the vigour and fearlessness of a scholar with a solid basis in one discipline applying his skills freely in another. What he sees, from the perspective of his own special knowledge, is a series of texts crying out, perhaps almost literally, for a reading that acknowledges one source of the pain to be the separation from goodness (the Mother) that is the lifelong curse of the sensitive mind. The readings he gives of the Beckett works dealt with are highly convincing and in places quite stunning. Beckett Studies, for me at least, will never be quite the same again.

My own interests are leading me towards a Beckett more tormented by God (an absent God, *bien entendu*) than once people thought he was, but perhaps that is no contradiction of the immense explanatory power of Keller's thesis; after all where else would Beckett's sort of God make himself, or, more accurately and fashionably, *her*self felt than in the endless departures and disappearances of the primal object?

There are many Becketts, but this may be the most fundamental of them.

Lance St John Butler
Pau, France

Introduction

For the listener, who listens in the snow,
And, nothing himself, beholds,
Nothing that is not there and the nothing that is.
            Wallace Stevens

Till feeling the need for company again he tells himself to call the hearer
M at least. (Samuel Beckett)

It is often said that the opening words of the psychoanalytical session
contain the totality of what is to come. Thinking this true of the
scholarly text, I find myself writing that this study is primarily about
love. This might seem somewhat odd for a reading of Beckett, but I
hope that in what follows the reader will gain an appreciation of what I
believe to be the fundamental emotional force that organizes his work –
a need for contact with a primary, loving other. I will suggest that
deeply embedded in his fiction and dramatic work is an enduring psychological struggle to engage the primal mother, in order to maintain a
complete, enduring sense of selfhood. Within his work, this struggle
and its consequences reflect universal experiences at the edge of the
earliest moments of human life, experiences that have at their core the
integrative qualities of maternal love.

The central argument of this study suggests that a fundamental
contribution of Beckett's work is its presentation of very early experiences in the formation of the human mind and, in particular, the
struggles of an emerging-self to maintain contact with a primary sense
of internal goodness. This struggle is highly complex, manifesting
throughout his oeuvre in variable, sophisticated ways, appearing in
character relations, imagery and the associative flow of the plot, and as
internal struggles within the narratives and monologues of various first-
person pieces, both dramatic and prose. I suggest a reading of the work
that assumes it is a production of a 'narrative-self', a virtual person who

produces it as a whole, and that we can approach an understanding of the feeling-states and central psychological organization of this narrative-self through a close study of the texts. Finally, I suggest the texts reveal the convergence of the experience of psychological birth, made possible through the loving mind of the mother, and the birth of fiction, of creativity, that is the heart of life.

Fundamental aspects of early, powerful states of mind manifest throughout the texts: a withdrawn, uninterested passivity that defends against powerful feelings of sadness and rage, feelings of envy directed at sources of goodness that could provide love and attachment, states of confusion between self and other that function to blur loss by forging a sort of primary contact, feelings of severe persecutory or annihilation-anxiety, and a constant, powerful struggle to remain authentic when faced with an overwhelming, consuming otherness. The core feeling-state, however, is one of profound loneliness and disconnection, predi-cated on the central feeling of being unwitnessed, or *felt*, in a loving way that would contain the earliest anxieties confronting an emerging-self. In this, Beckett's work is about the *possibility* of its own genesis since, as primal reader/auditors, we must maintain contact with the elusiveness that lies at its heart.

Beckett touched upon the centrality of emotional contact in his work when he said (allegedly): 'I'm no intellectual. All I am is feeling' (Graver and Federman, 1979: 217), a statement that fundamentally informs this study. There is no doubt Beckett's oeuvre profits from readings that make sense of its complex standing in the world of ideas – it has been successfully researched within a number of contemporary and historical paradigms. The present study takes Beckett at his word, by assuming there is something worth exploring in his work primarily about *feeling*. In this reading, I attempt to fill what I regard to be some-what of a lacuna in Beckett Studies: an undervaluation of the powerful, complex emotional states that form the foundation of his work. I will look at the *experience of being* that manifests in his oeuvre as a pro-foundly personal and compelling exploration of early mental life.

Although this is principally a psychoanalytical study, I have attemp-ted to avoid making it entirely theory-driven. In fact, I believe that Beckett's work can illuminate significant areas of psychoanalytical thought by opening new vistas of research into early experience. This reading developed from my own experience listening to others speak-ing about their lives and their own early experiences, directly, and not so directly. Though, of course, I have a general theoretical orientation, elaborated in Chapter 1, I try to be led by the textual material, rather than let theory lead the reading. For me, Beckett has been immensely valuable in elaborating primal experiences that lie at the core of human experience, and his work evaporates the boundaries between psychology and art. I hope the overall reading demonstrates a certain experiential reality in the texts, one that is not theory-dependent, but that encourages new theory-making. I make every effort to allow the text to speak for itself, to illuminate itself, and the very early experiences that lie at its heart.[1]

A crucial objection often raised against psychoanalytical readings is that the interpreter assumes the characters are 'real' people. I am taking a somewhat more complex attitude towards the text. I have worked clinically with a number of creative writers and have had an opportunity to witness the creation of a story from before its conscious conception, through its writing and revision, to its impact and place in the internal world of the writer after it is 'complete' (which it *never* is). In this study, I have certain core assumptions about the 'reality' of the text, based on this clinical experience. I read the text as if it were the production of what I call the 'narrative-self'. This is meant to be an underlying, coherent and persistent presence that we can at least discuss, through a patient and embracing reading of the entire oeuvre. I do not suggest that this self is to be in any way *equated* with the person that is Samuel Beckett, though of course, there is, and has to be, an intimate relationship with his internal world. It is the mediation of that internal world, through an active, sometimes conscious, often unconscious process, that leads to the creation of the fiction. The narrative-self cannot be known directly, though in Beckett's work, particularly in his later prose writing, there is a collapsing and condensation between the multiple and complex levels of narration. In this study, it suffices to conceive of the narrative-self as 'knowable' only through its manifestations, which can be in characters, imagery, the flow of the text, certain symbolism, and so forth.[2] I have always been amazed by the manner in which the writers with whom I work seem to have an actual relationship not only with the characters they imagine, but with the creative organizer of their work, the 'narrative-self', that is predicated on a real sense of both self and other. Although I often speak of characters as if they were 'real' people, I always have in mind that they are operating as aspects of a unified self. This also means that the dramatic pieces will be discussed as productions of the narrative-self, as an underlying coherent organizer.[3] I use the term 'narrator' to refer to the overt 'speaker' of a story or novel, which, in any individual piece, is a manifestation of the narrative-self. I develop the concept of the narrative-self in Chapter 1, since a fundamental suggestion of this study is that Beckett's work is a revelation of the psychological processes that occur during its conception and emergence in the early mind.

An equally important issue about a psychoanalytical reading concerns the possibility that it might 'pathologize' Beckett. If anything, I believe my reading presents a 'Beckett' that, far from pathological, is *more* human, more alive, and less odd, than often realized. Certainly, there is strangeness in Beckett's writing for many readers and on the most basic level it would be foolish to deny there is a representation of pathology in his work. Imagine a cocktail party at which a number of literary characters attended. One could certainly find Emma Bovary to be manipulating, aloof and a social climber, Lord Jim to be distracted and somewhat brooding, and any of a number of Anita Brookner's heroines to be resigned and demonstrating a false sense of cheerfulness. Surely, the average party-goer would see all of them as exhibiting characteristics that fall within the normal spectrum of ordinary human expectations. However, what would one make of Mr Knott should he attend, or of Pozzo and Lucky? On the surface, perhaps, that they are dysfunctional in some profound way? In purely medical terms, many Beckettian characters display schizoid, depressed, even psychotic pathology. Of course, one can read the characters as abstract representatives of universal themes or conditions. Lucky's speech, for example, can be seen as a reflection of a universal existentialist condition, or of the political aspects of his relationship to a materialist master. I read it, in line with the general thesis, as a deeply felt and *personal* account of an internal experience that is *real*, and that reflects an aspect of the narrative-self's relationship to the mother. I am looking at these texts with a psychoanalytical eye, less interested in diagnosis than in psychological *meaning*. Even at its oddest, Beckett's work is *not* pathological, but an expression of deeply internal meanings, from the long ruminative passages in *Watt* to the fragmented narratives of the later stories. Some of the features of the writing, whether dramatic or narrative, that tend to appear pathological, such as the fragmented style, the imagery and the uninterested tone, will hopefully seem far less so once some of these meanings are explored. My suggestion is that Beckett's style reflects the area of human experience he is exploring, where the earliest and most intense of relationships between the self and the world are played out.

Another feature of the study is the inclusion of clinical examples.

These are presented for a specific reason, and it is not to suggest a direct analogy between the feeling-states of the characters, their motivations, and so forth, and those of the patients. Rather, the vignettes are presented to elucidate the experiences I suggest dominate the narrative-self. To borrow from Wittgenstein (and Arsene), these vignettes are merely 'ladders', meant to help with an appreciation of particular experiential states within the work. So, for example, when we discuss the patient who would binge-eat in a manner similar to that of Mary in *Watt*, my intention is to bring to life the woman's experience as it connects to the behaviour, and it is this experience that I suggest comes close to the emotional heart of the novel. This, of course, must be demonstrated by the reading as a whole. The vignettes are meant as a gloss, and if one looks at the way psychoanalysis has grown as a field, I do not think it so unusual to include vignettes. Any applied psycho-analytical study uses vignettes, even if they are not overt, since all analytical theory derives from clinical experience. Using an idea of Winnicott to elucidate a text is a *deferred* way of using Winnicott's clinical experience. I have tried to bring this process closer to the texts, to develop integration between the texts and my own appreciation of them. In a sense, this is how psychoanalytical dialogue often progresses outside of the clinical situation. When discussing a case, using clinical material, analysts are often in a similar situation to the literary critic, since the actual 'self' under discussion is known only through a text, if the original analyst is not physically present (of course, the analysand never is). Yet, given that limitation, an informed and often clinically useful discussion can occur. I believe the same applies to the psycho-analytical study of art, since, as I have said, I think it is possible to at least play with the assumption that the text we read has a cohesive underlying psychological organization that can be knowable. It is my hope that if we allow for this assumption, we will be able to recognize certain aspects in Beckett's work that will make its entertainment worthwhile.

In this study, I use the word 'object', and this should generally be understood to suggest a concept of another 'person'. For the most part, as I have stated, I am concerned with the work as reflecting an internal world of objects. This is a highly complex area of psychoanalytical thought, and I will limit the idea here to the following notion.[4] I see internal objects (or 'imagos') as more than simple memory complexes or representations of external persons; following a Kleinian model I conceive of them as having a fundamental 'felt' reality within the mind that, in the deepest unconscious, equates them with actual beings that live within. With Beckett's work this is, perhaps, not so difficult a concept to imagine, since there are many descriptive experiences of the power and the felt reality of the presence of another within the self. I use the term 'self', in general, to refer to the totality of subjective experience, whether conscious or unconscious. The narrative-self is a core part of the human self, and is detailed below.

This study focuses on the earliest relations of the infant and mother. Often, in referring to this relationship, I use the term 'mother' to define the primary object of experience. Since I am concerned with aspects of early relating that require what is generally, sometimes specifically, a female function (intra-uterine experience, nurturing, primary mirroring, early sensations of touch, and so forth) I use the usually accepted analytical term 'mother'. Of course, a male parent or any caregiver can perform many of these functions, and it should be clear that in these cases I would still refer to the person as performing a 'mothering' function. I stress I am only focusing on this primary relationship, and do not intend to suggest that Beckett's work is limited to dyadic experience with the mother (though I do suggest it is dominant). I am looking at early experience as it manifests itself, often in situations that suggest a rupture in the primary bond. So, for example, a man, even a father, can be *felt* as a mother in terms of the elicited internal experience. I will never forget, during my analytical training, discussing a patient with my supervisor, and relating, over many months, how the man never seemed to talk about anything but his anger towards his father. My supervisor kindly pointed out that the reason the mother was apparently *absent* in the patient's monologues was because she was *present* in a much more fundamental sense, having been erased, but reincarnated in many aspects of the related tales of the father's failures. Along these lines, Morrison describes a part of *Avant Fin de Partie* (an early draft of *Endgame*) in which there is a story about a mother and a son. They are deeply connected, and when she disappears, only her son can find her. She is discovered, near death, but eventually recovers under the son's care. Morrison describes:

> the sense of terrible disaster and abiding loss [that] permeates the story […], (as if that moment of fear [i. e. the mother's loss] were perpetually present to him). These emotional elements are much like those in Hamm's chronicle, but the reversed roles and the alternate parent are significant differences. As Beckett finally chose to formulate the play, mothers are negligible and fathers are of central importance; and the

son's pain comes not from loss of the parent (by death) but from loss of the parent's *care* (which results in the child's death). (Morrison, 1983: 39)

In this study, I suggest the mother is *never* negligible in Beckett, or in human mental life; early experience with the mother infiltrates all subsequent relationships to an unparalleled degree. The predominant organization of the mind is predicated on what Morrison calls 'care', and which I call 'love', and it is not physical death that is of greatest concern to infantile-self: it is a *psychic death*, a primal catastrophe, in which the mind is ripped from its containment in the loving otherness that is mother. This fear *is* 'perpetually present' in Beckett, since when the internal cosmography of the infantile-self and mother, a cosmography of two, is dislocated, the universe comes to an end.[5]

Notes

1 Except for certain specific quotes in which Beckett comments directly on his own work, this study does not use any other biographical information (with the exception of Beckett's 'nest' game, described in Chapter 1). It is a textual study, and I hope this allows it to avoid the criticism levelled at other contemporary psychoanalytical interpretations, which Hill fairly sees as giving more weight to Bair's biography 'than Beckett's actual writings themselves' (Hill, 1990: 170). Of course, I hope my general thesis might be useful in ongoing research about the author's own experience with his early objects, reflected in comments to friends, letters, and so forth, and comparing these feelings to shifts in his writing over the years. Anzieu (1993) has written specifically about Beckett's writing as functioning as a self-analysis for the author.

2 Klein's paper 'On Identification' (Klein, 1988b: 141-75) was one of the earliest attempts to view characters within a text as aspects of the ego. In that paper, she developed her ideas about projective identification (see Chapter 1), by examining how the character Fabian projects aspects of his personality into others in order to take them over [in Julian Green's (1950) novel]. She discussed the fate of the core personality, which was left behind. J. D. O'Hara suggests that 'From An Abandoned Work' refers to a session of psychotherapy, and that what is abandoned is the therapy, which is never completed (quotation in Gontarski, 1995: xxvii). This is how I read the entire oeuvre, as a lengthy, complex psychoanalytical dialogue, between the emerging-self and an imagined other, whom it hopes can contain primal anxieties, much like the Auditor in *Not I*. I see the (temporarily) 'abandoned work' as directed towards the emergence of an authentic self in relation to a good internal presence. The oeuvre is also a message from an 'abandoned work', that is, from the unrecognized, emerging-self.

3 In this, I do not completely agree with Linda Anderson, who states 'the autobiographical self is a fictional construct within the text, which can neither have its origins anterior to the text, nor indeed coalesce with its creator' (Anderson, 1986: 59), since I believe that the narrative/autobiographical self, is *always* operative. Texts are always *transitional* records of its *ongoing* experience.

4 For a comprehensive review of internal objects, see Perlow, 1995.

5 A comment on the selection of texts: despite his 'minimalist' reputation, Beckett was, of course, a very prolific writer. It would be impossible to completely survey his work in a brief study. I have been selective in choosing texts to elucidate what I feel is a unifying quality observable throughout the oeuvre. I believe that the selection, though selective, is fairly representative, thus, there are detailed discussions of Beckett's dissertation, an early novel in English (*Murphy*), a later English novel (*Watt*), early French writing (the *Nouvelles*, and *Texts for Nothing*, which, for me, serve as abstracts for the Beckett Trilogy), a major play (*Godot*), and briefer, but, I hope, still substantial discussions of various late pieces ('The Lost Ones', *Footfalls*, *Ohio Impromptu*, and so forth). A future study will develop the themes of the present one, with a focus on the late work.

1

Preliminaries and *Proust*

This chapter presents a general outline of the psychoanalytical frame-work that forms the background of this study, followed by a reading of Beckett's dissertation on Proust.[1] I try to minimize the inclusion of theoretical references and material in the main body of the text; this may allow for a more direct response to the flow of textual material. The concepts presented here provide a framework within which the reading takes place but, in the end, the textual material must speak for itself. If the reader feels something in Beckett appears more interesting or exciting, though there is doubt about a theoretical notion I may have used to achieve this effect, I will have accomplished what I am setting out to do.

One of the core arguments of this study is that Beckett's oeuvre is a manifestation of a narrative-self whose universe is organized by a dominant feeling of precarious connection to a primary, good internal presence. I read the work as a record of purely internal experience, and do not wish to make claims about the actuality of early deprivation or hostility on the part of external objects. Certainly, there are many ways of viewing this aspect of Beckett's work theoretically: a fundamental source of controversy among competing psychoanalytical theories is the weight to be placed on endowment versus nurturing. I suggest the broad emotional appeal of his work is due to its elaboration of an early experience that is part of all internal development: the sense of disconnection from an early source of external love and nurturing.

A fundamental background concept of this study is *introjection*, which I use to mean the process through which external experience becomes part of the self. This is a fluid, ongoing process, but in its most basic form during early life, it involves the manner in which the emerging, nascent self begins to take into itself experiences of others, of the world, and of external relationships. In the earliest states of mind, there is a blurring between self and other, and boundaries shift and dissolve. A major focus of this study is the earliest, most fundamental sense of contact with a good mother, which I tend to view as a *primary* introjection. I follow Klein in assuming that the primary act of the nascent self is the introjection of a good internal object, around which the self becomes integrated, through feeling loved and supported against whatever hostile, depriving experiences (internal or external) may beset it. In the very earliest stages of life, a central focus of Beckett's work, there are alterations in the cohesiveness of the self, as it integrates and disintegrates.[2] These alterations are connected to the fragility of the internal sense of a good, enduring other, and the self depends on the actual appearance of the external good object. Simply put, as the infant feels a sense of terror, for whatever reason (cold, hunger, internal rage or nascent depression) it requires a containing object to allow it to begin to integrate such experience. The containment becomes, along with the object that contains, an enduring part of the self that allows for a feeling of vibrant, secure living. Thus, the continual presence of a good other allows this process to develop. Here we can see the relevance to Beckett, as, for example, when Watt begins to disintegrate when he is not in the *actual* presence of Knott, who acts for him as a wished for mother-container. We can look at Beckett's work in this way: as an exploration of the very early internal experience of disconnection from this primary object, which is fundamental in creating an enduring sense of self.

In trying to examine the internal experiences of such disconnection, I highlight certain imagery, symbols and other manifestations in the text. Of course, these are selective, but I hope they are not exclusionary. For example, in Chapter 2, there is an exploration of Murphy's 'theft' of tea from a waitress, who I suggest acts as an internally felt mother; in Chapter Five, I suggest the narrator of 'The End' expresses certain core feelings about himself (and about his primary object) in his defecation into his boat/womb, feelings elaborated in a statement by Klein:

> The phantasized onslaughts on the mother follow two main lines: one is the predominantly oral impulse to suck dry, bite up, scoop out and rob the mother's body of its good contents. The other line of attack derives from the anal and urethral impulses and implies expelling dangerous substances (excrements) out of the self and into the mother. (Klein, 1988b: 44)

There are surely other ways of reading the examples I have just given; my use of the theory is an attempt to demonstrate something about internal experience. In this example, I feel that Klein's description of the fantasies of rage, and its enactment in the robbing and soiling of the mother, are related in *some* way to the internal experience of the narrative-self as manifested in the text.

The narrative-self

When my twin daughters were about four months old, my mother came to visit us. One evening, around midnight, I wandered into our living room, and found my mother sitting in the near darkness, with one of the twins in her arms, their faces close. Neither of them took any notice of me, they were in a world of their own. My daughter was smiling, gurgling sounds came from her mouth, to which my mother responded 'Are you telling me stories? Tell me some stories!' They continued on, my daughter mouthing sounds, clearly in response to loving replies, and questions, from her grandmother.

This scene is central to the following study. The internal world of the infant *is* its first story – at the beginning of life, this world is a pre-verbal, archaic, unconscious. It is the mother's role, as a primary auditor, to recognize, to hear, to make sense of this world. This relationship is taken into the child, its stories/world flourish as it develops. To feel secure in the world, with a vibrancy and love of life, requires a sense of a loving, primary listener. These early moments of contact are primal fictions, primal truths, moments of primary-process thinking that eventually elaborate into the complexities of cultural and social life.[3] Within the mind, I see this core relationship as central to all creativity in life, it is a feeling that one is not alone, but heard and understood. It connects to the possibility of fiction-making as well, since the mother becomes the first part of the self that hears *itself* – she is the primal object of the internal narrative-self couple, in which the core, infantile-self is the subject.

Not long after seeing my mother and daughter that evening, I happened on a neurological journal, in which there was an article about stuttering. Recent research was described: it is thought that there are disruptions in the part of the auditory cortex in which we hear *ourselves* speak. This notion seems central to Beckett: his work struggles to have part of itself (the primary mother/auditor) hear the infantile-self. The struggle is directed at the reparation of a primary gap within; the stuttering staccato of *Not I* is a reflection of an early rupture within the mind, between an infant that is trying to be, and the self/mother that recognizes its being.

I am reminded of a patient, a woman whose early life was filled with disruptions, with a constant feeling of not being seen by her mother as existing. She once told me how, as a child, she would play a game with herself. She would cut a large, cardboard box into a television, and then set a chair in front of it. She would enter the box and play-act a show, or a newscast, at times breaking off the fiction to leave the box. There, sitting in the chair, she would pretend to be her mother, appreciating the shows, laughing, seeing and listening. She struggled to forge a connection to an absent part of herself, through a dramatic re-enactment of the very failure that disrupted her drama. In Beckett, the fictional world acts in this way. It is an attempt to connect to the mother, telling stories about the rupture between the self and the listener, hoping to be heard, seen, made whole, so that it can go on, for the first time, together, alone.

Baker touches upon these concepts in his discussion of sections of 'From An Abandoned Work' (Baker, 1998: 16–17). There is an overtly Freudian, associative movement in Beckett's text 'my mother white … enough of my mother for the moment … [then] a white horse followed by a boy' (130). The sun moves from the mother to the horse, suggesting an obvious displacement of the narrator's feeling. The narrator comments that he has always been adversely affected by white things, but after seeing the white horse he flies into a terrible, 'blinding' rage, 'the white horse and then the rage, no connexion I suppose' (132). He feels finished with the story, there is 'nothing to add', the day/memory has been 'sucked white, like a rabbit, there is that word white again' (134). Baker writes of these passages:

> [They are] an associative monologue about a split self, without full self-knowledge, pivoting around the mother. But even if the larger discourse behind this is psychoanalysis, the relationship is unstable. What role do such helpfully communicative pronouncements as 'the white horse and the white mother … please read again my descriptions of these' (134) play in an art 'too proud for the farce of giving and receiving' (Dj. 141) or an art that 'does not dabble in the clear, does not make clear?' (Dj. 94). (Baker, 1998: 16)

I suggest that the apparent undoing of meaning, primarily through the narrator's overt destabilization of psychoanalytical hermeneutics, is a defensive strategy to protect the self from mis-understanding, or from revelation in an abandoning, unheeding world. It is a dialogue between a core self and a not trusted, primary auditor/mother. The passages do suggest obvious 'analytical' meanings: a child's longing to be close to its mother, displaced onto a horse, against whom the child can then feel safe in raging against. However, in the undoing of these 'meanings', there is also a revelation of the genesis of the feelings. Like the narrator of *Disjecta* (i.e. 'Dj'), this narrator shuns the idea of sharing, there is nothing to add to the story, for us, for himself. The world is 'sucked white', a primal draining, though it is unclear whether this is purely aggressive, or is an attempt to keep something safe within the self, a wish for a primal nurturing (i.e. 'white' milk). Baker writes: 'the writer of *From An Abandoned Work* is already a reader, reading the inscriptions on his mind with a hopeless alienation from anything like a unified self. The text dramatizes the angry perplexity of a split subject reading his own psychic text ("there is that word white again") and failing to make sense of himself' (Baker, 1998: 17). I suggest the passages *can* make a terrible sense, not only to us, but also to the narrator. It is a plea for connection, by a self that is unifying, then fragmenting under the weight of non-recognition. The two aspects of the narrative-self are split; there is an un-bridged gap between infantile-self as creator, as storyteller, and the primal auditor/mother, the 'only white horse' that is remembered, un-remembered. As surrogate auditors, we are asked to read again, to hold the passage in our minds, to share the struggle of the self to connect and, in so doing, to connect with it. We are asked to *understand* that this art does make clear its ambivalence about sharing, about communication, and why there is such a terrible rage. It is a primal anger that rests behind a terrible fear of abject loneliness, in a world where a self is unseen, unheard, by a part of itself that is mother. In this way, Beckett's work also becomes 'about' the fundamental psychological nature of art. There is an ongoing oscillation in the artistic experience – as readers/viewers, we play the object, containing side of a virtual self, holding the text/self within our minds. Equally, our minds, our unconscious, infantile-selves are held by the virtual person, the virtual primal object, which the text becomes as we enter it.

I have said this study will be solely textual, and that I will only quote Beckett when he comments directly on his work. However, the one exception to this is a vignette from his early life that serves as central imagery for this study. Baker relates the vignette: 'Beckett told his friend Gottfried Buttner in 1967 that as a child he would pick up stones from the beach and carry them home, where he would build nests for them and put them in trees to protect them from the sea. He described his relationship to stone as "almost a love relationship, and associated it to death"' (Baker, 1998: 139). There are many references to stoniness in the oeuvre, and to suggest its connection to a Freudian death instinct, a wish for a return to inorganicity, is certainly fair. Along these lines, I once worked with a man who was deeply isolated from the world. He spent many long months as a youth in total seclusion, travelling in the far north on his own. As a child, there had been little connection to a loving mother, and he once related the following story. He was in a cabin and, as winter approached, he could see ice building up on the lake. The water was higher than usual that year, and as he walked along the shore he saw how the oncoming ice would soon encase the homes of the small animals that had built them, hoping for protection from the cold. These animals were the living, child parts of him, and though there is a description of the awesome power of natural decay, there is also a cry for helpful connection. This man lived in a world of frozen love, and he feared involvement with me, since the sea was his own destructiveness, as well as mine/the world's.

Beckett's autobiographical vignette suggests the core estrangement lying at the heart of the narrative-self, and its genesis in early feelings with the mother. The child protects the stones – reflective of his own internal, frozen, loveless state. The stones are also 'eggs', containing the hope for a re-emergence, a rebirth, as the child becomes a protecting maternal force in a world in which things that are born from a mother-sea (as stones are) are destroyed by it. It is a primal love relationship, between a child and the mother from which it comes; the nest becomes a maternal mind in which the child places these symbolic aspects of himself. In fact, the stones can also be the mother, depicting the child's experience of her as cold, unfeeling, and a wish to protect her from his *own* rage, feeling himself, and her, slipping into an unthinking, oceanic nothingness. This is a story about the birth of Beckett's fiction and drama as well, the frozen, stone-selves are placed in a nest, a primal text, in which they remain safe, hidden, yet apparent. Buttner serves as a containing other for the feelings related in the vignette, repairing the gap to the extent a text *is* generated, and as the story/nest opens, he learns about Beckett's primal love. The condensation within the vignette is dense, as the child blurs into the mother, hiding from her non-recognition of his need, building his own protective nest, and Beckett's written texts become nests in this way. Within them are aspects of an infantile-self with mother; in our reading we create a primal listener who will hear for the first time, moving away from destructiveness and hiding, into a sharing of early life.

The schizoid dilemma

The work of Harry Guntrip on schizoid experience informs this study, since I will be looking closely at the experience of a loving connection between the self and the primary object.[4] Guntrip felt that the desire to connect in loving relationships with other persons is the fundamental driving force of early mental life: 'the infant's first need is to love and be loved [and the] first object relationship is organized around this need. If the infant's need to love is rejected, it experiences the most painful emotional state: the feeling that its love is unacceptable' (Guntrip, 1968: 36). This is an important aspect of Beckett's world: the sense that one is unlovable and therefore will not be loved. There are a wide number of possible reactions to this experience, and many are found in the oeuvre: Murphy's sense of self-sufficiency, the disdain felt by the narrator of the *Nouvelles* for children and their happily dependent state, the imagery of, and desire to return to, a pre-object state, and feelings of rage and anger, often suppressed out of fear of damaging the needed love object. Guntrip formulated the basic schizoid dilemma as the inability to 'be in a relationship with another person nor out of it, without in various ways risking the loss of both his object and himself' (Guntrip, 1968: 36). Such a dynamic is an enduring aspect of Beckett's fiction, from Murphy's declarations to Celia to similar effect, the tramps' waiting for a figure they desperately feel they need, to the later texts where a relationship is maintained with a primary internal object (that is felt to be unloving) by the use of fictional fantasies as a means of displacing and hiding feelings of rage and sadness. To some degree, failures in early relating are part of all human experience, and it is this aspect of mental life that we can examine in Beckett's work. Few of us have had our fathers murdered by an uncle who then sleeps with our mother, but we can connect to Hamlet's internal states because such primary experiences are part of our early fantasy life, and become part of the substrate of our ongoing adult experience.

Guntrips's theory of the regressed ego illuminates the dominant psychological constellation of the oeuvre. Greenberg and Mitchell write that it is:

> constituted by a profound sense of helplessness and hopelessness. The depriving experiences with real others have produced a fear of and antipathy towards life so intense and pervasive that this central portion of the ego has renounced all others, external and internal, real and imaginary; it has withdrawn into an isolated, objectless state [... and]

seeks to return to the prenatal security of the womb, to await a rebirth into a more hospitable human environment. Thus, regression entails a flight and a longing for renewal. When the flight aspect is more prominent, the regression is experienced as a longing for death – relief from conflicted relations with external and internal objects. When the hope aspect is more prominent, the regression is experienced in connection with a return to the protection of the womb. (Greenberg and Mitchell, 1983: 211)

This ambivalence towards life is predominant within the narrative-self, manifested within the nature of the characters as 'real' people, the imagery, flow and associations of the text, and, in the later work, within the actual dynamic content of the narrator's words themselves. Murphy's longing for this objectless state, which contradicts his need for a deep and enduring love, Watt's hunger for containment and closeness to Knott, the images throughout the oeuvre of rooms that serve the dual function of protection and suffocation, these are all manifestations of this predominant self-state. The intense condensations of 'Fizzle 5' demonstrate this state quite poetically. It reveals a 'closed space' where 'all needed to be known for say is known' (236). It is a closure of the internal world to others, who are *all* needed, since all *that* is needed for the self *to be* is *to be known* by a loving other. But this is closed off in an internal void, as all (needed ideas, others) are already known: 'all needed [...] is known.' The ultimate journey is lonely, a world filled with the 'dead but not rotting' (237), as others, and the self, are neither alive nor dead, held hopefully/sadistically in this neither world. The road is 'just wide enough for two. On it no two ever meet' (237). The meeting that never occurs for Beckett, which is the source of so many failed endings, is a failed beginning, a failed meeting, a failed knowing between mother and child. Greenberg and Mitchell write further:

the helpless and terrified infantile ego, overwhelmed by unrequited longings and dread of abandonment, remains alive within the regressed ego, in the heart of the personality [...] In the face of the constant threat of depersonalization and disorganization, reasoned Guntrip, the ego continually struggles to remain attached to life. All mental life and involvement with others, real and imaginary, operates basically as a defence against regressive longing [...] the concept of the 'regressed ego' becomes a conceptual black hole, swallowing up everything else. Conflicted relations with others, and masochistic attachments to bad internal objects serve as the ego's protection against regression. Oral, anal, genital fantasies reflect 'a struggle ... to stay born and function in the world of differentiated object-relations as a separate ego'. (Greenberg and Mitchell, 1983: 212)

While I do not adhere to the concept that all fantasy or actual object-relations function solely in this regard, I think the central point of this argument is useful for this study. The 'struggle to stay born' is perhaps not fully appreciated in many readings of Beckett, since the retreat from life, manifested in cynicism, philosophical posturing, and so forth, can mask it. Further, the attachments of the fiction – Murphy to an idealized Endon, Watt to Knott, the tramps to Godot, the late narrators to clearly internal persecutors – are understandable as a way of remaining alive, since this is felt to be better than nothing.

Three positions

A dominant assumption of this study is that Beckett's work often reflects experiences within the 'Paranoid Schizoid Position', postulated by Klein as the first organizational framework of the psyche. For Klein, 'the early ego largely lacks cohesion, and a tendency towards integration alternates with a tendency towards disintegration, a falling to bits' (Klein, 1988b: 4). Building on what she felt was a pure Freudian psychology, by implicating both the life and death instincts in the formation of the mind she added a distinctive feature to its genesis. For Klein, it was the way the ego saw *itself* that was of the utmost importance and the nature and content of fantasy life became the predominant building blocks of the mind. She believed the infant's only avenue to rid itself of deeply felt anxieties about annihilation, or 'falling to bits', was by projecting them outward into the world. There, depending upon the reception they received by a containing other, the internal fantasies about the self would be modified, becoming either ameliorated or even more terrifying.

I suggest part of the narrative function in Beckett's writing is a projection of such anxieties into the texts-as-fantasies; exploring such manifestations makes understandable the nature of these anxieties, aspects of their genesis, and the strategies used to control them. I do not view the Paranoid Schizoid Position as pathological in itself, but as a vital, ongoing part of human experience concomitant with the later Depressive Position. Klein believed that achieving this position, developed later in the child, was the most monumental task in human life, since it completed the human psyche. It involves an appreciation of the *wholeness* of the other, and a toleration of the attendant anxieties that one has destroyed or damaged the object through earlier feelings of anger. Ogden has written that it is only upon entry into the Depressive Position that a full integration of the self occurs, with a corresponding sense of 'I-ness' that allows for a full experience of the world. He has brought together a concept of an even earlier state of mind that he calls the 'Autistic Contiguous Position', which he defines as being:

> associated with a specific mode of attributing meaning to experience in which raw sensory data are ordered by means of forming presymbolic connections between sensory impressions that come to constitute bounded surfaces. It is on these surfaces that the experience of self has its origins: 'The ego [the "I"] is first and foremost a bodily ego', i.e. the ego is ultimately derived from bodily sensations, chiefly those springing from the surface of the body. (Freud, Standard Edition, 19: 26, in Ogden, 1989: 49)

Supporting his concept with work from leading infant researchers, and the psychoanalytical notions of the 'second skin' and adhesive identification (discussed below), Ogden suggests such early experience of primal sensation is vital in creating the rudiments of the self. Of importance to this study is the fact that the primary maternal object plays the central role in these experiences through the contribution of her own body, her initiation and response to the child's bodily action and needs, and her innate understanding of their meanings. The importance of this position to the work of Beckett will be explored, since it is through this position that one develops a foundation of an internal 'home', a sense of 'I-ness' felt unconsciously as an actual 'place where one lives' (Winnicott, 1971). I see this search for a primary maternal home as a central struggle of the Beckettian narrative-self: an enduring search for a place of primary security and selfhood, in relation to a good, loving other felt to be an integral part of the self. The imagery (urns, garrets, houses), the searching for maternal objects and the difficulties inherent in these relations, and finally the relationship to the primary sensory qualities of language itself, all have an element of this profound, primary need for early contact. A vignette may integrate these concepts:

> Mr. D was fully in the Paranoid Schizoid Position when we began our work together. He felt I was envious of him and that I, like the world, held him in contempt, or had hostile intentions towards him. He lived in a darkened room, much like Murphy's garret, and spent his days in

abject loneliness. After a number of years of work, he had begun to experience me, in a very fragile way, as a caring, good mother. In one session, he hinted this process had begun. He evoked a Beckettian inner world, stating he was afraid to lose me, that I might die. He thought he would place me in an urn in the office where I could still be a helpful presence for him. Finally he spoke of 'mummifying' me, and then said 'But you are not a mummy at all. You are always there for me, not like Mommy. Oh, did you hear that!'

Here we are at the boundaries of the Paranoid Schizoid and Depressive Positions. The patient's placing me in an urn both kills me off (i.e. to protect himself against my envy and his fears of my retaliation for his envy towards me), but it also served a transitional, containing function through which he protected me, and kept me close. It further evokes a *relationship*, developed in the rest of the imagery. I became a 'mummy' that was dead, reflecting his experience of the internal primary object, but a 'mommy' that was also preserved and would not leave him.[5] Finally, the split becomes clear, as he experiences me as a good, integrative force within himself, unlike the bad 'Mommy'. His calling out to me, to ensure that I *heard* him, enacts the primary constellation within the narrative-self – I became a primary auditor, containing, recognizing his internal world, its anxieties, and the creative, symbolic, efforts of the emerging-self to heal its primal wounds. The complex fluidity of this sort of imagery, as well as the fluctuations in the experience of self, other, and self-with-other, will be explored in this study.

To maintain a sense of bodily and psychic integration, a person with a feeling of rupture in primary contact will engage in certain activities, many of which are reminiscent of Beckett. For example, Ogden lists: rhythmic muscular activities like bicycle-riding or walking, eating, rocking, (sometimes in a rocking chair), riding buses or subways and maintaining or perfecting a system of numbers or geometrical shapes (Ogden, 1989: 70). Throughout the oeuvre, there is a persistent, determined attempt to hold the self together against disintegration-anxieties in these ways; in the later work, it can be argued that the process of writing/speaking begins to serve this function more directly. It is my view that all of Beckett's work is deeply concerned with maintaining a coherent selfhood, and that this is primarily predicated on struggles within the earliest positions of mental life that are the foundations of experience. The late play ... *but the clouds* ... demonstrates some of these experiences. There is a lone, male figure on stage, and his (disembodied) voice provides a commentary. This figure is an internal part of the self, and the piece reflects a primary experience, within the narrative-self, of early relations with a maternal figure. The male voice says:

> Then crouching there, in my little sanctum, in the dark, where none could see me, I began to beg, of her, to appear, to me [...] For had she never once appeared, all that time, would I have, could I have, gone on begging, all that time? Not just vanished within my little sanctum and busied myself with nothing? Until the time came, with break of day, to issue forth again, shed robe and skull, resume my hat and greatcoat, and issue forth again, to walk the roads. (260)

This is the earliest part of the emerging-self, disconnected from a primary feeling of the mother, in a hidden part of the internal world. There has been *some* connection, allowing for the feeling that 'begging' is possible, since without any connection there would be no possibility of *any* experience at all. There are four possibilities regarding the relationship between the male figure and the woman: that she appears but vanishes 'in the same breath' (evoking a comparison to the play *Breath*), which allows for no experience of contact. Secondly, she lingers 'with those unseeing eyes I so begged when alive to look at me' (260). This allows for a more enduring sense of connection between an emerging-self and a mother, but one who is experienced as neither firmly established nor interested. It echoes a failure of primary recognition of the self, an experience this study will trace through Beckett's work. The third case has the female visage appear on the stage and speak 'inaudibly': '... clouds ... but the clouds of the sky ...' (261). This is the closest that the emerging-self can come to an integrated contact to the mother, and it explains the adaptations that are made by the figure, since the fourth case, the commonest, is the one that dominates internal experience:

> case nought [...] in the proportion say of nine hundred and ninety-nine to one, or nine hundred and ninety-eight to two, when I begged in vain, deep down into the dead of night, until I wearied, and ceased, and busied myself with something else, more ... rewarding, such as ... such as ... cube roots for example, or with nothing, busied myself with nothing, that MINE, until the time came, with break of day, to issue forth again, void my little sanctum [...] to walk the roads. [*Pause.*] The back roads. (261–2)

The internal adaptation to the experience or non-experience of the mother's love is appropriately called 'case nought' as the maternal figure approaches the unavailability of many that precede it in the oeuvre (e.g. Knott, Godot, Endon), a primal 'case' that precedes all experience. A slippage begins, into the autistic space Ogden describes, as the self struggles to maintain coherence, though there is a hesitancy before finally acquiescing to the more 'rewarding' obsession of the 'cube-roots'. There is also a retreat towards nothingness, but one that *still* must connect to a nascent experience of otherness, and one that is possessed ('MINE'), for this maintains a living connection until another 'issuing forth'.[6] This figure, like so many before him, will leave an 'unspeakable home' of internal loneliness, and wander as a shadow in the world, walking to maintain a physicality that contains the self. It is of special importance that we are given the qualifier – 'the back roads' – for without an internal sense of connection to a good mother, this figure feels undeserving of authentic contact and, like so many other Beckettian characters, wanders on the margins of the world. The final words of the piece are spoken by the male voice, which repeats the female's words, appearing to connect to what might be an early, fragmented memory of the mother. Thus, this aspect of self forms a tenuous identification with the mother, but this voice *also* fades, abandoning the figure to begin yet another 'issuing forth' off this internal stage, in search of a complete connection. This piece embodies much that is central to this study: the primary modes of coping with internal maternal unavailability, a sense of enclosure that reflects the deadness of the inner world, the experience of the core, emergent self as *both* an internal, depleted character *and* as an observing part of the narrative-self, and the nascent sense of hope reflected in the self-protection and wandering, an intention to 'go on'.

Projective identification and containment

Another central concept within this reading is *projective identification*. This is a complex, debated idea within contemporary psychoanalytical thought, and I will not attempt to do it justice in the following brief exposition.[7] For purposes of this study I use the term to mean the manner in which a cohesive self (or a self that is striving *towards* cohesion) unconsciously experiences aspects of itself as being *within* another consciousness (though it may also be within a cultural object, an inanimate object, and so forth). The self that places (projects) parts of itself into another maintains a strong, unconscious connection to those parts, even when they are experienced *as* other. In an object-relational reading, one could argue this occurs in all aspects of fiction: the characters and imagery of Beckett are no more aspects of an underlying self than any other writer. However, I suggest that within his writing this early process, by which the self attempts to defend itself against anxiety, to maintain a connection with another, or to control another (for example, the 'puppets' of *Murphy*) is exposed to a degree and with a clarity not found elsewhere. Beckett's work is *about* that which makes fiction, and authentic life, possible – the primal projective texts/identifications with the mother/auditor.

Another closely related psychoanalytical concept that forms a central piece of this study is *containment*. Hinshelwood writes that 'the notion of 'containing' [...] derives from Klein's original description of projective identification in which one person in some sense contains a part of another. This has given rise to a theory of development based on the emotional contact of infant with mother and, by extension, a theory of the psychoanalytical contact' (Hinshelwood, 1991: 246). Essentially, the concept of containment suggests a primary relationship between one person and another. The embryonic self requires the mother to accept aspects of its internal world that for one reason or another are experienced as distressing. Thus, Rosenfeld writes about a patient who 'showed that he had projected his damaged self containing the destroyed world, not only into other patients, but into me, and had changed me in this way. But instead of becoming relieved by this projection he became more anxious, because he was afraid of what I was then putting back into him, whereupon his introjective processes became severely disturbed' (Rosenfeld, 1952: 80–1). In other words, the patient's internal world (the fundamental universe of self and others that reflect his total experience) was felt to threaten his own self-cohesion. It was necessary to attribute aspects of this universe (in this case a 'damaged self') to Rosenfeld. The patient's continued anxiety stemmed from the fact that *without an understanding acceptance and interaction from* Rosenfeld, there remained a fear that this damaged experience would be returned to him in an even more dangerous incarnation. This meant the patient became even more unable to take things in from the world, since he feared that what he had tried to rid himself of (bad internal feelings and experiences) would come back to haunt him. By understanding the patient's terror and his need to rid himself of these bad aspects of his inner life, and returning them with a non-hostile, calm acceptance, Rosenfeld maintained a contact with the man that allowed for mutative change.

It is in the work of Bion that these ideas reached their earliest mature form. He began to connect these concepts to very early experiences between the child and its mother, experiences in which a child's most fundamental annihilation anxieties need to be accepted and transfigured by his most important other:

> The analytic situation built up in my mind a sense of witnessing an extremely early scene. I felt that the patient had witnessed in infancy a mother who dutifully responded to the infant's emotional displays. The dutiful response had in it an element of the impatient 'I don't know what's the matter with the child.' My deduction was that in order to understand what the child wanted the mother should have treated the infant's cry as more than a demand for her presence. From the infant's point of view she should have taken into her, and thus experienced, the fear that the child was dying. It was this fear that the child could not contain. He strove to split it off together with the part of the personality in which it lay and project it into the mother. (Bion, 1967: 103–4)

Again, it is important to stress this is not necessarily a pathological process, but a *fundamental early interaction between an infant and its mother*. Because of the infant's early sense of fragmentation and powerful fantasy life, there is not necessarily any reasonable failure on the part of the mother. Thus, Hanna Segal would write:

> When an infant has an intolerable anxiety, he deals with it by projecting it into the mother. The mother's response is to acknowledge the anxiety and do whatever is necessary to relieve the infant's distress. The infant's perception is that [...] the [mother] was capable of containing it and dealing with it. He also introjects an object capable of containing and dealing with anxiety [which then becomes part of the self, as an aspect of the internal world]. The containment of anxiety by an external object capable of understanding is a beginning of mental stability. This mental stability may be disrupted by two sources. The mother may be unable to bear the infant's projected anxiety and he may introject an experience of even greater terror than the one he projected. It may also be disrupted by excessive destructive omnipotence of the infant's phantasy [i.e. its inability to accept the need for contact with another who could be helpful]. (Segal, 1981: 134–5)

The 'container' is not limited to the psychoanalyst or mother; anyone able to listen to, and tolerate, such primary anxieties can function in this way (Langs, 1978). I suggest that apart from the manner in which certain characters in Beckett (e.g. Endon, Knott, Godot) are sought out to provide this function, the fictional process itself can provide it. Later

Beckettian narrators use the creation of a fictional universe more explicitly as a means of containment. In the early work, there is often a sense of containment in symbols or imagery, as rooms, houses, hospitals, and so forth, provide this function; there is also a manner in which words themselves offer a containing function. In Bion's description of the failure of words to contain, we get an eerie echo of an experience perhaps most clearly presented in *Not I*. Thus, Hinshelwood writes about a 'man who stammers so that the words which should contain his emotions become engulfed and squeezed by the force of the emotion into a stammer or babble. The word is in this sense a container affected and disrupted by the emotion it is supposed to contain' (Hinshelwood, 1991: 250). In this sense, the Auditor in *Not I* is an overwhelmed, internal mother-container, who cannot process the sudden eruption of repressed feeling that 'she' verbalizes as a nascent part of the self.

Catastrophe

Beckett's work reveals a constant struggle to maintain contact with a good internal object, a contact that allows a nascent self to avoid the feelings of disintegration and annihilation. A search for the core anxiety of humanity dominates psychoanalytical history. Freud felt the early danger situation varied with the stage of development: the loss of the breast, the loss of love and ultimately the threat of castration were central to his thought. Klein's work with young children convinced her the predominant and most central anxiety was that of personal annihilation, or a complete, catastrophic destruction of the self and its psychic universe. This view was consistent with her belief in the dominance of the death instinct in human life, especially at the earliest moments of existence, and she saw the threat of its overcoming the self as the predominant anxiety of human experience. Ernest Jones, Freud's close colleague, had written earlier about a notion of catastrophic loss, *aphanisis*, by which he meant the deprivation of all possible connection to pleasure, and therefore the loss of existence (Jones, 1927: 459–72). Such a catastrophe, a final loss of *all* internal objects, is the dominant threat experienced in Beckett's work. Some of the mechanisms by which the self protects itself from these anxieties (i.e. during states when it does not feel contained by a meaning-making mother) are through a sense of *omnipotence* (i.e. others are not needed as I am all powerful), *projection* (i.e. others are attacking me; the generally hostile world often seen in Beckett), *idealization* (another external object is perfect and will protect me; e.g. Murphy with Suk or Endon) and *splitting* (keeping good and bad internal objects separate). Many of these strategies manifest in the texts.

One consequence of this is the overwhelming influence the dread of annihilation can have on the human experience. Bion felt this threat was present throughout life, and that this spectre of a primal catastrophe haunted all movement within the psyche. He believed the creative process of the mind, in its broadest sense, involved an engagement with this sense of primary loss and catastrophe, since the dismantling fragmentation inherent in change threatens the internal sense of containment engendered by a certain set of beliefs. There is a constant movement throughout life between the fragmenting anxieties of annihilation of the Paranoid Schizoid Position, and the integrative aspects of the Depressive Position (Bion, 1963). Thus, he conceived of a non-pathological move back towards the Paranoid Schizoid Position, which he coupled with the idea that at times projective identification was normal, useful for communication and understanding. Such movement, between early annihilation anxieties and the anxieties inherent in accepting an integrated completeness of an idea or person (which is transitory), forms the basis of normal mental life. This touches upon those interpretations of Beckett's work that see it as primarily about the process of artistic creation, since movement between these mental positions, and the danger inherent in it, is the foundation of creativity. The collapse of the artistic world *is* the collapse of internal mental *life,* if imagination becomes dead for ever. If the retreat into earlier psychic spaces is tolerable due to the security of an internal universe of good others, then rebirth occurs, since imagination was only dead in fantasy.

Looking at the consequences of primal anxieties that result from early failures of containment elucidates aspects of the Beckettian universe. Pervasive throughout the work is a sort of 'nameless dread', a threatening, haunting fear of non-existence engendered either by abandonment or by a usurpation of the self.[8] Bion developed the concept to describe a meaningless fear (or fear of meaninglessness) that besets the infant in a state where its primary anxieties are not contained by the mother. In these circumstances, the infant takes into the psyche, not a good mother able to understand and make chaos meaningful, but an object that destroys meaning (by being experienced as insane, or forcing the self to withdraw into insanity), and which abandons the self to a dangerous, meaningless world: 'In practice it means that the patient feels surrounded not so much by real objects, things-in-themselves, but by bizarre objects that are real only in that they are residues of thoughts and conceptions that have been stripped of their meaning and ejected' (Bion, 1962: 116). The narrative-self in Beckett struggles to survive this central difficulty, from Watt's travails with the unnamable 'pots' in the house of an uncontaining Knott-mother, to the tramps whose perceptions and memories become clouded in an increasingly meaningless world presided over by an uncontaining Godot-mother. Perhaps, the Unnamable most endures this dread (the title of the novel can equally refer to a state of being, i.e. an *unnamable* dread), struggling in abject isolation, save for a feeling of containing, within itself, what can be best described as 'an internal object that strips meaning [and gives rise to] a superego [i.e. a primary internally felt other, or group of others] that issues meaningless injunctions about behaviour' (Hinshelwood 1991: 354). In this light, the experience of a self that is 'neither' revolves around the meaninglessness inherent in an 'impenetrable self' and 'an impenetrable unself'. This is predicated by a failure of containment, by the otherness implicit in the world behind the perpetually closing doors of the short piece 'neither' (see below).

Winnicott provides an alternative model of early annihilation anxiety that is useful to this study. His notion of *impingement* focuses not so much on maternal abandonment *per se*, but on ruptures in the infant's illusory sense of omnipotent being. He felt the mother was required to support the infant's notion of independence, by providing basic needs in a timely fashion that allowed the infant to continue to believe it was autonomous, until such time that it could gently tolerate the reality of its actual vulnerability. Thus, Winnicott shifts the origin of the annihilation anxiety from a Kleinian internal object to actual external failure. My position will be to examine the work from an internal perspective, though within this it is possible to trace feelings of impingement. Thus, Watt's feeling of duty towards Knott, the tramps' 'requirement' to stay and wait for Godot, and the sense of internal, unnamed demands within the self of later narrators, can all be viewed as breakdowns in the development of an autonomous sense of self due to an experience of an internal other who does not allow for the development of self-esteem.

Winnicott also developed the notion of a primal catastrophe. In one of his last papers, he grapples with his own feelings about death, and describes the fear of annihilation or breakdown as the fear of a breakdown that has *already* been experienced. (Winnicott, 1973). Phillips elaborates on this:

> The death [Winnicott] describes [...] as having already happened is the psychic death of the infant, what he calls the 'primitive agony', of an excessive early deprivation that the infant can neither comprehend nor escape from. This intolerable absence of the mother was beyond the infant's capacity to assimilate. It was included as part of the infant's total life experience, but it could not be integrated, it had no place. Beyond a certain point [... the infant] could not hold his belief in his mother's existence alive in his mind [... These] events without context, they had merely happened [...] What was registered, unconsciously in Winnicott's view, was an interruption, a blanking out, an absence in the person's self-experience. [The Unconscious] is a place where deprivations are kept. (Phillips, 1988: 21–2)

It is this space, or non-space, that dominates the internal world of the Beckettian narrative-self. This study examines the experience of this non-experience, as it manifests in imagery and associations, and as it is structured within re-enactments of primal scenes of disconnected agony. These notions connect to the well-known story of Beckett's fascination with the lecture of Carl Jung, during which he described the case of a girl who was not 'fully born'. In his discussion with an actress playing May in *Footfalls*, Beckett stressed the need to understand that May was never 'born', but 'just began' (Knowlson and Pilling, 1979: 222). Beckett, like Winnicott, was preoccupied with a sense of not truly beginning, and perhaps this is why there are so many attempts to start again, to be born properly, as the fictional process mirrors the psycho-logical. The convergence of Beckett's artistic exploration and the psychoanalytical approach I am developing is echoed in the statement of Phillips, that for Winnicott: 'One of the aims of psychoanalysis was to re-establish continuity with whatever constituted the patient's "personal beginning". At the end of his life Winnicott was preoccupied by the final experience he might be unable to have, and by under-standing the earliest deprivations that could make people feel that they had not begun to exist' (Phillips, 1988: 22). These are the struggles of the narrative-self, whose greatest fear is not to be alive enough to die properly, as an autonomous, real presence in the world.

Following closely on the concept of containment is that of *mirroring*, which also forms part of the background approach of this study. In Winnicott's understanding, the baby sees *itself* when it looks at the mother:

> What does the baby see when he or she looks at the mother's face? I am suggesting that, ordinarily, what the baby sees is himself or herself. In

other words the mother is looking at the baby and what she looks like is related to what she sees there. All this is too easily taken for granted. I am asking that this which is naturally done well by mothers who are caring for their babies shall not be taken for granted. I can make my point by going straight to the case of the baby whose mother reflects her own mood, or worse still, the rigidity of her defences. (Winnicott, 1971: 112)

The infant receives from the mother something it has *already given* in its own look, and this will help to consolidate its own internal experience: 'The infant's first image of itself includes a connection with the mother; by the mother's look, the infant *knows that it is seen*' (Summers, 1994: 142, italics mine). There are a number of other conceptions of mirroring, but Winnicott's captures the essential point.[9] Regardless of one's specific beliefs about what the mirroring, or in more recent terminology 'empathy' or 'attunement', achieves for the internal self-state of the child, there is the central fact of a *recognition* experienced as somehow *real*. When Murphy does not feel *seen* by Endon, when Krapp does not feel *seen* in the punt, and when Vladimir, in a near panic, asks the Boy whether he is *seen*, the important thing is the *experience* of recognition, and its implied effect on the development of a secure, stable internal world and sense of self. Certainly, different theories present divergent opinions on the results of such recognition and its failures, but all agree that it is a vital part of self-experience and growth. My major concern in using the concept is that it provides a general framework within which certain recurrent experiences, that are manifested in the texts, can be understood as reflecting a primary state of connection, or disconnection, from the mother during early experience. Winnicott also developed a concept related to mirroring, and this, too, informs this study. This is his notion of *holding*, or the means by which the mother anticipates and protects the child's emerging-self. For Winnicott, this included not only an appreciation of the continuity of physical dependency that occurs after birth, but also of the importance of psychic contact.

An unspeakable home

Another important element of very early experience related to containment, and which forms a foundational background to this study, is the nature of the function of skin and touch. In the early 1970s, Esther Bick began to use sophisticated techniques of infant observation to develop the concept of 'adhesive identification' (Bick, 1968, 1986). This related to the very earliest moments of the child's extra-uterine life, its experience of its first object (the mother), and the introjection of this object into the psyche. Bick found that in situations where there was some problem in connection between the infant and the mother there is a developmental difficulty in which the infant cannot project its experience because of the absence of a developing internal space. In essence, the self is in its most primal, unintegrated state, seeking a maternal object, through touch: 'Bick proposed the notion of a "psychic skin" which ideally serves to bind together the experiences or "parts" of the nascent self, on their way toward integration into a cohesive sense of self' (Mitriani, 1994: 67). This notion connects to Freud's concept of the primal ego as a bodily ego, a projection of surface. For Bick, the 'psychic skin' is dependent on a primal other, an undifferentiated object composed of 'experiences of continuous interaction between a physically and emotionally "holding" and mentally "containing" mother, and the surface of the infant's body as a sensory organ' (Mitriani, 1994: 67). Bick hypothesized that 'later, identification with this [psychic skin] function of the object supercedes the unintegrated state and gives rise to the [ph]antasy of internal and external space [… and] until the containing function has been introjected, the concept of space within the self cannot arise [and] construction of an [internal containing] object [… will be] impaired' (Bick, 1968: 484). Within Beckett, these are central experiences, which find expression in a constant search for otherness, and in endless retreats into the self. The search is primarily for a containing object, a primal mother, 'a light, a voice, a smell, or other sensual object – which can hold the attention [and hold] the personality together' (Bick, 1968: 484). It is often forgotten how important touch is to the creation of textual meaning. Children begin to understand the symbolic potential of letters through touch, by handling their little wooden letters and puzzles, by making their erratic little crayon markings and, finally, when sitting nestled in the lap of a loved one, by touching words in their story books. Letters/texts are the primal Beckettian shape that holds the world, and the self, together, as a sort of proto-mother, and ruptures in this first contact are evident throughout the oeuvre. Mitriani discusses a young female patient, for whom early maternal presence was fleeting, fading; she experienced her patient as trying to make meaning out of her mother's absence:

> [She was an infant] who must have been continually obsessing about whether or not she had cried too loud or perhaps not loud enough.

Maybe the pitch of her cry was too high or maybe too low. Maybe she should continue to cry out or perhaps she should stop at once, and if so, for how long? [She wondered] if mother was ill or asleep, or perhaps she had finally left forever. Was mother dead? Or was she? (Mitriani, 1994: 75).

This describes the feeling-state of non-recognition central to the Beckettian voice. The texts are not only an expression of this state, but serve to counterbalance it. As Mitriani writes of her patient: 'although [her] material was quite communicative, it became apparent that her ruminations were not really thoughts connected to experiences, but rather an agglomeration of words which provided a cocoon of sensation within which she could wrap her precarious self for protection' (Mitriani, 1994: 75).

Aspects of this very early sense of disconnection between the emerging-self and the mother are apparent in Beckett's work from the beginning. The failure to develop internal space, predicated on ruptures in this early connection to maternal touch, is evident in the pervasive sense of enclosure. This manifests in the smallness of rooms (e.g. in *Murphy*, the Trilogy), the condensation of space in *How It Is*, *Endgame*, and *Waiting for Godot*, and the compression reflected in the density and self-enclosure of the prose (beginning in *Watt*, and extending through *Texts for Nothing*, and the later short prose and short dramatic pieces). The complex, complete encirclement of internal space reaches its heights with the late stories (e.g. 'The Lost Ones'), and in dramatic pieces like *Not I*. The main point about this self-enclosure is its relation, in the very earliest instance, to a failing primary connection to the internal mother. There is a double quality and function to such enclosure, the British child psychotherapist Frances Tustin (1980) postulates 'autistic objects' which serve to protect the child from early experiences of rupture from the world that is mother. The Beckettian world, and its textual incarnation, is filled with barriers (rooms, clothes, and words) that serve both to protect the self from invasion by functioning as a carapace, and to prevent a leakage of the self into a boundless world.

In Beckett's late piece 'neither', one finds a highly condensed expression of these experiences:

To and fro in shadow from inner to outershadow
from impenetrable self to impenetrable unself by way of neither
as between two lit refuges whose doors once neared gently close,
once turned away from gently part again
beckoned back and forth and turned away

> heedless of the way, intent on the one gleam or the other
> unheard footfalls only sound
> till at last halt for good, absent from self and other
> then no sound
> then gently light unfading on that unheeded neither
> unspeakable home (258)

This is a highly condensed metaphor of very early experiences of primary disconnection.[10] The wanderer of the piece can be seen as a core, emerging-self trapped in an enclosed space, between an unaccepting outer world and an undeveloping internal world, which are both felt to be shadowy and inhospitable. There is a sense of hostility or lack of interest in the self, as there appears to be an active sadism (or mechanical deadness): the doors open, seemingly beckoning the wandering self, only to close as it approaches.[11] The notion of refuge within a place or behind a door is symbolic for containment within a maternal mind, or within a mental space in which such a presence is felt. This is often echoed, in *Watt*, for example, where the house of Knott is continually seen as a refuge. The 'unheeded' neither-self is not recognized, and unheard, and this forms the core of the difficulty as containment becomes impossible, leaving the emerging-self wandering in the in-between world explored in Beckett's fiction. It is an 'unspeakable home' *before* words, before a sense of time, existing only on the margins of the earliest moments of life. It is 'unspeakeable' in its primal horror, a motherless space that should be the first home, the first place of welcome.

Meltzer developed these ideas of closed internal spaces and failures of early containment. He describes a child who 'tended to draw pictures of houses, in which there was a house on this side of the paper, and there was a house on the other side of the paper and when you held it up to the light, you saw that the doors were superimposed, you know, a kind of house where you open the front door and step out the back door at the same time' (Meltzer, 1975: 300). It is this collapse of space that we see in 'neither', as the houses, representative of internal and external worlds, collapse into a space in which Guntrip's 'regressed ego' struggles to move, balanced between complete withdrawal and a struggle to go on living. The wanderer in 'neither' moves within the space that is *between* the two sides of the picture; both sides are necessary for life, one side the inner house that is the internal world of the self, the other the world of living others that begins with an experience of the interiority of the mother.[12] For this child, as for the Beckettian narrative-self, there is a condensation of this space into a near nothingness, a space it keeps from total collapse by its *own* creation of space, through fantasy and speech. There is something within this early experience of an absent mother, reflected in the adhesion of the child's drawings of houses, which suggests the need for containment within another. The houses also represent the child-*with*-mother, the buildings are symbolic of inner worlds that the child must glue together in order to maintain contact. There is something of this quality in the entangled, adhering relationships one finds in Beckett, from the attachment of the servants to Knott, to the tramps attachment to each other and to Godot, to the tight, airless representations of inner room/worlds in the late fiction. Bick called one of the outcomes of this sort of experience a 'second-skin' formation by the infantile-self, a means of holding itself together when contact is uncertain: 'Disturbance of the primal skin function can lead to the development of a "second-skin" formation through which dependence on the object is replaced by a pseudo-independence, by the inappropriate use of certain mental functions, or perhaps innate talents, for the purpose of creating a substitute for this skin container' (Bick, 1968: 484). An example of a second-skin is the precocious development of speech, through which the child contains itself by the sound of its own voice, an important aspect of the Beckettian monologue. She also describes a certain muscular rigidity that contains and quiets sensation, something evident in a number of characters (e.g. the hero of the *Nouvelles*, Clov and Hamm) whose bodies are rigidified into postures that entrap, but also contain. There are many other examples of second skin functioning in Beckett: the jar that contains the Unnamable serves both to contain him and entrap him, and the many urns, rooms and enclosed dramatic spaces serve such a function for the narrative-self.[13]

Winnicott's notion of *potential space* is also germane to this discussion. Potential space has to do with an arena of imagination developed within the infant's mind through a loving connection to a patient, playful (and play-allowing) mother; potential or transitional space is one in which:

> we are neither inside the world of dream and fantasy nor outside in the world of shared reality. We are in the paradoxical third place that partakes of both these places at once. So while the boundary between the 'me' and the 'not-me' is of fundamental importance in the attainment of integration, health and indeed sanity, the potential space, 'the place where we live', transcends this boundary. (Davis and Wallbridge, 1981: 160)

This space is often enclosed within Beckett, and it is one *into* which the narrative-self struggles to emerge. Again, it is in the compressed in-between place of 'neither', where genuine adventure or exploration is shut off, so that the journey of life becomes encased within the early states of mental being. Late stories demonstrate movement into this world of transitional space through their internal fiction-generating, as do later dramas such as *Footfalls*, in which a repressed character/part of a unified self struggles to create *within* a context of internal enclosure (i.e. within the play proper).

There are similarities between these concepts and the Winnicottian notion of the 'false self' (Winnicott, 1965: 148). Winnicott felt an experience of premature separation from a vital primary object engendered sensations of severe annihilation anxiety. To counter this overwhelming sense of internal fragmentation a false self develops, in which a set of personality characteristics emerge that are not authentic, but designed to conceal the lack of true being, and to allow for rudimentary acceptance by the world. The Beckettian world is filled with experiences of premature ruptures from important objects, and the sense of a false self floats throughout, from the mimicry of Watt and the hero of the *Nouvelles*, to the withdrawn compliance of the heroine of *Not I* and the struggles of the late narrators for identity and their sense of the usurpation of their authenticity. Bick also comments on another aspect of the false self phenomenon: 'the catastrophic anxiety of falling-into-space, and the dead end [which] haunts every demand for change and which engenders a deep conservatism, and a demand for sameness, stability and support' (Bick, 1986: 299). The anxiety about change, this love of sameness, is a familiar one in Beckett. However, the deadened 'dead end' is one the narrative-self refuses to accept, as it continues to create, to start again, hoping for a change that will bring primal contact.

A lorn land

The central thesis of this study is that Samuel Beckett's fictional/dramatic universe is organized by an emerging-self attempting to maintain an enduring contact with a good primary object/mother, and that his writing explores the experience of this self, its genesis, defences, and reactions to failures of such contact. One of the characteristic features of the Paranoid Schizoid Position is a loss of contact with the most despairing, depressed parts of the self, since annihilation anxieties and feelings of rage dominate the internal world. Such withdrawn/depressed parts of the self are often in relation to unconscious early fantasy figures, and often the relationship centres around primary feeding experiences that reflect the earliest ways in which one engages the world. Beckett's fiction/drama often displays a sense of primary self-disruption, in the imagery and expression of starvation and feeding. This suggests an emerging-self caught in a 'neither' world on the edge of life, struggling to love and to be loved.

The internal sense of security that allows the infant to engage the world in a productive, creative fashion begins to develop from the earliest moments of life. This development is intimately connected to the primary nursing situation the child enjoys with its mother, a composite of feelings of being nourished, held, kept warm and touched. It is through this experience that the child begins to develop a sense of trust in the possibility of love, and begins to expect, through the repair of inevitable frustrations, that an interaction with a non-hostile world is possible. This is why, at the core of the paranoid state, we often find experiences of disruptions in the feeding experience. Hardy's poem 'The Puzzled Game Birds' illustrates the dramatic paranoid shift that occurs when the birds realize they are being *killed* by those who have *also* loved and fed them:

> They are not those that used to feed us
> When we were young – they cannot be -
> These shapes that now bereave and bleed us?
> They are not those who used to feed us,
> For did we then cry, they would heed us.
> – If hearts can house such treachery
> They are not those who used to feed us
> When we were young – they cannot be!   (Hardy, 1994: 31)

Here is the struggle to maintain a Depressive Position, which would allow the birds to accept the traumatic reality that they are, in fact, being killed by those whom they love, and who they feel have loved *them*. There is a sense of dissociation as the others become depersonalised 'shapes', and the deepest level of the birds' attachment centres around the mother's recognition of the needs of the infantile-self: the birds were heeded, and fed, when they cried. The splitting of whole objects remains intact to the end, as the birds maintain with ever more vigour that those who would feed and love the young *cannot* be the same as those who would now drain them of life.[14] The birds' poetic statement reflects the internal experience of the infant who is confused ('puzzled'), terrorized, and raging at the world/mother for her absence or misattunement to his needs, and who feels that this is tantamount to her killing him, either directly or in retaliation for his own anger.

In another poem from this period, 'Winter in Durnover Field', Hardy elaborates the sense of hostility that is the centre of the paranoid state, and which hovers around the notion of a more generalized world-as-mother who withholds food from the infantile-self. Three birds walk under a grey sky, across a field in which recently sown wheat has frozen:

> Rook. – Throughout the field I find no grain;
> The cruel frost encrusts the cornland!
> Starling. – Aye: patient pecking now in vain
> Throughout the field, I find ...
> Rook. – No grain!
> Pigeon. – Nor will be, comrade, till it rain,
> Or genial thawings loose the lorn land
> Throughout the field.
> Rook. – I find no grain:
> The cruel frost encrusts the cornland!
>
> (Hardy, 1994: 31–2)[15]

Here, the birds are starved by the *world*, experienced as a barren, frozen place, a barren world/mother reminiscent of many Beckettian settings, from the world of mud in *How It Is*, the 'bog' and 'Cackon' country of *Waiting for Godot*, to the grey nothingness of *Endgame*. The voice of the Rook, with its constant refrain of 'no grain', reflects the deepest, most despairing part of the self, engaged with an 'encrusted', unavailable mother-'cornland' whom he feels is dead, starving him. The Pigeon's hopeful, and (perhaps) realistic, musings go unnoticed, as the Rook is stuck in a paranoid stance: the time is now, and now is always; I am hungry, and world/mother is dead to me. In 'Birds at Winter Nightfall', Hardy makes the mother more human: 'the flakes fly faster/the berries are all gone/Shutting indoors that crumb-outcaster we used to see upon the lawn.' (Hardy, 1994: 31). The nurturing mother remains unavailable, inside a house that represents an excluding maternal mind, and there appears to be an emotional, withholding *agency* on the part of the world. The primacy of dependence, in the face of such a harshly experienced world, is the centre of the mother–infant universe at the beginning of life, and is the beginning of love. It is within the early nursing situation that the central relational dynamics that organize the internal world are developed, and it is here that Beckett's fiction often elaborates the foundations of human emotional life. In his writing, these issues receive an intensive fictional investigation, with this sense of a depriving, uninterested world/mother forming a consistent internal background. This sense of disconnection is often expressed as a primary state of anxiety, depression, or paranoia, and there are numerous examples where this state is entwined with images of feeding or primary nurturing. The state that ensues will be a confused one, where boundaries are unclear, as the infantile-self is uncertain about the origins of the rage, loneliness, and anxiety that it feels. In *Watt*, the primal importance of words in Beckett becomes explicit, as their relation to early nurturing situation comes into focus. Watt's endless internal ruminations serve as autistic objects, protecting him from the frustrations, invasiveness of a hostile/unavailable maternal world; they act as a 'second skin' that becomes a sensual and containing presence. As the narrator of 'Heard in the Dark 2' states: 'Simple sums you find a help in times of trouble. A haven ... [E]ven still in the timeless dark you find figures a comfort' (250–1).

One of the functions of the seemingly endless internal monologue created in some of Beckett's non-dramatic work, and in certain dramatic pieces, is to act as a nurturing, maternal containment. This protects the self, and re-creates (or creates for the first time) a 'haven' that approaches primary containment. It is *within* the enclosed monologues that the nature of the early ruptures can be found. Beckett alluded to these fundamental qualities of words while speaking to an actress who played May in *Footfalls*: 'Words are as food for this poor girl ... [T]hey are her best friends' (Asmus, 1986: 339). Words become primal nutrients for the narrative-self, allowing an ongoing engagement in a creativity that replaces, and strives for contact. In Beckett's work, the infantile-self struggles to engage the world, torn between a turning away from the mother/other, and an emergence into a realm of experience and risk. The opening words of 'The Image' condense this core experience of emergence/retreat poetically, and within the framework of an early nursing relationship with the world/mother: 'The tongue gets clogged with mud only one remedy then pull it in and suck it swallow the mud or spit question to know whether it is nourishing' (165). This is the underlying image that dominates the internal world portrayed within the texts – a struggle between emergence and hiding, despair and hope, predicated on a sense that the world, being unknowable, *may* be as dangerous as it *may* be nurturing.

Proust

In his dissertation on Proust, Beckett describes a constellation of experiences at the heart of the Paranoid Schizoid Position, and gives a hint as to their genesis. This section examines those aspects of his study relevant to this reading – in particular, the fundamental importance of a containing, maternal mind in organizing a cohesive, calm, internal world.

In *Proust*, Beckett writes of the bizarre, even inhuman quality of experience in what is clearly a primal state of mind: 'I would describe men, even at the risk of giving them the appearance of monstrous beings, as occupying in Time a much greater place [...] extended beyond measure, like giants plunged in the years, they touch at once those periods of their lives – separated by so many days – so far apart in time' (2). The experience of temporal self-continuity with a coherent, stable set of internal objects is inadequately achieved during the earliest moments of life, when the psyche struggles with cognitive immaturity and powerful physical needs. The 'monstrosity' that Beckett suggests to be part of mankind's natural endowment is just that: the fundamental connection to the world proceeds as a *struggle* to maintain wholeness (of others and the self), and to maintain a coherent sense of time and change. This passage describes the immense boundlessness of potential experience, which would overwhelm the self, *were it not for primary maternal containment*. In the Paranoid Schizoid Position, change is felt as inherently dangerous, since self-integration has not been achieved: 'There is no escape from yesterday because yesterday has deformed us, or been deformed by us [... it] is within us, heavy and dangerous. We are not merely more weary because of yesterday, we are other, no longer what we were before the calamity of yesterday' (2–3). This equates the primary dangerousness of time and change to an attack on identity. In early states of experience, internal needs and desires that depend on a primary other for fulfillment can, when unfulfilled, cause serious disturbances in identity, and in the constancy of the object. The good mother, loving and helpful, disappears, replaced by a bad, withholding or absent mother. The sense of self is equally disrupted as internal calm becomes dominated by panic and rage. Since the mother holds the self together, making the infant continuous, this state disrupts complete connection to the world, which becomes terrifying in its inconsistency: 'The aspirations of yesterday were valid for yesterday's ego, not for to-day's. We are disappointed at the nullity of what we are pleased to call attainment. But what is attainment? The identification of the subject with the object of his desire. The subject has died – and perhaps many times – on the way' (3). This is an expression of experience within a Paranoid Schizoid state: there is a sense of depletion due to the constant struggle to maintain connection to a perfect object, a struggle engendered by inevitable fluctuations in early attunement between mother and infant. The universe seems populated by mysterious, unknowable others who arbitrarily attend to the self, along a spectrum ranging from loving to uninterested, withholding, and hostile. However, in successful early relationships, this struggle can lead to, not the death of the subject, but of otherless narcissism; the mother becomes as whole as the infantile-self that experiences her. Beckett goes on to consider:

> a mobile subject before an ideal object, immutable and incorruptible [...] Exemption from intrinsic flux in a given object does not change the fact that it is the correlative of a subject that does not enjoy such immunity. The observer infects the observed with his own mobility [...] we are faced by the problem of an object whose mobility is not merely a function of the subject's, but independent and personal: two separate and immanent dynamisms related by no system of synchronisation. So that whatever the object, our thirst for possession is, by definition, insatiable. (6–7)

Again, this passage describes experience within the Paranoid Schizoid Position. There is the sense of an ideal object that can form a predominant, defensive constellation with the self, against the realities of change and frustration. Further, this object is somehow damaged ('infected') by the nature of the self and its demands. The impossibility of perfect 'synchronization' is dangerous, since in this primal state of mind dis-connection carries the weight and terror of eternity. There is a need for total possession of the mother, and it is this need for domination that is projected, creating a terrifying, engulfing world. It is not surprising that the primary sensation is of an 'insatiable' 'thirst'; the mother and the breast can never be adequately introjected in this state, since time fragments them into part-objects that are hated when they fail. Beckett's statement, that all that an 'I' can realize 'in Time [...] can only be possessed successively, by a series of partial annexations – and never integrally and at once', is a perfect description of experience in the Paranoid Schizoid Position.

It becomes increasingly clear that such experience is dominated, for Beckett, by considerations regarding the nature of love, seen as a powerful, complete incorporation of the other. The following reflects struggles within this primal state:

> Even suppose that by one of those rare miracles of coincidence [...] realization takes place, that the object of desire [...] is achieved by the subject, then the congruence is so perfect [...] that the actual seeks the inevitable and, all conscious intellectual effort to reconstitute the invisible and unthinkable as a reality being fruitless, we are incapable of appreciating our joy by comparing it to our sorrow. (3–4)

These words describe another primal anxiety constantly explored in Beckett's writing. If, in these primary states of mind, the other becomes congruous with the self, there is a loss of potential and of growth, since there is a collapse into narcissistic otherlessness. The self, which can only *be* by existing in time, faces elimination, as 'aspiration' (i.e. psychic change and life) is destroyed, the world collapsing into a determinism founded by the primitive belief in omnipotence ('the actual seems inevitable'). The most fundamental need of the mind, to connect to a living other, remains unattained, since it demands frustration and misattunement. It is the mother who primarily modulates the possibility of change and surprise (i.e. the 'invisible and unthinkable') by placing herself just outside the infant's experience, but not so far as to be lost altogether. If the mother is absent, or if the infant does not allow her presence, the foundations of living feeling are destroyed, and no effort of the intellect can reconstitute them. One is neither alive nor dead, a grey, changeless world becomes predicated on the loss of feeling, as joy and sorrow become one.

In *Proust*, there is a glimpse of the type of primal relationship that generates such experience. The 'future' seems hopeful, the self is calm, 'smug' in its will to live until '[its] surface [is] broken by a date, by any temporal specification allowing us to measure the days that separate us from a menace' (5). Beckett gives examples: Swann's distressed fragmentation upon realizing he will be separated from Odette, and the narrator's panic, triggered by the realization Albertine is scheduled to be with her aunt the following evening. Of the genesis of these states of panic Beckett writes: 'the tacit understanding that the future can be controlled is destroyed' (6), reflecting the fractured disorganization of an infantile-self confronted with an inevitable failure to remain omnipotent. The urge to devour the world, to make it part of the self, conflicts with a need for the otherness that is life. In an attuned early environment, this experience is mitigated, mediated by the mother's love and patience, but for Beckett's Proust: 'No object prolonged in this temporal dimension tolerates possession, meaning by possession total possession, only to be achieved by the complete identification of object and subject' (4–5). Through enduring relations with a loving other, this statement, instead of evoking loss and defeat, could be read as a prerequisite for authentic living, and self-integration. Sense could begin to be made of the world, as the feeling that others are simply 'separate and immanent dynamisms related by no system of synchronization' diminishes through authentic contact (7). Again, there is a dual implication to the statement that 'the creation of the world [does] not take place once and for all time, but takes place every day' (8). Though change is necessary for life, it need not be *catastrophic* change in which all that comes before is forgotten or destroyed. It is through the endurance of the self, predicated on a good, stable set of early internal objects, that life becomes both continuous and surprising. Rather than the 'compromise between the individual and the environment' (7) being felt as a 'dull inviolability', it becomes a living, though sometimes confrontational, engagement with the *whole* world. For Beckett's Proust, the response to this situation becomes engagement with the world through habit, which in a dislocated experiential world is a 'generic term for the countless treaties concluded between the countless subjects that constitute the individual and their countless correlative objects' (8). Habit becomes the ultimate protector of the self, guarding against an endless series of shifting others. This situation is inalterable, since the 'periods of transition that separate consecutive adaptions (because no expedient of macabre transubstantiation can the grave-sheets serve as the swaddling clothes) represent the perilous zones in the life of the individual, dangerous, precarious, painful, mysterious and fertile, when for a moment the boredom of living is replaced by the suffering of being' (8). A central, subjective sense of the narrative-self manifests here, as life becomes dull, devoid of genuine engagement and vitality. The despair is typically condensed; there is disappointment that life cannot be avoided, since one cannot be born into the grave-sheets, yet the life that remains *retains* the same futility. Moments of being without the mother, which in a healthy environment serve as times of internal structure building, here become filled with a vitality of danger, pain and mystery. However, there is no balance, these times are full of 'suffering', as if 'being' can mean nothing more than lonely isolation. There is no possibility of 'being alone in the presence of the mother', when the child is contained, secure within its mother's mind, feeling that securing recognition within itself so it can go on alone, yet not alone. Here the alternatives are suffering, akin to a form of disintegration anxiety, a loss of internal objects, or a bored engagement in life. This boredom seems to be a consequence of the intractable mutability of human engagement: in a world where others are constantly changing and unknowable, boredom serves a protective function, protecting the self from the severe trauma of an endless series of ruptured engagements. It also reflects the inability of the self to maintain an enduring experience of maternal containment; there is an endless sense of waiting for a mother who will make the self whole and life meaningful. Real engagements are condemned to be lifeless, as the ego or self becomes as a 'minister of dullness', a protective 'agent of security' (10):

> When it ceases to perform that [security] function, when it is opposed by a phenomenon that it cannot reduce to the condition of a comfortable and familiar concept, when, in a word, it betrays its trust as a screen to spare its victim the spectacle of reality, it disappears, and the victim, now an ex-victim, is exposed to that reality – an exposure that has its advantages and disadvantages. It disappears – with a wailing and gnashing of teeth. The mortal microcosm cannot forgive the relative immortality of the macrocosm. The whisky bears a grudge against the decanter. (10)

The self is limited to its role in organizing reality into the 'comfortable and familiar', to protect the 'individual' from the 'spectacle' of reality; this ego-function is essentially a Freudian one. However, there is a sense this also entails a realization of maternal otherness, since the mother's unique personhood cannot be controlled, reduced through an omnipotent control. A sense of smallness haunts the nascent self, one evinced in 'grudging' anger at the mother's 'immortality', the containing 'decanter' whose mind must hold her growing child, allowing a gentle integration into the world. In Beckett, this situation is often reversed; the self often experiences the maternal mind as overly engulfing, unable to tolerate its need for both containment and separation.

Beckett's own illustrations from Proust elucidate the consequences and the nature of a self that is isolated, compliant, withdrawn from the beauty and danger of the world, and drugged by a life-draining habit. He describes Proust's narrator, on vacation with his grandmother, staying at the Grand Hotel (12–13), feeling 'feverish and exhausted', but unable to calm himself to sleep in the 'inferno of unfamiliar objects'. He is 'defensive', 'vigilant', 'taut', and as 'painfully incapable of relaxation as the tortured body of La Balue in his cage, where he could neither stand upright or sit down'. That Beckett chooses this scene is important, for within it lies the essential experience that organizes his oeuvre. In fact, the adjectives are appropriate to his own work: a world in which characters are defensive, vigilant, and taut, strangers in strange lands, often unable to sit (in welcome), or to stand (to leave). The world becomes a storm of 'sound and agony' that the Proustian narrator cannot quell, objects are threatening and violent, and he is amidst 'wild beasts'. His grandmother comes in, and 'comforts him', helping him prepare for sleep as if he were a child. She helps him to 'unbutton his boots', undress, and 'puts him to bed', and comes again in the night, when he needs her. In a sense, the narrator exists no more; he is fragmented and dissociated, and 'there is no room for his body' in the room. In his terror, he fills the space with an inner dread, creating a 'cavern' of monsters. In a very real way, this is reminiscent of early childhood terrors, in fantasy and dream, and it is not surprising that when the maternal figure comes to him, he is calmed again. Separate, alone, he suffers primary separation anxiety, and is incapable of re-organization without the mother. The experience brings to mind Bion's description of the 'bizarre objects' that occur when the self is fragmented, extruded into an unbounded world, becoming prey to a world filled with its own 'beasts': 'Each particle [of the self] is felt to consist of a real external object which is encapsulated in a piece of the personality that has engulfed it [...] The object, angered at being engulfed, swells up, so to speak, and suffuses and controls the piece of the personality that engulfs it: to that extent the particle is felt to have become a thing' (Bion, 1956: 344–6). Proust's narrator experiences such an internal disruption, entering the same state that threatens the narrative-self throughout the oeuvre, as he 'rids himself of the apparatus of conscious awareness of internal and external reality [achieving] a state which is felt to be neither alive nor dead' (Bion, 1956: 39). The arrival of a maternal object binds the chaos, allowing for the re-integration of a living self. A second vignette that Beckett chooses reinforces the importance of maternal presence; having telephoned his grandmother, the narrator hears her voice:

> now for the first time, in all its purity and reality, so different from the voice [...] of her face that he does not recognize it as hers. It is a grievous voice, its fragility unmitigated and undisguised by the carefully arranged mask of her features, and this strange real voice is the measure of its owner's suffering. He hears it also as the symbol of her isolation, of their

separation, as impalpable as a voice from the dead. The voice stops. His grandmother seems as irretrievably lost as Eurydice among the shades. Alone before the mouthpiece he calls her name in vain. Nothing can persuade him to remain at Doncieres. He must see his grandmother. (14–15)

The strangeness of the telephone-voice creates a dislocation in his experience of grandmother as an internal, living presence. Regardless of the woman's real feelings at that moment, the narrator experiences a disturbing disconnection from a primary maternal presence within himself, one that connects to the primal experiences of touch (i.e. the voice is 'impalpable'). This creates an internal deadness predicated on separation from an integrating, inner mother, to which he must reconnect by seeing the woman in person. A number of patients have had this experience with me during conversations on the telephone. Not being able to see me in person ruptured a primary sense of containment, creating an overwhelming panic, and a feeling that all goodness and love was lost. Beckett's understanding of the episode in the hotel elaborates on this: 'But this terror at the thought of separation – from Gilberte, from his parents, from himself – is dissipated in a greater terror, when he thinks that to the pain of separation will succeed indifference, that the privation will cease to be a privation [...] *when not only the objects of his affection have vanished, but also that affection itself*' (14, italics mine). This world is both terrifying and potentially beautiful. The only defence against separation anxiety becomes habit, but it is a life-killer, since it destroys the hope that the individual might survive the terror and be able to organize the world. The will for authentic living is lost, 'an idle tale' suffocates the vibrant narrative of human life, as a far worse anxiety ensues. The individual loses not only the loved internal persons, but also the *capacity to love, and to be loved*. This is the ultimate catastrophe, the world becomes a dead world, as the self collapses into a defensive position that protects against the pain of separation. It is better than no world at all, however, and this place is home to the narrative-self, as it struggles to engage a loving other.

In this world, the self is fragmented, devitalized, either doomed by habit and intellectualization to a deadened existence or, alternatively forced to face a strange, de-realized world of terrifying loneliness and 'wild beasts'. It is a world without the possibility of hope, love has been stillborn, blocked by a fear of engulfing otherness, or by rage. Beckett's quoting of Proust suggests the inevitability of such a state: 'How have we the courage to wish to live, how can we make a movement to preserve ourselves from death, in a world where love is *provoked by a lie* and consists solely in the need of having our sufferings appeased by whatever being has made us suffer?' (38, italics mine). This is a world deprived of joy, of mutual attunement and sharing, it is a world of loneliness. Love becomes mere manipulation, an attempt to force the mother-as-contemporary figure to repair an early, basic fault, felt as a narcissistic wound.[16] An awareness of this never-ending search, and the impossibility of filling the inner void, leaves the Proustian narrator disillusioned and suicidal, and Beckett is in close agreement with these feelings: 'Surely in the whole of literature there is no study of that desert of loneliness and recrimination that men call love posed and developed with such diabolical unscrupulousness' (38).

Love, for Proust (writes Beckett), is 'our demand for a whole' (39), a statement that lies at the heart of both men's work. For Proust, a remembering of the past is an attempt to create a more cohesive self, to repair a self ruptured and fragmented by the loss of an internal, maternal figure. In Beckett, there is an even more desperate attempt to hold a world together, when the basic ability to reach the world, to love, is lost within the earliest states of experience. Beckett's world teeters between a complete, final withdrawal in hopeless despair to an isolated, but safe, internal sanctuary, and a faint, almost imperceptible cry, to be born again, to go on, to a mother who this time will love, recognize, hear. For Proust, and for Beckett, others exist in discontinuity, 'And not only "I", but the many "I"s'. For any given Albertine there exists a correlative narrator, and no anachronism can put apart what Time has coupled' (43). This is the Paranoid Schizoid experience, as a sense of wholeness of self and other is eternally beyond reach. As the speaker of *A Piece of Monologue* states: 'No. No such thing as a whole' (260). Tottering on the edge of the Depressive Position, this speaker's world is fragmented, too. Things went wrong from the beginning of psychic birth – at the first 'suck' began the 'first fiasco', a primal sense of rupture in the nurturing, loving bond. The first steps, between mother and nanny, were felt as unaffectionate (the speaker was 'bandied about' between neither-doors), as life became a march from 'funeral to funeral', with a false self 'ghastly grinning' (265). Like Watt with the Knott-mother, the speaker wanders in darkness, unable to bring forth a sense of love, always 'almost' saying 'loved ones', but unable to tolerate the depressive anxiety, to integrate something that cannot be whole. The piece is full of imagery of primal connection: 'Birth. Parts lips and thrusts tongue between them. Tip of tongue. Feel soft touch of tongue on lips. Of lips on tongue. [...] Stare beyond through rift in dark to other dark. Further dark. [...] Nothing stirring' (268). This is a primal disconnection that begins with a failed psychic birth, reflecting the sensations of failing touch between the mouth and the breast, across a primary gap ('rift') to the mother's body and mind, as an uncontaining darkness envelops the internal world, as nothingness stirs, still. The inner world becomes a vast darkness full of 'ghosts': 'Ghost light. Ghost rooms. Ghost graves. Ghost ... he all but said ghost loved ones. Waiting on the rip word' (269). The 'ripping' that so kills the emerging-self, preventing wholeness from developing, is the tearing away from the mother's presence, from the touch of lips and breast, creating a gap in the self that leaves one's words meaningless and void. As well, there is a wish to tear oneself away from this dead, encasing feeling of primary failure, a wish aborted by the terror of premature separation.[17] Like May, in *Footfalls*, this speaker has only one concern, one thing that is 'it all': there is 'never but the one matter', a need to repair an internal connection that leaves him wandering in a world where there are only '[t]he dead and gone. The dying and the going. From the word go' (269).

Without an enduring sense of maternal presence, of containment within a loving, recognizing maternal mind, there can be no enduring self. Proust's narrator seeks the mother in disparate figures, and failing to find her, attempts to hold himself together by searching in the past. The Beckettian narrative-self manifests this fragmented searching continuously through the oeuvre, as characters fight boredom and despair in a place where there is 'nothing to be done'. It is a search for an attuned, recognizing mother, who holds the primal self; it is a search that continues because *one desires to be understood because one desires to be loved, and one desires to be loved because one loves* (46, italics mine). This is the motive for the search of Proust's narrator, and the motive behind the faint voice of Beckett that 'must go on'. Only in speaking can the narrative-self hope to be heard, to be understood, and fulfill its need to love, and be loved, by the part of itself it first touched in the mother. Love for Proust, and for Beckett, becomes a 'function of sadness', founded on inescapable isolation, rather than any enduring inter-relatedness. Communication is impossible, to attempt to share oneself with another is a 'human vulgarity', or 'horribly comic, like the madness that holds a conversation with the furniture' (46). Others are unreachable, but it is *because* of the inner deadness, engendered through maternal unavailability, that the world appears filled with lifeless things. The first piece of 'furniture' was the absent mother (in the

infant's eyes) and, in her eyes, the infant. The child takes this relationship into itself, beginning the death of love. The risks implicit in hope,
in the wish to communicate are immense, and the need to be loved,
and to love, is easily held at bay by a fear of re-traumatization. If there is
no world but that of 'furniture', one has nothing to regret, there is no
real loss. In such a world, one must be alone, either hopelessly
misunderstood: '[our] speech and action are distorted and emptied of
their meaning by an intelligence that is not ours', or enacting a false-
self: 'we speak and act for others – in which case we speak and act a lie'
(47). These are the two poles of Beckett's despair: the loss of the self –
either by abandonment to an unempathic world, or by a forced
compliance, a capitulation. In this, one finds the final cause of self-
estrangement and disconnection from authenticity: 'One lies all one's
life long ... especially to those that love one, and above all to that
stranger whose contempt would cause one most pain – oneself' (47).
This quotation, from Proust, demonstrates the damage to the core self
created by the sense that the other's love is either dangerous or
unavailable, and that self-deception is the only means to survive.

Therefore, for Beckett's Proust, isolation is rationalized, made
appropriate. Resignation rules, withdrawal is accepted as inevitable;
loneliness and disconnection are held at bay, for the moment: 'the artist
is active, but negatively, shrinking from the nullity of extracircum-
ferential phenomenon, drawn into the core of the eddy [...] we are
alone. We cannot know and we cannot be known. 'Man is the creature
that cannot come forth from himself, who knows others only in
himself, and who, if he asserts the contrary, lies' (48–49). Like Sam and
Watt, who come together, only for a moment, before forever parting,
Beckett and Proust come together here. In his sharing of a deeply held
understanding with an artist he admires, Beckett, in a way, undermines
his whole thesis. For Proust's art held a profound communication for
Beckett, a shared state of loneliness and fragmentation, which was
clearly important for him. Perhaps it was this deeply felt experience of
understanding Proust and, in a sense, of being understood by Proust,
that helped lay a foundation for Beckett's own artistic exploration of an
internal state where one is indeed alone, almost entirely without hope,
where to hope for love and understanding would be to lie. Hope would
contravene a law of nature for the Beckettian narrative-self, though it
hides within the texts, within the primal text-making, waiting for an
auditor. Yet, the myth must remain, there is no one beyond the self, at
least no one who will respond with an empathic understanding and

with love; there cannot ever be, for she who would have allowed for such a feeling was never felt as being there.

Notes

1 Material from a number of general references has been helpful in developing parts of this section: Laplanche and Pontalis, 1988; Moore and Fine, 1990, 1995; Bacal and Newman, 1990; Summers, 1994; Hinshelwood, 1991; and Rycroft, 1988.

2 Early in her career Klein suggested, following Freud, that the ego's first act was to deflect outwards (project) the death instinct, and to subsequently face the difficulties of introjecting a now poisoned and dangerous world. The death instinct is a highly problematic concept in psychoanalysis, but is one that could be applied to Beckett's work. I have tended not to speak of it in the study, preferring to view the continual struggle to remain alive as a consequence of a feeling of internal disconnection from a primary object.

3 Freud felt primary-process thinking was his greatest discovery. It uses *condensation* (the combination of two or more images to form a composite, which is invested with meaning from both) and *displacement* (the shifting of interest from one image, thought, or object to another). Thus, images can become fused and readily replace or symbolize one another. Within primary-process thinking, there is no concept of space or time, and there can be the use of hallucination to fulfil needs.

4 Simon (1988) and Brink (1982: 87–100) examine *Endgame* in terms of schizoid object relations.

5 Citing the work of André Green, Baker (1998) explores the introjection of the 'dead mother' in Beckett.

6 See Meares (1986: 545–9) for a discussion of the sense of possession.

7 For some recent thinking, debate, and criticism of the concept see Sandler, 1987, Grotstein, 1985, and Ogden, 1993.

8 Karin Stephen first used the term 'nameless dread' to refer to early infantile anxieties centered on 'a dread of powerlessness in the face of instinct tension' (Stephen, 1941: 178–90).

9 Kohut felt that a vital part of the self was a grandiose aspect that required admiration. The mother (or other caregiver) provided this function to help the development of the self (Kohut, 1971). For general criticisms of concepts of mirroring, see Stern (1985: 144–5), who develops more sophisticated terminology based on infant research. Since I am not attempting to tie Beckett's literature to any specific psychoanalytical theory, I use the term to reflect the importance of maternal recognition of the child in the general sense outlined above.

10 There are clearly religious references in the piece, and I do not mean to suggest that my interpretation is definitive. The images of the closing doors may have been those referred to in a conversation between Beckett and the playwright Israel Schenker. Schenker relates how he spoke sadly to Beckett of his realization that an image he had used in some recent writing, of a door closing, had been accidentally borrowed from Beckett's writing. Beckett, according to

Schenker, pondered gently, and then said: 'Shit, I stole it from Dante m'self!' (*Waiting for Beckett*, BBC television, 1995, dir. John Reilly)

11 There are echoes of this in many places; in *Godot*, for example, the sending of the Boy functions as an opening door, and can be viewed both as sadistic, as well as kindly.

12 In this light, various 'expulsions' in Beckett (e.g. in 'The Expelled', *Watt*, and so forth) take on a certain meaning – there is a rejection by the inner world of the containing mother (within the self) and an expulsion into a rejecting, external world-mother.

13 Schmideberg reported the importance of clothing in serving a containing function for the child, and clothes serving such a function for a number of Beckettian characters, for whom clothes provide a shielding and containing function (Schmideberg, 1934: 245–64).

14 The sense of 'puzzlement' that engulfs the birds in this state of maternal disconnection can be seen in the tramps' confusion in *Waiting for Godot*, or in Watt's regression in *Watt*. It also often acts as a defence against overwhelming feelings of rage.

15 A patient brought this poem into analysis following the analyst's vacation. It was connected (by the patient) to a university lecturer who had discussed it in a class the patient had attended years before, whose nickname among the students was Dr Death (for his allegedly grim demeanour). It was only after the session had ended that the patient realized that he had experienced sadness during the analyst's silence in the session. He related this, in a later session, to a feeling of emotional starvation and internal death during the analyst's vacation.

16 See Kohut (1977: 181–2) for a self-psychological discussion of this Proustian search for a reparative maternal object.

17 Morrison (1982, 349–54) sees the speaker's story as a displacement from his own experience, which he cannot own, and that the 'rip' word reflects his evasion. I suggest the speaker is an aspect of the self that speaks of its own self-state in the monologue. The reason for the displacement is also evident in the sense of primary 'ripping' from the internal good mother. The 'ripping' also suggests the raging infantile response to the disconnection (much like Murphy's raging attack, see below), as well as its fear that the mother will respond violently.

2

No Endon sight: Murphy's misrecognition of love

Murphy, Beckett's first novel, centres on the title character's search for a tranquillity born of nothingness. A deeply schizoid, middle-aged man, Murphy lives in dire poverty and, when first encountered, has recently begun a relationship with Celia, a prostitute who wants them to begin a life together. He feels the world is hostile, offering him nothing but, at Celia's coaxing, he finds a job in a mental institution. Attracted to the erasure of reality he believes to exist within the schizophrenic mind, he is drawn to one patient, a Mr. Endon. Soon after imagining this man does not value him, Murphy dies in an explosion in his garret-room, leaving unanswered the question to what degree his death was a suicide. Some critics have examined the underlying philosophical themes of *Murphy*, a work rich in allusions to Descartes, Leibniz, and other early modern thinkers (e.g. Mintz, 1959, Morot-Sir, 1976, and Levy, 1980). It has also been read as satire (Kennedy, 1971) or comic parody (Kenner, 1961). This reading focuses specifically on the *experience* presented, viewing the narrative flow, the characters, and imagery as reflective of the narrative-self that organizes the fiction. Levy writes:

> The book, then, is concerned far less with Murphy as one character than with the construction of a closed narrative system everywhere reflecting the abandonment or absence on which it rests. Every element in the novel either reflects Murphy or reflects other elements, which in turn reflect Murphy [...] who is just a means of reflecting the experience of Nothing. The narrator has only to step forward, as he will in the later novels, and reveal that he has built this narrative system in order to reflect his own strange experience in it and thereby gain some expression of his identity. (Levy, 1980: 25)

This reading suggests the *narrative-self* is reflected everywhere, as in a dream or psychoanalytical session, and the 'text' is a manifestation of the self and its owned, and disowned, parts. In this sense, then, the narrative-self is *always* stepping forward. The fundamental experience that dominates the narrative-self, supplying the work's emotional force is, as Levy points out, abandonment and absence, but in a highly *specific* sense. At its heart, *Murphy* suggests an early experience of disconnection from the good mother, her containing love and her joy with her infant.

Speaking of *Waiting for Godot*, Beckett said 'If you want to find the origins of *En attendant Godot*, look at Murphy' (Duckworth, 1966: xiv). An aspect of this is the sense of completion Murphy seeks within the gaze of a maternal, containing object (though he mistakes his motive in this). Robinson (1969: 86) points out that the other major characters have an absolute dependency on Murphy, much as the tramps need Godot. The most glaring example of this is the elaborate sub-plot in which Miss Counihan, Neary, and their group, embroiled in a complex romantic and amorous melange, need to find Murphy to satiate their desires. Murphy functions, like Godot, as an object whose absence motivates and organizes the others' lives, but there is a more central function of their obsessive quest. Early experiences of maternal absence permeate the work's underlying emotional state, manifesting within Murphy as feelings of worthlessness, inadequacy and alienation.[1] The entire escapade to track Murphy down is a counterweight to this self-experience, as Murphy becomes an idealized object that must be possessed for others' happiness to be possible. This rights a depleted, despairing-self, and expresses a rage born out of neglect. It is now the *others* who cannot connect to the vitally needed Murphy, whose affirmation they require to secure happiness. Murphy, caught up in his own priorities, neglects them, reversing his *own* sense of primary abandonment, and in this way functions as a sort of proto-Godot, reflecting that part of the narrative-self that is abandoning and resentful itself.[2]

The organizational framework of this chapter will be the notions, outlined in the introduction, of the centrality of early experiences in the development of a secure inner world, which allows the self to engage others in a productive, living fashion. Levy writes that Beckett's fiction is preoccupied with self-consciousness. He wonders whether it is the self-consciousness of the 'artist trying to grasp his own creative act or [...] that of a person withdrawing form the world of others, either through insanity or sheer impotence' (Levy, 1980: 1). In *Murphy*, we see the answer to this question embraces it as a whole. The narrative-self, in speaking, *is* attempting to live, to restore a primal, maternal connection within itself. This *is* the most fundamental, primary act of life, which allows for later creativity, and is one that must be undertaken *within* the world of (m)others.

A room without a view

Murphy's opening line 'The sun shone, having no alternative, on the nothing new' (1) perfectly reflects the internal world of the title character, a closed, lifeless system. No authentic life or growth is possible in this world (i.e. nothing 'new under the sun'), since the sun loses its generative power in both a physical and emotional/metaphorical sense. Having 'no alternative', this source of all life becomes merely a mechanical servant of universal, meaningless laws. This feeling of hopelessness pervades Murphy himself, locked into this deterministic disconnection, living 'as though he were free' in a mew, where 'he had eaten, drunk, slept, and put his clothes on and off, in a medium-sized cage of north-western aspect, commanding an unbroken view of medium-sized cages of south-eastern aspect [...] for the mew had been condemned' (1). Murphy's lifestyle reflects the dehumanized, robotic essence of his internal experience, exposed here as repetitive and meaningless. The outer landscape reflects the dark cynicism that pervades Murphy's inner world – homes are reduced to 'cages' that are part of the same dismal, monadic world of lifeless others. This imagery is reminiscent of a passage in Klein, where she describes the mourning process of a patient, Mrs A., who had recently lost her son:

> In the second week of her mourning Mrs A. found some comfort in looking at some nicely situated houses in the country, and in wishing to have such a house of her own. However, this comfort was soon interrupted by bouts of despair and sorrow. She now cried abundantly, and found relief in tears. The solace she found in looking at houses came from her rebuilding her inner world in her fantasy [... and in] getting satisfaction from the knowledge that other people's houses and good objects existed. Ultimately this stood for her re-creating her good parents, internally and externally. (Klein, 1988a: 358)

Unlike Mrs A., Murphy cannot experience the re-integration that comes from mourning. His internal world does not contain any enduring good objects – all the houses that surround him are crumbling, his condemned flat itself can be seen as the body/mind of a damaged internal mother, failing to contain him. He has no sense of connection to a good mother (there is no mention in the novel of any actual experience with a loving maternal presence). He is, in effect, an emotional orphan (there is only a vague and mysterious relative, a Godot-like figure, who supplies Murphy with minimal sustenance). Whereas for Klein's patient the houses represent an experience of reparation, restoration, and re-connection to a loving internal presence, these opening landscapes reveal Murphy's barren, decaying inner world and its connection to his primary struggle to connect to life.

In 'The Calmative', these symbolic aspects of houses recur: the narrator wanders, towards the end of the piece, through dark, deserted city streets as an outcast in search of peaceful anonymity. His gait, 'slow, stiff [...] at every step solv[ing] a stato-dynamic problem never posed before' suggests his rigid adhesion to life in a world where change is difficult, and recognition unlikely: 'I would have been known again (i.e. by the gait), if I had been known' (75). Stopping in front of a butcher's shop he sees a tableau that reflects a dying part of the self, 'the dim carcasses of gutted horses hanging from the hooks head downwards', and he tries to retreat into nothingness by 'hug[ging] the walls, famished for shadow' (75).[3] He fails to call to mind memories of a woman who had some affection for him, but a little girl appears within the building, and he sees her long enough 'to try and have her smile, but she did not smile, but vanished down the staircase without having yielded me her little face' (75). Excluded from a loving interaction with the child, he represents a withdrawn part of the narrative-self, yearning for contact, perhaps with his own infantile-self (represented by the child).[4] Alone, feeling shunned, he has to stop, propping himself up against a house, where he feels nothing, then slowly: 'a kind of massive murmur [...] That reminded me that the houses were full of people, besieged, no, I don't know [...] many of the rooms were lit [...] the sound was not continuous, but broken by silences possibly of consternation. I thought of ringing at the door and asking for protection till morning. But suddenly I was on my way again' (76). The narrator, deflated by his failure to connect with the child, suddenly experiences a connection to the house, itself symbolic of the (m)other's inner world. He is 'reminded' that houses are for people, and so they become, as they fail to become for Murphy, full of hope and the possibility of engagement. There is another thought – the house/person is 'besieged' (a reflection of the narrator's own internal state of alienation from a loving internal presence), and there may be alarm within the house, a result, perhaps, of his *own* presence at the door. This scene demonstrates the dynamics within the narrative-self: depletion due to a lack of internal goodness, feelings of longing for others, and a sense that others see the self as dangerous, unworthy of contact. The narrator is enlivened by his engagement with the house-that-is-other and, walking along, becomes more aware of the living world, admiring the bright colors of other house-minds, with their beautiful, varied windows, eyes that see and are seen. This is a yearning for a connection to the world and, more fundamentally, for an enriched internal universe that, like the houses, might be filled with light and love. This narrator re-enters the space where Murphy resides, lying ignored, he is walked over on the street, and 'reality' comes back to him as he drifts into a 'blinding void' (76) of lonely disconnection.

Murphy's initial presentation reflects this predicament: he is encountered strapped into a rocking chair of 'undressed teak, guaranteed not to crack, warp, shrink, corrode, or creak at night' (1). It is a secure, reliable object that never leaves him, functioning as the only thing that can soothe him by allowing freedom from persecutory torments. It is a *maternal* object, but one infused with an autistic aura, he is securely held by the chair (as a child would be held by a mother), strapping himself in when the world becomes too overwhelming and frightening. The chair is not a person, however, but primarily a defensive escape, the rocking less akin to the calming sways a child experiences at the breast than to the self-contained rhythms of the autistic child. Like such a child, Murphy rejects the world:

> Somewhere a cuckoo-clock [...] became the echo of a street cry [...] These were sights and sounds that he did not like. They detained him in the world to which they belonged, but not he, as he fondly hoped. (2)

> Slowly the world died down, the big world where [...] the light never waned the same way twice, in favour of the little [...] where he could love himself. (6-7)

> Slowly, he felt better, astir in his mind, in the freedom of that light and dark that did not clash nor alternate, nor fade and lighten. (9)

Sensations become hostile persecutors for Murphy, he cannot experience the goodness to which Klein's patient reawakens as she overcomes her depression through re-connection to her good internal objects. Murphy is only alive in his mind, where he can love himself, striving to disengage from life. This is, perhaps, a manifestation of the death instinct, a hatred of life itself, exemplified by his mentor, Neary, who could willingly stop his heart, withdrawing from the world particularly at those very moments when desire was at its height.[5] One of the anguishes of the 'big world' is clearly its foundation on change, 'the light [that] never waned the same way twice' – the world is incapable of creating a sense of ongoing goodness, it is dangerous and unpredictable.

This is opposed to the changeless 'little world' where there is no 'fad[ing] nor lighten[ing]', and this suggests a Paranoid Schizoid attitude, where there is freedom from ambivalence within the 'light and dark that did not clash'. The isolated 'room' part of Murphy's mind becomes paradoxical, as it does for all Beckettian characters – it is a sanctuary from a hostile world, but it also protects that world from the rage of its inhabitant. It imposes an imprisoning loneliness predicated on opposing views – on the one hand, one does not love and is therefore unlovable and, on the other, that one is unlovable and has no hope of having love accepted. Murphy returns repeatedly to his 'little world', for only there is a feeling of being loved, and loving, possible. The highly intellectualized reasoning that provides alternative motivations for withdrawal remains subordinate to this core need that Murphy, and all Beckettian characters, share with humankind.

Murphy's only true obstacle to total psychic withdrawal is Celia's love for him, and *his* embryonic love for her.[6] The small room they rent from Miss Clarridge, to begin their new life, has an exquisite floor that delights Murphy, and 'Celia because it delighted Murphy' (63); Celia, like a good mother, shares Murphy's inherent joy, making it her own. The room symbolizes Murphy's failing engagement with life; at one point, Celia sits within it, waiting for him to return, rocking in his chair:

> There was not much light, the room devoured it, but she kept her face turned to what there was [...] it was never quiet in the room, but brightening and darkening in a slow ample flicker that went on all day, brightening against the darkening that was its end. A peristalsis of light, worming its way into the dark.
>
> She preferred sitting in the chair, steeping herself in these faint eddies till they made an amnion about her own disquiet. (67)[7]

The light suggests a life-force in constant, wavering engagement with death and darkness, it is a sense of contact with a loving mother who brings her infant into the world with attentive, nurturing care as a sun that shines on the something new. There are complex non-engagements, since the room, with its living and dying lights, reflects both the schizoid nature of Murphy's inner world and of Celia's isolation, as well as their intersection in an interpersonal space where their experiences meet. A light of life is 'worming its way into the dark' – this is Celia's love for Murphy, her wish to help him love her, himself, and perhaps a child.[8] Celia has entered Murphy's darkened room, disrupting him by generating a conflict: to love and lose his total control, to risk a devastating, re-traumatizing disappointment, or to die. Sitting in a darkened room, in his chair, she is in touch with her own struggle to go on living in a world where she has no one, save for a crumbling grandfather and, perhaps, Murphy. Her love, willingly offered, is devoured by Murphy in his love-hunger, just as the room 'devours' the containing light as she sits in it, quietly waiting. These changing lights make 'an amnion about her own disquiet', which somehow gives her, like Murphy, a sense of primary intra-uterine holding, allowing her to understand and fear a world where life has become 'an end to a means' (67). She realizes Murphy may be lost to her, that his 'light' will not 'worm' its way into her world, because of his assertion that to move forward with her would destroy him. Sitting in his chair, Celia is drawn to the final retreat that Murphy seeks, but refuses it, since for her it is her beloved himself, the possibility of a relation with another, that makes the choice of life possible. Celia and Murphy are twinned, but she resists a complete regression from life, while Murphy, as a despairing part of the narrative-self, sinks away from the world into a fantasy of connection, the meaning of which he does not recognize.

Get thee to the chandlery

The novel's early imagery (i.e. the enclosed rooms, fading lights, and decaying world) suggests an experience of disconnection from core, good internal objects, as does Celia's desperation to connect to an elusive other. However, the novel expresses more than a retreat into despair, as Murphy clearly attempts engagement with the world. He was born under a bad sign: the obstetrician knew, as he cried for the first time, that he was not meant for this world: 'the infant Murphy was off the note [...] His rattle will make amends' (71). Life is a cursed undertaking; even at birth Murphy is out of harmony and alone, but there is a defensive quality to this alienation, it makes Murphy special, an attitude found in those seeing themselves uniquely tortured by 'bad fate'. Yet, to a degree perhaps unappreciated, Murphy does not go down without a fight: 'The only thing Murphy was seeking was [...] the best of himself' (71). It is hidden, but Murphy does seek engagement despite an overwhelming feeling the attempt will lead to ridicule. His reliance on the magic of Suk notwithstanding (he will not act without the grace of this astrologer[9]) and prompted, at the very least, by his sexual need for Celia, he seeks a job – this crucial act demonstrates, to some degree, an attempt to change. A patient, Mr B., avoided engagement with the world by not working. Like Murphy, there was fear (and a possibility) of ridicule, for Mr B. had not worked for many years, and accepting a low-level position was humiliating. Working also meant engagement with a changing, unpredictable world and, like Murphy, this man hated change, which he felt is always for the worse. He also sought absolute guarantees, which were possible only if the world did exactly as *he* wanted. Finally, a job meant a deepening commitment, on a genital level, to his partner and, as for Murphy, this opened his deepest fears of abandonment and engulfment. Murphy, however, overcomes these feelings, attempting to placate Celia and engage life, but on the 'jobpath' he experiences a humiliation that enrages and shames him. 'Stalking about London in a green suit' (73) he looks ridiculous and out of place, the suit encasing him in airless isolation: it was 'entirely non-porous. It admitted no air from the outer world, it allowed none of Murphy's own vapours to escape' (72). It is an enclosing second skin, containing him, holding his fragile self together, as it holds his body like an exoskeleton. He faces the world armoured, protected within its concrete-like rigidity, but it also prevents the circulation of life from entering, forestalling any genuine contact by acting as a hard shell/autistic barrier that only allows detached experience. This is reminiscent of a patient who would don expensive clothes to shield against imagined attacks by the world. He felt rage, projected this outward, believing his 'suit of armour' would protect and camouflage him. The containing function of Murphy's suit is condensed: the vapours it encases suggests a self feeling threatened by dissolution into the world, a sense of contained hostility *towards* the world (i.e. the vapours as a stench, such as Miss Clarridge gives off), as well as a feeling of being disgusting to others. Primarily, it serves a protective function, containing Murphy's own rage, a sort of straight jacket that holds him physically and psychically, preventing an eruption of violence that will kill the world/mother, leaving him alone. Murphy is as afraid of killing the world as of being killed by it: his cutting, devaluing humour, and his passive, sadistic toying with Celia, are as much muted manifestations of the rage within as they are defensive manoeuvres to fend off his dread of dependency.

Murphy's one sincere attempt at engagement is pivotal, occurring when he decides to leave the ambivalent margins of life. He nervously presents for the position of 'smart-boy' at the chandlery rather than 'expos[ing] himself vaguely in aloof able-bodied postures on the fringes of the better-attended slave markets' (76–7). A re-enactment of early trauma follows this initiative, making clear the genesis of his internal withdrawal:

> The chandlers all came galloping out to see the smart boy.
> ''E ain't smart,' said the chandler, 'not by a long chork 'e ain't.'
> 'Nor 'e ain't a boy,' said the chandler's semi-private convenience, 'not to my mind 'e ain't.'
> ''E don't look rightly human to me,' said the chandlers' eldest waste product, 'not rightly.' (77)

The narrative-self reveals its ambivalence, identifying with *both* Murphy *and* the chandlers. Sadism is directed at Murphy who, though frightened and withdrawn, comes out of his shell to take a chance on life and love (he subtly undermines any chance of this, of course). The chandlers mock him by metaphorically dis-naming him: he is *not* smart, he is *not* a boy, and he is *not* human. Ms A., a patient who felt her mother held a deep, envious hatred of her attempts to engage life, presented a dream that reflects a similar experience: *she had tied her mother down and wrote on her (i.e. the mother's) body in an indelible ink: 'I am not stupid, I am not speechless, I am able to think' over and over again.* This patient legally changed her name several times, attempting to disidentify with her past, to separate from her internal mother's envy and from her own rage and depression. In the dream, the same mechanisms operate as in the chandler exchange, where Murphy's humanity is dis-named. Ms A., in her dream, reverses this dis-naming by writing on her internal attacker, expressing her rage, making clear what she *is* – in complementary fashion the narrative-self *also* takes Murphy's side: rage is directed at the chandlers, for *they* are named as inhuman (i.e. a 'semi-private convenience' and a 'waste product'). The narrative-self undoes their slurs, revealing an empathic closeness and affection for Murphy. This ongoing dialectic is central to the Beckettian world ('It is a quick death. It is not'), where life cannot be fully engaged because of a fear both of retaliation, and of one's outwardly directed rage. The boundaries blur in this passage: the narrative-self feels tortured, as Murphy does, but it *also* tortures him, as do the chandlers. The door to life locks after this episode: having nervously 'presented' himself he faces a universe where there is 'nothing to be done' that can change his sense of alienation. His rejection is a re-enactment of disconnections from goodness that have led him to develop as a schizoid, raging recluse. It seems Murphy expects no less, being 'too familiar with this attitude of derision tinged with loathing to make the further blunder of trying to abate it' (77). He accepts himself as an object of ridicule, feeling there is no point challenging this internalized perception. It is an identification with the aggressor that develops from early ruptures in primary bonds, becoming in later years a 'cold, cruel world' that is a monadic, despising other. It engenders and justifies retreat to the small spaces, the rooms, where there is no chance of attack, no reason to fear one's desire to exert a catastrophic counter-attack that would leave one all, all alone.

This confrontation with harsh, ridiculing aspects of the early psyche leaves Murphy exhausted and confused, looking for somewhere to sit, but 'there was nowhere' (77). He is trapped in the space of 'neither', no longer in the 'big' world, not yet safely withdrawn into the 'little' one either: 'There had once been a small public garden [...] now part of it lay buried under one of those malignant proliferations of urban tissue known as service flats and the rest was reserved for the bacteria' (77). This statement demonstrates the change in Murphy's internal world: the character and narrative-self blur as the garden, a symbol of life and growth, a place where Murphy presumably would have found sanctuary and maternal containment, is gone, there can be no place for him in the world. It is dead and 'buried', just as Murphy's sense of goodness is destroyed, replaced by a cancer (*both* a manifestation of a hostile world *and* his own rage) devouring the beauty of the landscape. This is central to the underlying self-state of the oeuvre: it is reflected in the barren landscapes of *Godot*, the 'zero', ashen world in *Endgame*, the 'mud' of *How It Is*, and the grey worlds of the later plays. There is a connection between this central self-state, its manifestation in Murphy and one type of experience that engenders it: an aggressive, devaluing attack by the other, which mirrors a self-loathing, and sets off a vicious circle of rage, fear, withdrawal, and despair. After realizing there is 'nowhere' for him, Murphy yearns 'for five minutes in his chair' (78), and to be in an:

> embryonal repose, looking down at dawn across the reeds to the trembling of the austral sea and the sun obliquing to the north as it rose, immune from expiation until he should have dreamed it all through again, with the downright dreaming of an infant, from the spermarium to the crematorium. [...] he actually hoped he might live to be old. Then he would have a long time there dreaming [...] before the toil up hill to Paradise. (78)

The anguish of life drives Murphy to '[this] most highly systematized [fantasy]' (78), which operates as a psychic retreat, a secluded, separate part of his self-experience where he can relish it 'just beyond the frontiers of suffering, it was the first landscape of freedom' (78). The fantasy is triggered by his decaying inner landscape – on the one hand he yearns for a sort of re-birth, dreaming with the possibilities of the infant, yet this infant's experience is deadened and condensed, as it collapses into a brief ride from 'the spermarium to the crematorium'. The inner struggle of life and death continues: he wishes to live long, even in the hell he inhabits, so that he can longer enjoy the respite of watching his life in a 'post-mortem situation', seemingly less tortured, but no less isolated and despairing than that of *Play* or *The Unnamable*. His refusal to accept a 'good prayer' by a 'godly chandler' (78), which might shorten this ambivalent state, highlights his loneliness. The chandlers' importance in triggering this whole sequence is clear: Murphy devises a counterpart to their badness, reflecting the infant's primal sense of the world-as-mother split into two halves, the good and the bad. Now so filled with hate he cannot engage either, his ultimate journey to Paradise will be difficult, the hill is of an outrageous gradient.

The chandler-experience is a central one, reflecting the core psychological state of the narrative-self, ambivalent about engaging the world. At the centre of this storm of self-devaluation and rage, Murphy feels weak and defeated, wishing for the autistic security of his mother-chair, so he can 'cease to take notice and enter the landscapes where there were no chandlers and no exclusive residential cancers' (79). The chandlers become the symbolic representatives of the primal bad object, reactivated by his real rejection, they now persecute him as horrible, sadistic beings that inhabit a cancerous, Murphy-killing world. He must escape these diseased inner landscapes to a place, a psychic retreat, where he can be alone with 'only himself improved out of all knowledge' (79) – that is, his *specific* knowledge of a painful, unloving world, and his corresponding rage and depression.

Crying over cowjuice

After leaving the chandlers, Murphy attempts to repair his damaged, disorganized internal world through a re-enactment of early nurturing. He decides against visiting a park, which would 'reek of death' (mirroring his internal state almost hallucinogenically), or a return home, for fear of disappointing Celia. He feels the only solution is to eat his lunch, 'more than an hour before he was due to salivate' (79), a Pavlovian allusion that reveals the mechanistic nature of his internal world. Lunch is a daily 'ritual vitiated by no base thoughts of nutrition' (80), functioning as a complex drama through which he enacts internal struggles centered on early disconnection. Feeling undeserving, Murphy believes he must steal from the world to get anything at all; the theft must be *secretive*, to avoid a destructive counter-attack. His choice of the arena of food and drink to wage this battle is not surprising – it is through nurturing the infant first feels the goodness of the world-mother, and begins to believe it contains goodness within itself, as the good feed. It makes exquisite sense for Murphy to turn to a food ritual at a time of deepest self-disorganization and despair, when he feels the emptiest. Advancing into his seat at the diner, he enjoys the sensation of being touched since '[he] did not so often meet with these tendernesses that he could afford to treat them casually' (80), and this rare 'caress' helps him slip back into an early state of mind. Murphy can only experience this 'caress' through inanimate objects, like his chair or this stool, being fundamentally disconnected from a loving sense of touch, though he appears to experience his sexuality with Celia as moving dangerously in this direction. Seated, he begins a primal re-enactment with the mother – feeling unloved, he feels unreal: 'The waitress stood before, with an air of such abstraction that he did not feel entitled to regard himself as an element in her situation' (80). The actual waitress/mother's lack of interest reflects early disruptions in the mother/infant bond that have generated Murphy's withdrawal, he must steal from this withholding, uninterested mother to exact revenge on his past, as well as on a world whose abusiveness he experiences in the present. He seduces the waitress with scientific charm: it is *she* who is now seen by *him* as inhuman, a mere object upon which he can apply the behaviourist theories of the 'Kulpe school' (80). *She* becomes the victim, the inhuman target of dehumanizing slurs, with Murphy-as-chandler now in the active role. He manipulates her into giving him a free cup of tea by claiming he had ordered 'China' not 'Indian', getting it refilled with hot water by saying: 'I know that I am a great nuisance, but they have been too generous with the cowjuice' (83). Murphy reorganizes his shattered self by stealing, without detection, from the mother: 'No waitress could hold out against their mingled overtones of gratitude and mammary organs [i.e. the words 'generous' and 'cowjuice']' (83). His awareness of the way to this woman's heart reveals a raging need to exact revenge on a stand-in in this primal re-enactment, a mother unable to resist a 'grateful' child who stirs up her own feelings of love and nurturing. He deceptively subverts her anger, as she becomes an early 'waitress-mother' who suppresses feelings of exploitation by a needy, ever demanding newborn that fails to recognize her as an independent being, but merely as someone there to *wait* on him. The following clinical vignette demonstrates a similar experience:

> Ms F., a university student, was in analysis to deal with a severely self-critical attitude and bulimia. She once described a ritual she conducted every Monday morning before classes. Entering a local café, she would order a cappuccino, and since she was a favourite of the young male waiters she became automatically 'upgraded': they would give her a large instead of a medium coffee, or a larger cup for more foamed milk. She felt awkward about these episodes, since she acted manipulatively in order to get special treatment. On another level she felt the extra coffee or milk was of fundamental importance, because she believed she could never get enough from the world, and it was only through seductiveness or trickery that she could get enough to survive. This echoed her feelings towards both her parents, especially her mother, whom she felt had implanted this notion in her as a means to keep her close.

This woman's world-view approximates Murphy's, her morning class acting in a chandler-like fashion, since she felt the other students mocked her fundamental unworthiness. The extra coffee functioned to 'fill her up', creating a reversal; it also allowed a feeling of connection to a nurturing mother (in the form of the waiters), though one she had to seduce and rob.

Murphy's reversal of the chandlers' sadism changes his self state: he feels better about himself and his prospects, having gone from being a passive victim to a manipulator by 'defraud[ing]' a 'vested interest' (84), but his sense of himself as an outsider who must steal remains and he feels hated by the world. At this point, a job at the psychiatric hospital becomes a possibility for Murphy, and he feels he can become special and valuable, but only by fulfilling a pre-ordained retreat from life. At a critical juncture, he hovers between life and death, closing his eyes he is "in an archaic world [...] he tried to think of Celia's face [...] but his skull felt packed with gelatine and he could not think of anything' (95). This archaic world is both pre-verbal and deeply withdrawn, Murphy has trouble connecting to the living one, his ability to engage his good internal object (i.e. Celia/mother) is impaired, and his cognitive functions are destroyed. Those forces that operate within him to kill life are ascending, derailing any possibility that his employment can be a rewarding move towards life and love. At the park, Murphy settles down to enjoy one of his few pleasures, the eating of his biscuits, and this meal becomes another attempt to reconnect to primal feelings of nurturing. His usual habit, of eating his favourite first, his least favourite last, seems strangely inadequate, and only by being 'free' enough to eat the five cookies in any of the one hundred and twenty possible random combinations will stop his 'violat[ion of] the very essence of the assortment' (96). This erasure of desire, manifested as his preference for differing biscuits, furthers his flight from life and, as the ability to choose is lost, all 'under the sun' becomes wooden and without uniqueness. The joy of his original sequence (eating his favourite first) was balanced by the displeasure of eating the least favourite last, and by the banality of the intervening 'indifferents'. In this choosing, Murphy was energized by an engagement with possibility, but in his deepening withdrawal there can be no difference to stir his inner fires as the infantile experience of favouring foods is lost.[10] A deformed woman, Miss Dew, arrives to feed the sheep that wander in the park; these animals 'were a miserable-looking lot, dingy, close-cropped, undersized and misshapen. They were not cropping, they were not ruminating, they did not even seem to be taking their ease. They simply stood, in an attitude of profound dejection, their heads bowed, swaying slightly as though dazed. Murphy had never seen stranger sheep, they seemed one and all on the point of collapse' (99–100). These pathetic creatures symbolize Murphy's own feeling-state; like the woman who would feed them, they are deformed outcasts on the world's margin, prefiguring the patients with whom Murphy will soon be in contact. Deeply depressed, they 'turn their broody heads aside from the emetic, bringing them back into alignment as soon as it passed from them' (100). Nutrition, seen here as poison (i.e. 'emetic'), loses its ability to nurture, both physically, and as an experience that connects to loving maternal relations. This is reminiscent of a bulimic patient who said that her purging made her feel strong, allowing her to punish herself (for a variety of fantastic failures) by symbolically aborting life from within her body. Miss Dew, as good mother, hopes to feed these hapless creatures, whose rejection of nutrition is reminiscent of severely depressed infants. Murphy sees things differently, being 'absorbed […] in the ecstatic demeanour of the sheep' (100), and the animals' emaciated stoicism is an encouraging confirmation of his attitude. He employs a manic defence to counter his rejection by the chandlers: he denies his own despair, as well as the clear anguish of the sheep, he devalues Miss Dew's attempt to bring joy to herself and the animals, and he solidifies his position of triumph over a hostile world by identifying with the sheep, whom he idealizes as heroically sensible in their withdrawal (as he will do with the psychiatric patients). There is an underlying rationalization – it is clearly better never to have been born or, having been born, to protect oneself with a denial of one's rage and despair with a slow move towards death. But the sheep *are* Murphy, and Miss Dew *is* Celia, and this scene represents a lost opportunity to experience the world's goodness – the reality that love *is* available – because one's inner world is held hostage by malevolent and attacking monsters, and this is despair in its coldest form.[11]

Even in so hopeless a despair, Murphy cannot fail to be warmed by such a pure, selfless love. He continues to sit, speculating on Miss Dew and the sheep, trying to relate the incident to his own feelings for Celia: 'In vain. The freedom of indifference, the indifference of freedom, the will dust in the dust of its object, the act a handful of sand let fall [...] all was nebulous and dark, a murk of irritation from which no spark could be excoriated' (104–5). His mind is a torrent of ambivalence, he is locked in a struggle between life and death. Celia's love throws a spanner into the works, jolting his emotional and cognitive templates of the world as hostile and unloving, challenging his fatalism. Indifference is his theme, a withdrawal from the choices that fuel life and give it meaning – no cookie is different from any other, we are all misshapen sheep waiting for death in a cold and will-less world with no real possibility of authentic relations, our will merely 'dust in the dust of [our] object' (105). The possibility of change is too much for Murphy – his ability to give meaning to the world is disabled, his ability to be excited, 'sparked', is extinguished. He moves away from life, into himself, and away from 'the gross importunities of sensation and reflection' (105). He has been 'unavoidably detained' in the world, but 'nothing can stop him now [...] nothing did turn up to stop him and he slipped away [...] from Celia, chandlers, public highways, etc., from Celia, buses, public gardens, etc., to where there were no pensums and no prizes, but only Murphy himself, improved out of all knowledge' (105). The world does not intervene – it fails him in this way – there is no caress to hold Murphy, but he is still rife with ambivalence, for as he slips from external sensations into his internal world, he is orbited (as the Unnamable will be in his own time by Murphy himself) by representations of key persons and symbolic places. Celia, the most important figure in his world, drawing him out with love and caring, is mentioned twice, as if she is invested with more feeling, and so is harder to be free of. The chandlers are there, as hard in their own way to leave, in that they, as the bad mother, represent the mocking of a world he hates, but also wishes to seduce. His buses are there, and long rides he cherishes (for Murphy, being human, *is* capable of joy), as are the public gardens, maternal places where he feel safe (when they are not destroyed by a cancerous world). It is from this inner conflict, this struggle of good and bad, of loving and hating, that Murphy must withdraw, for to engage it means to confront emotions he cannot tolerate. The intensity of love is overwhelming, he experiences it as a compliant dependence, leading to an abandonment that *must* lead to a raging destruction of a needed person. His need for Celia leads him to expose himself to the chandlers, and it is their ridicule, emblematic of a mocking world, that mirrors his feelings of unworthiness. Murphy opts to retreat from this cold and vicious circle – to love is to be failed is to hate is to kill is to be alone. Better to be alone from the start and spare oneself the suffering.

A metaphor of mind

The sixth chapter of the novel is an exposition of Murphy's 'mind', or rather, and most importantly, his *fantasy* of mind: 'what it *felt* and pictured itself to be' (107, italics mine). It is important to recognize the fantasy nature of this exposition (although Murphy experiences it as real and inevitable), and how it supports the notion of a rupture between his core self and primary object. As a symbolic representation of his own experience, Murphy's mind becomes a place structured by his relationship to the world. That Murphy's 'mind' can step back and have such a self-experience means the fantasy is not inevitable, but open to deconstruction and change. The unfortunate consequence of Murphy's schizoid withdrawal is that he so idealizes the fantasy (and the world it requires) that no alternatives exist. Again, there is defensive self-aggrandizement, he becomes *too* unique for the world *because* of his alienation.

Murphy's picture of his mind operates as a manic defence, allowing an escape from the devastating depression of interacting with a complete world, where the *same* people, particularly Celia, are both loved and hated. Murphy's mind 'pictured itself as a large hollow sphere, hermetically closed to the universe without [...] [n]othing ever had been, was or would be in the universe outside it but was already present as virtual, or actual, or virtual rising into the actual, or actual

falling into the virtual, in the universe inside it' (107). Fantasizing in this
way, Murphy escapes depression and rage, by closing off a world he
believes cannot love him. He denies that anything has been lost (he is
not 'impoverished') since he contains the entire world, completely
under his control, effecting a triumph over it. External reality is lost, as
the 'virtual' (i.e. wishful fantasy) and the 'actual' are collapsed. What is
also lost, however, is the possibility of growth, change, and surprise, for
this inner world is lit by the dead sun. There is no possibility of altering
external reality, which simply reflects an already known inner world –
the chandlers merely confirm what *must* be. Further elaboration of this
fantasy 'mind' suggests a genesis within a core experience of unworthiness, depression and rage: 'There was a mental fact and there was a
physical fact [...] he distinguished between the actual and the virtual of
his mind [...] thus the form of kick was actual, that of caress virtual'
(108). This is Murphy's central psychic reality: he retreats to an *idealized*
inner world, aspiring to a deeper, thoughtless realm with no possibility
of personal experience or selfhood. He accepts the reality of this inner
world, with its one unalterably privileged fact: experience of the
physical world, of external reality, can never be as pleasant as the
experience of the inner. This feeling of independence is an illusion, one
he does not recognize, which ultimately rests on an idealized internal
object – a good mother that will become manifest in the person of
Endon. The inner world cannot come into being without an interaction
with external reality, and what Murphy believes is inner freedom is
really a response to a *particular* experience of reality – where the mental
meets the physical is the 'kick', or the experience of the aggressive
retaliation of the chandlers. This is 'actual', Murphy's basic organizing
principle, his way of experiencing the world, and it contrasts with the
'virtual' experiences he knows only through fantasy. The 'caress'
(feelings of being held, contained, or loved), which has at its root the
mingling of the needs of the child and the selfless devotion of the
mother, has not been part of Murphy's 'actual' experience – with this
schism in operation he retreats inwards to search for the reparation of a
loving relationship, something he has been unable to attain with his
mother, the chandlers, Endon, and, sadly, has been unable to accept
from Celia.

The organization of Murphy's subjective universe is clear: the world
outside his control will 'kick', mock, abandon, and reject him; in fantasy
he yearns for 'a Supreme Caress', but without a sense of internal good
he cannot evoke this experience by himself, and takes the further step

of complete withdrawal: 'His mind was a closed system, subject to no principle of change but its own, self-sufficient and impermeable to the vicissitudes of the body' (109). This enclosure protects him from expected disappointment, but also destroys the opportunity to bring in the good experience that creates self-value, something which could change his ability to interact, by making the 'actual' world amenable to further good experience. There is a metaphorical exposition of this frozen, unchangeable schizoid state:

> [O]ne part of him never left this mental chamber [...] because there was no way out. But motion in this world depended on rest in the world outside. A man is in bed, wanting to sleep. A rat is behind the wall at his head, wanting to move. The man hears the rat fidget and cannot sleep, the rat hears the man fidget and dares not move. They are both unhappy, one fidgeting and the other waiting, or both happy, the rat moving and the man sleeping. (110)

This echoes other passages – Murphy's non-engagement with Celia's love, and the chess-encounter with Endon, where there is an inverse relationship of desire and avoidance. It encapsulates a key relational experience: a sense of invasiveness, with one party's existence impinging on the being of the other. It is a paradoxical dilemma at the heart of the schizoid constellation – a child who feels its mother does not experience it as separate, and who feels treated, alternatively, as a desperately needed part of her, leading to an overwhelming sense of invasiveness, and then, when not needed, as dispensable, creating a feeling of abandonment (the mother, of course, may experience early relations with the infant in exactly the same manner). It is an immobile inner world reminiscent of a Chinese-handcuff that closes tighter regardless of which finger one tries to withdraw. The man grows to know the rat, and vice versa, to expect its movement in an entwined symbiosis that leads to non-movement and waiting. This is apparent throughout the oeuvre: with Vladimir and Estragon awaiting a man who will not come while they are waiting, or with Watt 'tied' himself to a bell that his master will ring – a rat in his own head. There is a tone of persecution, an atmosphere of encased slavery: of the server and the served, but who is who? Clov and Hamm, the tramps and Godot, May and her mother, the men who come and the man who writes in a room, all are variants on the rat and the sleeper, but who is the enslaved? The answer is both, and neither: it is a schizoid, enmeshed form of dependency, where waiting means 'waiting on' in a dependent, fearful servitude in the anticipation of love and recognition. With whom is Murphy identified with in this passage? – with *both* the man and the rat, for each perceives himself as the persecuted, but each is also the persecutor. The following clinical vignette provides a perspective on this, and the notion that within Murphy there exists a dominant anticipatory relationship that reflects an earlier relationship that shapes his current experience:

> Mr C. had a history of violent physical and emotional abuse by his father; as an adult he would spend his time within his room, sleeping, or watching television. He remembered (in connection to my interpretation that his untidy room reflected a painful, disorganized inner world) that as a child he would hide in his room, a sanctuary from his father. He had protected himself from painful feelings as well, by building an inner, hidden room that could also protect his father from his own rage. He was locked in an inner experience where he was bad, and needed to hide to escape punishment (his father's attacks), but also protected his father from his own rage by becoming imprisoned himself, in a physical jail (his adult room), and an internal one (by being unable to experience his depression and rage). Mr C. developed raging fantasies, and feared he would end up in a real prison. He recalled his work as a prison guard, in which he occasionally would be aggressive with prisoners. He accepted he was his own jailer – his real room was a metaphor for his internal experience, of the need to hide a living part of himself away from his internal father, who embodied all of the memories of early abuse and violence. Paradoxically, the room was a container and a sanctuary for his disrupted sense of himself, but also a prison, protecting *both* him *and* the world from violent destruction.[12]

This vignette relates both to *Murphy*, and to the oeuvre as a whole. Murphy, like Mr C., fears the world, feeling attacked by it – he hides within an internal room, as much to protect himself as to protect it. Like the rat, he is small and powerless in the face of the tyrannical father/sleeper, but like the sleeper, he is imprisoned in a room, anxious because of an unseen, invasive intruder.

Murphy cherishes the freedom to move among the treasures of his mind's three zones, which reveal a fantasy life predicated on rage and deprivation. In the first zone 'the elements of physical experience [were] available for a new arrangement' (111). The pleasure here is 'reprisal, the pleasure of reversing the physical experience. Here the kick that the physical Murphy received, the mental Murphy gave. It was the same kick, but corrected as to direction. Here the chandlers were available for slow depilation, Miss Clarridge for rape by Ticklepenny, and so on' (111). Experience becomes compartmentalized, this initial psychic retreat is dominated by reversal or revenge, as Murphy copes with the world by turning passive experiences into active ones. This is a classic Freudian defence (demonstrated by Mr C.'s becoming a prison guard to reverse his own early experience) and Murphy controls the world in imagination by turning his experience of the world-as-'physical fiasco' into a fantasy of 'howling success' (111). This psychic retreat is a fantasy playroom, similar to those discovered by Klein in her work with small children. When allowed to play uninterrupted with toys children would use them, on occasion, to enact wildly violent dramas often involving parental figures, and Klein concluded these dramas were enactments of the child's inner world. The first zone of Murphy's 'mind' is a Kleinian playground where he moves objects into postures and combinations that reverse perceived attacks: 'the light contained the docile elements of a new manifold, the world of the body broken up into the pieces of a toy' (111). The world is fragmented into fantasized parts, which Murphy manipulates and, like Klein's children, these sadistic fantasies have a vibrant reality. They shape his anticipated experience of new encounters: Murphy, it will be remembered, *anticipates* ridicule by the chandlers in his dress and general attitude, shaping his world as much as he is shaped by it.

In the second zone, pleasure is contemplation – Murphy still experiences a sense of self, feeling 'sovereign and free' to move from one 'beatitude to another' (112). It functions to counterbalance the sadistic fantasies of the first zone: in this fantasy space, all is (not)-chandler, and all is good, or 'states of peace'. It is in the third zone ('the dark'), with its fantasies of self-annihilation, that Murphy feels most at home, '[all] was a flux of forms, a perpetual coming together and falling asunder of forms [...] neither elements nor states, nothing but forms becoming and crumbling into the fragments of a new becoming, without love or hate or any intelligible principle of change. Here there was nothing but commotion' (112). Murphy fantasizes ultimate freedom, alone and protected from the dark forces of life, but even here does not give up on the world. The descriptions of this zone imply a fantasized pre-cognitive space, without thought, beyond the pain of reality. It is also a pre-emotional space, without love and hate, without states of mind of any kind, a realm of pure potential without commitment. It is beyond engagement with the world, and so, paradoxically a place of death, though here Murphy feels most alive and safe, a 'mote in the dark of absolute freedom' (112). He clings to 'being-ness' while moving close to self-annihilation: 'He did not move, he was a point in the ceaseless unconditioned generation and passing away of line' (112). This fantasized space comes close to Winnicott's description of the unknowable, protected self, forever hidden from the world, protected in its viability, vitality, and authenticity. It approaches Guntrip's deeply regressed ego, desperately fleeing from the perceived destructiveness of the world, clinging to a fragile hope that conditions will change so a rebirth can ensue. This darkest zone is Murphy's most hallowed inner room, where he exists beyond life, affection, sexuality, sustenance, and beyond his belief that love is unknowable. In the first zone rage is expressed as revenge, 'spitting at the breakers of the world' (113); in the second there is a fantasized move towards reparation, 'where the choice of bliss introduced an element of effort' (113). In the final zone 'more in the dark, in the will-lessness' (113), Murphy is fixed on the misguided belief it is only by escaping into nothingness that he can avoid annihilation by the world when, in fact, the annihilation is threatened from within. He abandons engagement with life, unknow-ingly clinging to the hope of rebirth within the love of a new mother, who will manifest as Mr. Endon, an idealized figure that he believes has attained this idealized state of existence.

Footfalls

Miss Clarridge's house, where Murphy and Celia reside, is an internal stage of schizoid relationships, in which Celia's reaction to the suicide of the 'old boy' takes on particular importance.[13] As a representation of attempts to connect with an absent, primary figure, these scenes encapsulate a fundamental experience at the heart of the oeuvre, prefiguring the isolation of Molloy in his mother's room, Vladimir and Estragon's hopeful/less wait, and the haunting embroilment of the heroine of *Rockaby* as she becomes the (not)-mother herself. The suicide seals Murphy's fate, convincing him of the impossibility of love, and creating a final, envious cynicism within him.

The old butler's footsteps, sounding in the room above, grow to comfort Celia, giving her a sense of contact during her long hours waiting for Murphy. As in the late play *Footfalls*, these sounds are a connection to a troubled, unknowable other, and to an aspect of herself. That play is a highly condensed metaphor of an internal space built upon primary dyadic failure – it centres on the repetitive pacing of a woman, May, in her forties, caring for an aged mother. There are three sequences: in the first May and her mother have a conversation suggesting great pain in the younger woman's life, for which the mother asks forgiveness. In the second, the mother appears on stage to observe her daughter's pacing, commenting on May's isolation since childhood, and her daughter's need to revolve 'it all' in her head. In the final section, May presents a narrative about a Mrs Winter and her daughter Amy, which can be read as a displacement of her own experience of a frigid internal relationship with her mother/self.

A major aspect of this play is its exposition of the nature and consequences of early experiences of the infantile-self's disconnection from the mother. The play is an internal, unconscious representation of a primary feeling-state, the characters are aspects of the same unified, narrative-self, but since this level of unconscious representation operates within the primary process, there is a fluidity of identity. Thus, May can be viewed as a deeply regressed, hidden part of the narrative-self (much like the wanderer in 'neither', the man in ... *but the clouds ...*, Lucky, and so forth), while the mother represents a primary maternal imago. Since May *also* acts as nurse to her aged mother, she herself takes on maternal, caring attributes, while the mother acts as a helpless, dependent part of the self. This type of self-object blurring is a fundamental aspect of unconscious fantasy, which helps to explain powerful attachments to early figures, which are *both* self *and* other.[14]

Beckett's own comments, to an actress who played May, supports the idea of the primary constellation being centered on May as a deeply regressed part of the self:

> She interrupts herself in the sentence '"In the old home, the same where she – (*Pause.*)" and continues "The same where she began" because she was going to say "… the same where she was *born*". But that is wrong, she hasn't been born. She just began. It began. There is a difference. She was never born.' (Quotation in Knowlson and Pilling, 1979: 222)

There has never been a full psychic birth of the infantile-self within the home of the mother's mind, and the play is an expression of that self *in its relation* to the mother. May lives primarily in the Autistic Contiguous position: her pacing helps provide a physicality that holds her fragile self together, much like Murphy's long walks or bus rides, Molloy's sucking stones, or Malone's pencil. She is clothed in a 'wrap' that, like Murphy's suit of armour, serves a containing function, preventing spillage of the nascent self into a boundless world. As Gidal states: 'The figure on stage in *Footfalls*, wrapped, is never a figure inside a wrap. It is, as a whole, a wrap' (Gidal, 1986: 163). This reflects the rigidity of the self that May represents, as she slides towards oblivious withdrawal from life, from 'it all', clinging desperately to a sense of connection through autistic pacing.[15] This pacing is not enough, however, and she demands her mother remove the carpet so she might hear the sounds of her own footfalls on bare wood. This is another self-containing strategy, one that creates a primary sense of being-with-the-mother, since one of the earliest methods mothers use to calm their infants (and themselves) is by carrying them while pacing. May can self-calm by creating just such a connection, as she becomes *both* mother *and* child, walking *herself* in a soothing, rhythmic dance, as the footfalls sound a beat of otherness like so many other repetitive sounds that calm the infant (presumably because they mimic a primary connection, *in utero*, to the mother's heartbeat and movements). There is a suggestion that the sounds calm her mother as well:

> M: Mother. [*Pause. No Louder.*] Mother.
>   [*Pause.*]
> V: Yes, May.
> M: Were you asleep?
> V: Deep asleep. [*Pause*] I heard you in my deep sleep. [*Pause.*] There is no sleep so deep I would not hear you there. (239)

It is the play's condensation of the early mother–infant relationship that is central – its representation of an unconscious fantasy of early experience, but further, one encapsulated *within* a cohesive self. This ambiguity gives the play its power, but leads to confusion about its being internally or externally referential. In expressing an internal, encapsulated part of experience, May and her mother are aspects of a unified self, and May's calling her mother (in the above passage) out of the darkness reflects the internal nature of the mother, reminiscent of the male figure and voice in *… but the clouds …*. A primary failure of connection between the infantile-self and mother dominates this experience, and the couple blurs, since *both* enact mothering and dependent roles. The narrative-self identifies, at times, with the *mother*, as a helpless, drug dependent part of the self that feels it is dying, but it also remains connected to a distracted, pacing mother-as-*May*, who provides a measure of physical nurturing to her mother, but without any continuity of attention. In light of this, the third part of the piece, in which May recites a narrative displacement from her own actual experience, takes on an additional significance, mirroring the mechanisms operating within the underlying narrative-self. May displaces aspects of her grief, loneliness, and disconnection from the mother into the 'fiction' *just as* the narrative-self itself is fragmented within the play proper, its own feelings of disconnection and loneliness enacted within the condensed relationship of May and the mother. The core of May's fiction relates a rupture between a daughter, Amy, and her mother, Mrs Winter. May begins

> What is it, Mother, are you not feeling yourself? [*Pause.*] Mrs W. did not at once reply. But finally, raising her head and fixing Amy – the daughter's given name, as the reader will remember [...] she murmured, fixing Amy full in the eye she murmured, Amy did you observe anything ... strange at Evensong? Amy: No, Mother, I did not. [...] Just what exactly, Mother, did you perhaps fancy this ... strange thing was you observed? [*Pause.*] Mrs W: You yourself observed nothing ... strange? Amy: No, Mother, I myself did not, to put it mildly. Mrs W: What do you mean, Amy, to put it mildly, what can you possibly mean, Amy, to put it mildly? Amy: I mean, Mother, that to say I observed nothing [...] I saw nothing, heard nothing, of any kind. I was not there. Mrs W: Not there? Amy: Not there. Mrs W: But I heard you respond. [*Pause.*] I heard you say Amen. [*Pause.*] How could you have responded if you were not there? (242–3)

A primary rupture between the self and its good internal object explains May's need for displacement, something, which manifests in the fiction. It becomes the mother who, like May in the play proper, is distracted and disconnected from the other.[16] The tone is paranoid, suggesting a blurring between the two figures that echoes the condensation in the play proper, where both May and mother are aspects of a coherent self. The same mechanisms operate in both instances: May condenses and displaces an experience of early disconnection into her story, just as she herself is a manifestation of such an experience in the play proper. In both the play and the narrative, the mother and child enact complementary, reversible roles, something that can help explain some of the 'confusion' of the play. Knowlson and Pilling (1979) write:

> In *Footfalls*, however, the many parallels and repetitions, together with the analogies that exist between the mother and daughter both in the drama itself and the story which is set into the drama, serve to create a play in which we can never be sure of what we are looking at or to what we are listening. We realize, perhaps only after the play has ended, that

we may have been watching a ghost telling us a tale of a ghost (herself), who fails to be observed by someone else (her fictional alter ego) because she in turn was not really there. (227)

If the 'ghost' is viewed as the narrative-self, some of the confusion can be explained, as the dominant experience becomes a primary disconnection between emerging/infantile-self and the mother. The play *must* be confusing, the sense of self and other *must* blur, since it operates in a primary process mode of thinking, where the characters are both self and other at the same time, and this experience is enacted in form, content, and mode of presentation. It expresses this dominant feeling of disconnection *within* itself, since May's experience of the internal mother's absence, expressed within her 'fictional' story as a mother who appears insane, reflects the dominant experience that the narrative-self displaces into the play as a whole. May's 'fiction' reflects the *process* that *generates* the whole play itself, the process of becoming a creative narrator within a mother–infant matrix. There is a collapse of internal and external: May's experience of being unwitnessed takes the form of being experienced as an hallucination (and the ensuing paranoid interrogation), in the fiction, something due to a sense her mother is not there in the *actuality* of the play proper. May's narration creates a sense of externality (i.e. May is a *real* person), but May also represents an *internal* part of a cohesive narrative-self, unwitnessed by another part of itself, *a disconnected internal mother*, who feels unwitnessed herself (by a distracted or unloving infant). The experience of the play (for the audience) reflects its working within deeply enmeshed, condensed experience of a self struggling with feelings of disconnection from a primary maternal object needed to help integrate experience.

Returning to *Murphy*, there is a similar sense of blurred maternal identification in Celia's experience of the old boy, and a suggestion of its genesis. It is the 'man and rat' metaphor, with a twist: Celia is calm only when she hears the butler's pacing, he is unhearing and unheeding; much like May, he seems never to have 'done with it'. Like an anxious mother listening for sounds of her infant in the night, or the child for whom the sounds of the parent is a containment against anxiety, Celia becomes used to the old boy's footsteps as a connection that counters her lonely despair:

'Oh, Miss Clarridge, is that you, I am so worried about the old boy, there has not been a move or a stir out of him all day.' [...] 'I have got to expect it,' said Celia, 'and listen for it, and this is the first time I haven't heard it' [...] Celia was in a state indeed, trembling and ashen. The footsteps overheard had become part and parcel of her afternoon, with the rocking-chair and the vermigrade wane of light. (133–4)

The footfalls create an inner presence, reminding her the old boy, though suffering, is still alive; she identifies with his pain, manifested in his pacing, just as her own anguish is revealed by her rocking in Murphy's chair, and both movements mitigate isolated suffering through rhythmic self-containment. In fact, the old boy has committed suicide, driven by despair to a gruesome, lonely death, prefiguring the play *Eh Joe*, apparently hounded to death by merciless inner demons. He is locked in the most impenetrable prison-room in this inner stage, where there is no contact with the world: his food is taken in on a tray, and he is never seen. While Molloy and Malone turn to writing to express this world, the old boy turns to the razor, as the most unambiguously despairing character in the oeuvre. This sense of retreat, and its connection to suicidality, is reflected in the following vignette:

A female university student suffered from bulimia and a severe inner voice that continually attacked her aspirations. This was identification with early parental imagos, reflecting the actual parents' need to destroy the child's esteem so she would not separate. One session, around the time she was making great progress in her studies, she spoke of her great despair the night before. She curled up in her room as sadistic thoughts circled in her head, shouting: 'You're no good! Who do you think you are! You are stupid! It is a joke to think you can study at Cambridge one day!' After telling me this, the patient related a fantasy of crawling into a dark closet and staying there. I suggested that it would indeed be very quiet in the womb. She laughed and said she had been at a café before our session, and had seen some small children playing. She became sad, wondering in awe that they were once only small eggs within their mothers' bodies. I suggested that her climbing back into the closet/womb was not an actual wish for a lifeless state, but a hope for a sanctuary where she could rest before being born again. She said that, yes, this was so, though she felt she would like to rest for a very long time. She described desperation during the periods when she binged, and her feeling she had to vomit to get the food out of her. I interpreted that this was a powerful enactment of what we had been discussing. She fed herself in an exaggerated nurturing by bingeing, only to rob herself of life, in accordance with the inner demons, in a symbolic emptying/abortion.[17] She said yes, that in this way she could remain a little girl for ever.

This vignette demonstrates the manner through which rooms become metaphorical spaces within the mind, connected to a state of being that fluctuates between representing sanctuary within the mother, and death. This woman felt a retreat from the world/mother (a projection of her own inner harshness) was the only way to survive, the images of conception and of children playing represented her sense of being able to give life to others (and to enjoy life herself), and the powerful impact of early feeding experiences, and their role on later states of mind, is demonstrated in her struggle with bulimia.

The metaphorical impact of the old boy's death is complex. Following the discovery of the body, for example, Miss Clarridge's main concerns are herself, and how to deal with the death without being 'a penny out of pocket' (136). Celia is deeply traumatized and, to comfort her, Murphy expounds: 'On and off, angrily, the unutterable benefits that would accrue, were already accruing, to the old boy from his demise. This was quite beside the point, for Celia was mourning, like all honest survivors, quite frankly for herself. [...] So far from being adapted to Celia, [Murphy's speech] was not addressed to her' (136). This enacts a central dynamic – there is a lack of empathic connection and, although he rightly surmises that Celia is mourning for herself, Murphy cannot get past this. In his attempt to comfort her, he compounds her grief, since he cannot recognize (or allow himself to recognize) its depth or its genesis. On the surface, his angrily 'expounding' why the old boy is better off dead is selfish narcissism – a mere pretence to preach his own form of nihilistic cynicism. But there is more to it, since part of what generates Murphy's anger is his own rage at Celia for not attending to *his* need for empathy: he is *jealous* of the old boy. His anger confirms his inability to love her, but it *also* reveals his own need for love. Murphy feels 'annoyed' by Celia's behaviour, she is only periodically aware of him, in a 'kind of impersonal rapture', and even his 'proudly casual' announcement that he has obtained employment 'excited her to the extent of an "Oh". Nothing more' (137). Murphy goes into an extended tirade about his struggles to find work, then telling a joke that was 'not addressed to her. It amused Murphy, that was all that mattered' (139). His outburst may be merely self-serving, but its intensity suggests Celia's lack of attention and concern for the old boy is genuinely hurtful to him. This seems to repeat an early dyadic pattern for Murphy, he now experiences, in Celia's withdrawal, a reawakening of disconnection from his mother. Murphy is unable to recognize that in Celia's pain are the roots of his own: that as

he will be with Endon, so she is attached to a distant, depressed figure in
the old boy, who provided her with a remnant of the only security she
has known. Her isolated vigil in the room below the old boy may be a
re-enactment of earlier experience when, as a child, she found herself
separated from her primary maternal figure (apparently her grandfather) by the bars of her crib. Her inner world, lonely and unloving,
becomes manifest in the outer, as a lonely self hides in quite anticipation of an uninterested figure whose footfalls sound both the
torments of primary separation and of embryonic connection.

These scenes reflect the pain of early separations: Celia's eyes,
usually 'clear and green', now roll and evert like an 'aborting goat's'
(137), Murphy sarcastically compares her mourning to the loss of an
entire family of fourteen children, and he experiences the disappointment of the affair in the same, overwhelmingly traumatic way that a
child does when denied maternal love, comparing his state to the dying
withdrawal (i.e. 'marasmus', 138) of infants cut off from all emotional
contact. Their anguish is unimaginable, Murphy's own internal impov-
erishment blinds him to a chance to empathize with Celia, so much like
himself in her suffering, and needing his love now more than he can
possibly allow himself to know.

The depth of Murphy's hurt can be gauged by his reaction to this
scene. He has Celia dress him like a child (reminiscent of the scene in
Proust in which the narrator's paranoid regression is contained by
maternal care), and announces he is leaving, uncertain when he will
return. When Celia expresses interest, Murphy sits down 'in order to
torment at his ease this tardy concern […] He still loved her enough to
enjoy cutting the tripes out of her occasionally' (140), expressing an
infantile rage at being abandoned. Secretive about the job, he leaves her
with the possibility open that they will soon be together again.
Watching him from the window, she sees only his hand, clutching a rail
as he walks along, being mocked by a group of boys: 'multiplied in their
burlesque long after her own eyes could see him no more' (143). The
last Celia sees of Murphy alive blurs into a caricature that mirrors his
trace in the 'big world', as the mocking of the youths acts as an echo of
the hostility and derision that has been his experience in a world of
chandlers.[18]

The direction they now take moves them towards contact with the
mother, and demonstrates that Celia and Murphy are twins born of
absence. Murphy will fall in love with Endon, and Celia continues her
mourning for the old boy: '"Are you in trouble?" said Miss Clarridge

[...] I hear you moving about in the afternoon just like the old boy' (144). Celia longs to get into the old boy's room, and does move into it. Her understanding of Murphy becomes clearer as she, too, seeks a pre-partum space, and in this womb/room she approaches the old boy/mother, identifying with him, caring for herself (and him) within his space, as she also identified with the absent Murphy/mother by rocking in his chair. Like Watt, Hamm/Clov, Vladimir/Estragon and many other characters, she remains in tight orbit around the absent mother, without whom there is a nothingness that would dwarf her current despair. She can lose herself in this place, undressing to rock in the chair: 'She closed her eyes and was in her mind with Murphy, Mr. Kelly, clients, her parents, others, herself a girl, a child, an infant. In the cell of her mind, teasing the oakum of her history. Then it was finished, the days and places and things and people were untwisted and scattered, she was lying down, she had no history' (148–9). She *becomes* Murphy as she rocks, growing close to him and the absent mother whom he represents, finding herself filled with images of others in a space that is no longer suffocating, but now calm and full. She is close to the essence of what she is, in being herself-with-other, moving unfettered in time, beyond her own infancy. The 'cell' of her mind no longer just a 'prison', but a primal sense of potential being, Celia appears to be reorganizing herself, repeating this sequence over the days to follow, mourning her own life: 'the coils of her life to be hackled into tow all over again, before she could lie down in the paradisial innocence of days and places and things and people' (149). She is in the place that Murphy so cherishes – a place without people, and therefore without pain; a calm, but also, lonely place, where in her isolation she can feel a sense of autonomy and authenticity.

Celia functions as a part of the self more directly engaged with life, able to tolerate feelings of despair, and to connect to her loneliness in a way that motivates her to act. Having left the room while the char cleans it, she is roused from her withdrawal, and longs to see her grandfather. Waiting for him in the park, she watches a child flying tandem kites, mere specks high in a darkening sky. The loneliness of this vanishing dyad is not lost on Celia as she stands close to, but apart from, the child who, in his joy, is a younger version of her grandfather (or herself). She calls out to him as he leaves, but is herself mere absence, and the boy does not hear her (he is singing), foreshadowing the disconnection between the lost narrator of 'The Calmative' and the child-self he observes through the window. Cold, tired and discouraged from her visit to the world, she returns home where 'there was nothing to go back to, yet she was glad when she arrived' (153). The nothing that waits in the empty home is a nothing that welcomes her into her past, into her sense of belonging, however slight, and to her longing. Watt, Vladimir and 'she' will know of it, wandering as shadows in worlds filled by an absence that is their only hope of contact; and as Godot, Knott, and Krapp's women are manifestations of early absence, so too are the old boy and Murphy for Celia. She returns to them from her walk in the world, to re-find the nothing that makes her glad to be home. Walking up the stairs after learning that Murphy has come and gone, knowing he will never return, her hand grips and slides along the rail in the darkness, as his did when she saw him alive for the final time. Gone where she cannot follow, she connects to his shadow though the sensuality of touch and imitation. It will be her place in the novel to live a while longer in this world of absence and sorrow.

An Endon sight

Murphy does not feel part of a secure, loving world, a feeling engendered by disconnection from a good, internal presence. Earlier sections have explored how his fantasy of mind demonstrates this core part of himself, how his failed attempt to engage the chandlers triggers a regressive, despairing retreat, as well as reparative enactments in nurturing, raging attacks on the mother, and how his need for love is thwarted by a perceived neglect on the part of Celia, who is mourning a part of herself in the dead old boy. This final section examines Murphy's last days, and his most important attempt to engage a maternal figure in the guise of the psychiatric patient Mr. Endon. This relationship is the novel's climax – in seeking to find nothingness, Murphy awakens in himself a dormant self-esteem and need for attachment, but fails to recognize that through this he has found the means to escape the deadly disconnection that dominates his inner world.

Starting his tenure as nurse, Murphy is told his duties do not include any affection for his charges: 'All you know about them is the work they give you to do' (162), anticipating many Beckettian characters that take on primary maternal functions in caring for an infantilized other. Murphy *is* a good mother who relishes his work, and has an innate affection for the patients, 'They caused Murphy no horror [...] his immediate feelings were respect and unworthiness [...] the impression he received was of that self-immersed indifference to the contingencies of the contingent world which he had chosen for himself' (168). This respect allows an empathic immersion into their states of being, opening their worlds to him. They trust him as no other, several developing an embryonic love for the man, but Murphy refuses to recognize this, remaining fixated on the idealized belief that, like Miss Dew's sheep, the patients are ecstatic rather than tormented. They are 'lost ones' that fulfil his purpose – a 'race of people he had long since despaired of finding' (169), but he does not realize they also represent a split-off/depressed family within himself, much like the inhabitants of the houses that Klein's patient re-connected to, and brought back to life. Though he recognizes the affection that emerges, he suppresses it: 'Nothing remained but to see what he wanted to see [...] He would not have admitted that he needed a brotherhood. He did. In the presence of this issue (psychiatric-psychotic) between the life from which he had turned away and the life of which he had no experience, except as he hoped inchoately in himself, he could not fail to side with the latter' (176). Determined to enact an idealized withdrawal from life, Murphy sees the world only as *he* wants to see it. His refusal to admit a need for love reflects his retreat, his stagnation, within an omnipotent stance that blocks an integration of the world's complexity. The 'inchoate' experience is exactly what he denies, not some abstract world of nothingness, but an early experience of togetherness with, and absence from, loving primary objects. He empathically understands that the patients' communications and actions describe an internal state of suffering, despair, and a deep wish for loving contact, but sees any attempt to reach them as unnecessary: '[his] *experience* [...] *obliged* him to call sanctuary what the psychiatrists called exile' (177–8, italics mine). He describes the rationale for seeking kinship with the patients, 'It was not enough to want nothing where he was worth nothing' (179), nor to renounce the world outside of his intellectualized self-love. Disconnected from feelings of worthiness, Murphy finds himself in an abstract intellectualized retreat that gives him a sense of superiority over an unloving world; he projects an imagined, idealized state of non-being into the patients, in order to have something to aspire to, failing to recognize it is *because* of his attachment to them that his (and their) sense of being lovable has developed. He must deny clear evidence that his suppositions are wrong, and disregards the frequent expressions of patients' anguish, distorting their meanings to suit his own needs. He sees the 'absolute impassivity of the higher schizoids' (180) as evidence of their ability to willfully disconnect from a life not worth living, and is encouraged by their enclosed 'cells': 'The three dimensions, slightly concave, were so exquisitely proportioned that the absence of the fourth was scarcely felt [...] No system of ventilation appeared to dispel the illusion of respirable vacuum. The compartment was windowless, like a monad, except for the shuttered judas in the door' (181). These rooms, like the third zone Murphy aspires to, are timeless, withdrawn sanctuaries on the edge of experience, yet he also requires them to be part of the living world – not simply a final suicidal withdrawal, they allow for respiration, though *appearing* to be vacuums. These rooms, parts of the mind that act as a boundary to existence, are the stages of Beckett's later work that reflect ongoing dynamics between contact and withdrawal – they are internal spaces felt within the narrative-self as hovering on the 'neither' boundary of life and death, between the mother within and the world without.

Murphy's intuitive understanding of the patients is demonstrated by their fondness, respect, and trust for him. One patient refuses exercise without his involvement, another will not rise in the morning unless Murphy invites him to, a third refuses all food unless Murphy feeds him with a spoon. Murphy is an empathic, containing mother who respects the patients as living, sentient beings whose inner worlds are valid and understandable, and they engage the world *through* Murphy, demonstrating the love he himself deems impossible. These deeply disturbed men *trust* him, his love shifts their internal worlds and, as projections of terrorized hostility are muted, they take in new experiences, feeding on the good food given by mother-Murphy. He recognizes the importance of what is happening, and it begins to alter his internal landscape: he doubts the pre-determined nature of his life, feeling instead that his ability to connect to the patients is more a meaningful part of his own nature than a mere correspondence to astrological designs. He feels that *he* has value, despite massive attempts to withdraw from a place where he believes this to be false, as he rejects a sense of himself as subordinate to an overreaching, deterministic system of another's making. He does not fully recognize, however, that rather than his system being 'closed around him', it is actually expanding as he finds lost, hopeful aspects of himself *within* the patients that *he* helps to restore and bring to life. He responds to the patients' minds as Klein's patient did to the houses – both begin to recover a connection to the world. He recognizes in them what he begins to recognize in himself, that he is a living, sentient being who *creates* meaning in the world through a loving attitude that allows an ongoing rebirth into a safer, more secure world. Ultimately, he cannot appreciate the consequences of this, seeing his achievement as a step towards a world the patients strive to escape: 'His success with the patients was a signpost pointing to them [...] they felt in him what they had been and he in them what he would be [...] nothing less than a slap-up psychosis could consummate his life's strike' (184). This is his terrible misrecognition, and it reflects the tenacity of his tie to a cold, unloving mother/world.

It is Mr. Endon for whom Murphy develops the most positive feelings, being bound to him 'by a love of the purest possible kind [...] they remained to one another, even when most profoundly one in spirit, as it seemed to Murphy, Mr. Murphy and Mr. Endon' (184). Through this connection, Murphy engages the world, and the experience approximates the earliest mother–infant bond. The love he imagines they share is beyond contingency, founded on a mutuality and sense of oneness predicated on respect (i.e. *Mr.* Murphy and *Mr.* Endon). The chess games they play, though they actually sit together at the board quite rarely, operate as transitional objects that allow him to feel the presence of a loving other, even with a physical separation.[19] It is in the long evenings, during their separations, that he feels the absence like a small child: 'fac[ing] the twelve hours of self, unredeemed split self' (188). His isolation seems unbearable, he feels disconnected and fragmented as the stars seem veiled by 'cloud or fog or mist', and the night sky appears 'dirty' (189). His recently found attachment highlights his loneliness, and his old coping strategies fail. He can no longer come alive in his mind and, though he blames this on fatigue: 'it was rather due to the vicarious autology that he had been enjoying since the morning, in little Mr. Endon and all the other proxies' (189). This again misses the point by continuing to misattribute his positive feelings to an identification with an idealized nothingness, failing to recognize that it *because* of their mutual interaction that Murphy has begun to change. He dreams of Celia, his love unharnessed from schizoid despair, but ultimately is unable to overcome the life-destroying parts of himself: 'the self whom he loved had the aspect [...] of real alienation. Or to put it perhaps more nicely: conferred that aspect to the self whom he hated' (194). His night-time separation from the patients becomes a time of increasing loneliness, since there 'was no loathing to love from, no kick from the world that was not his, no illusion of caress from the world that might be' (240). He misses the contact, failing to recognize that they are actually awakening in him a sense that a 'caress' may be possible in the big world, just as they have a sense of *his* caress. His night-time separations create an overwhelming 'unintelligible gulf' (240) that the infantile-self experiences as catastrophic, and Murphy responds, not by recognizing the possibilities of connection, but by maintaining an idealized retreat to an inner void where connection is lost.

Murphy's final, ill-fated chess game with Mr. Endon is the natural climax of the novel. On night rounds he stops to look into Endon's cell, and is gratified to see his friend's face upturned towards him through the judas:

> Mr. Endon had recognized the feel of his friend's eye upon him and made his preparations accordingly. Friend's eye? Say rather Murphy's eye, Mr. Endon had felt Murphy's eye upon him. Mr. Endon would have been less than Mr. Endon if he had known what it was to have a friend; and Murphy more than Murphy if he had not hoped against his better judgment that his feeling for Mr. Endon was in some small degree reciprocated. Whereas the sad truth was, that while Mr. Endon for Murphy was no less than bliss, Murphy for Mr. Endon was no more than chess. Murphy's eye? Say, rather, the chessy eye. Mr. Endon had vibrated to the chessy eye upon him and made preparations accordingly. (241–2)

This highlights Murphy's misrecognition of his own nature, since he feels joy and self-worth because his 'friend' notices him, reacting with some pleasure to his existence. There is a sense of early mother and child relating, since as the child begins to become more aware of the mother as a whole presence, there is a move into the Depressive Position with the possibility of genuine integrated love. The mother feels increasingly valuable as her child relates to her as a whole person instead of a series of part-functions. In the passage, there is a cynical attitude towards these developments that reflects Murphy's idealiza- tion of non-contact with nothingness. Endon would be 'less' not more, if he could feel a sense of belonging and love, and Murphy somehow superior if he did not hope for contact with Endon as a person. Again, there is something not recognized – the clear indication that Endon is responding to Murphy in a vital, authentic fashion. An experience of my own may elucidate this:

> When my infant daughter first began to walk, she immediately became engrossed with the suddenly unlimited opportunities for exploration that appeared. The first few months saw her so absorbed in these activities that she took little notice of anyone in her play area as she practised. One day, after about two months of her blissful 'ignorance' of me during her walks, she stopped, picked up a small headband, and

walked over to me with a look of remarkable anticipation and excite-
ment. I put on the headband and she broke out into peels of delighted
laughter. Next she brought a small jar of plastic letters, that she could
not open, to me for opening, as she patiently waited.

These are the beginnings of a *whole* contact with the outer world,
and a direct echo of Murphy's experience with Endon. Just as my
daughter moved from a state in which, through feeling protected, she
appears withdrawn and uninterested in persons, to a state where she
requires others to interact with her for feelings of joy, so Endon has
begun, with the empathic attunement of Murphy, to look forward to
his chess matches. This engagement waxes and wanes: my daughter
would use me at times as a part-object – for example, as 'the letter-
container opener' – but there is a distinct progression towards whole-
object relating. It is the quality of early relationships that allows a child
to feel this movement is possible and safe. Endon's seeing Murphy as
'the chessy eye' is not a rejection of Murphy as a person, it is the first
step towards genuine connection and love for both. There is a
contradiction between Murphy's expressed and actual needs: he is
depressed because Endon does not recognize him as a person, and
immediately represses this feeling in order to maintain a belief that he is
actually depressed because this fact *closes* off his approach to the nothingness he imagines Endon blissfully inhabits. It is Endon's burgeoning
connection to Murphy, and the latter's sadness that this is not complete
enough, that demonstrates the illusory nature of this world and its
benefits. The final scenes with Endon are highly condensed, Murphy re-
experiences, as child, a sense of disconnection to a withdrawn mother.
This also makes sense of his own withdrawal, since he becomes *like* that
mother in an attempt to stay close to her. In other words, his entire
obsession with attaining an Endon-like state of withdrawal is explain-
able by a need for recognition, by Endon-as-mother, of this achievement. This is the central paradox, to be loved and recognized by the
absent-mother for becoming like her, when this necessarily means
recognition is not possible. It is in his failure to recognize Endon's
underlying wish for connection that Murphy loses contact with this
very part of himself. Their fatal chess game acts as a transitional, primal
text upon which Endon writes of his isolation and of his nascent
awareness of the other Murphy fails to become.

Murphy's final chess game with Endon is a complex dance of
isolation and attempts at engagement.[20] Realizing the seemingly endless quality of this game of approach and withdrawal, Murphy surrenders

in deep sadness, absorbed by the image of Endon until he begins 'to see nothing, that colourless which is such a rare post-natal treat, being the absence (to use a nice distinction) not of percipere but of percipi' (246). Murphy cannot contain Endon's isolation, much as he was unable to tolerate Celia's mourning, her sense of primary loss. Though they are actively engaged in playing (i.e. Endon *needs* him as a partner) Murphy withdraws because his *own* need for connection is unmet. The world dissolves into an objectless nothingness, as Murphy regresses into an other-less place, his disappointment masked, yet again, by the illusory feeling that *not* to be recognized (or not *wanting* to be recognized) is his highest ambition. Later, Murphy will enter Endon's bedroom and kneel by his bed, nearly touching his face, and sees himself 'stigmatised in those eyes that did not see him', while he hears within himself words demanding to be spoken to Endon:

> 'the last at last seen of him
> himself unseen by him
> and of himself'

A rest.

'The last Mr. Murphy saw of Mr. Endon was Mr. Murphy unseen by Mr. Endon. This was also the last Murphy saw of Murphy.'

A rest.

The relation between Mr. Murphy and Mr. Endon could not have been better summed up than by the former's sorrow at seeing himself in the latter's immunity from seeing anything but himself. (249–50)

Murphy comes to Endon needing contact, and in this final non-engagement his earliest internal drama is enacted. The patient develops a nascent awareness of Murphy, and this triggers the latter's spiraling despair, since he assumes it will allow him entry into the narcissistic nothingness he fantasizes to be the patient's state. He idealizes Endon as a primary object – it is the relationship itself that is crucial – for Murphy not only wants to be *like* Endon, but to be *loved* for it. In fact, Endon's withdrawal, like that of the other patients, is assuaged through Murphy's kind interest and, in this final scene together, Murphy compounds his mistake. It is *Murphy* (as a failing mother) who does not really *see* Endon, viewing him solely as an object through which he will gain access to a withdrawn world. *He* attempts to use *Endon* far more deleteriously than his imagined use by the patient during the chess games, which were embryonic attempts to connect with another person. Murphy fails Endon-as-child, because he cannot tolerate the changes occurring within his own internal world, changes which require the acceptance of loving feelings and a move away from absence. What Murphy sees in Endon's eyes is not himself unseen by Endon but, rather, *himself unseen by himself*. He cannot recognize his own need for a loving, living attachment, nor his ability and worthiness in the world; and so is looking into his *own* 'immunity from seeing anything but himself'.[21]

This final rupture generates a raging despair. Retreating to his room/mind for his last moments of life, Murphy undresses and lies down, trying 'to get a picture of Celia. In vain. Of his mother. In vain. Of his father (for he was not illegitimate). In vain. It was usual for him to fail with his mother; and usual, though less usual, for him to fail with a woman. But never before had he failed with his father' (251). Murphy again fails to maintain contact with a good internal presence, but his attempt demonstrates his desire to remain within the world. His primary disconnection from a good mother is evident in the *unexceptional* nature of his failure to find her within him, though there appears to have been some sense of primary attachment to the father, as, perhaps, a figure of reparation. He continues in desperation, as his internal world abandons him:

> He saw the clenched fists and rigid upturned face of the Child in a Giovanni Bellini Circumcision, waiting to feel the knife. He saw eye-balls being scraped, first any eyeballs, then Mr. Endon's. He tried again with his father, his mother, Celia, Wylie, Neary, Cooper Miss Dew [...] with the men, women, children and animals that belong to even worse stories than this. In vain in all cases. He could not get a picture in his mind of any creature he had met, animal or human. Scraps of bodies, of landscapes, hands, eyes, lines and colours evoking nothing, rose and climbed out of sight before him, as though reeled upward off a spool level with his throat. (251–2)

Murphy is deeply enraged, and fantasizes the destruction of the very organs that fail to recognize him, from abstract general orbs to the specific eyes of Endon; in fact, if one can imagine him trying to repair *cataracts* by his scraping, he is trying to reverse the non-recognition and make himself visible to the mother that Endon represents. His feeling of abandonment is compared to circumcision, the mutilation of a child's body (reversed by cutting the maternal figure of Endon), and he regresses into a primal position, where there are no whole objects, but only meaningless fragments. He is terribly alone, rage having destroyed his inner world, and he attempts to assuage his disintegration by dis-placing his suffering into 'worse stories'. The internal world withdraws, as shards of otherness, 'reeled off a spool', an echo of Freud's fort-da game, in which a small child threw a spool and pulled it back towards himself, in order to maintain a connection to his absent mother. Murphy's others are not to be pulled back – he draws up the ladder to his garret and ties himself into the chair, beginning a final rocking before an explosion occurs within the gas system, but in these final moments there is a desperate struggle. There is a moment of possible change, based on a recognition of his own rage and the intensity of his narcissistic withdrawal from the world. His ambivalence is clear: he has the intention to return to Celia '*if* he felt better' (252) in the morning, but at the same time cuts off the world by withdrawing his ladder. And so, in the final analysis, it becomes an intractable internal conflict, and an attachment to a disconnected internal state, that enwombs/entombs Murphy to his end.

After Murphy's ashes are accidentally scattered amidst the vomit and sawdust of a pub floor, Celia takes Mr. Kelly to the park to fly his kite, and sees the child she once attempted to greet, who had not returned her call. This time she does not hail him, she has lost her hope for joy in the world, tied again to absence in the figure of her grandfather. Mr. Kelly's kite breaks free, another ruptured dyad, and he chases it, 'a ghastly, lamentable figure [...] the ravaged face was a cramp of bones, throttled sounds jostled in his throat' (282). The living world collapses for Celia as well; as an infant:

> Her cot had a high rail all the way round. Mr. Willoughby Kelly came, smelling strongly of drink, knelt, grasped the bars at looked at her through them. Then she envied him, and he her. [...] Sometimes he sang:

> > *Weep not, my wanton, smile upon my knee,*
> > *When thou art old, there's grief enough for thee,*

etc. Other times:

> > *Love is a prick, love is a sting,*
> > *Love is a pretty, pretty thing,*

etc. Other times, other songs. But most times he did not sing at all. (235)

Celia's inner world completes an enclosing circle, just as the dying sun sets on the world of the novel, a complement to the frozen shining that opened it. She has lost Murphy, but that part of him that was full of self-absorbed, despairing cynicism lives on in the Mr. Kelly of her own early life, as an absent, envious, and sarcastic other, whose songs reflect an inability to contain infantile anxiety. She remains, a part of the self that struggles against all odds to remain attached to life, as a 'last exile' in a world of 'puppets'. The final image has Celia closing her eyes, as the rangers clear the park with their cry of *'All out'*, and this final expulsion from a place of joyous freedom stands as a stark, fitting finale to a novel that circles endlessly around the experience of banishment from primary love within the maternal mind.

Notes

1 Murphy is the central figure who dominates the novel: 'All the puppets in this book whinge sooner or later, except Murphy, who is not a puppet' (122). He represents the core of the narrative-self, with the other characters (most centrally Celia) acting, on the whole, as the world/mother, though Celia can be seen as an abandoned part of the core dyad, being left by Murphy.

2 Hill (1990: 111–13) notes the dichotomous relationship of Murphy and Neary, the latter seeking withdrawal, as the former seeks connection (to Miss Counihan through Murphy). Neary's search is a split-off, infantile quest for maternal connection, as he needs the mother to make sense of confusion and chaos. He tells Murphy that 'life is all figure and ground', and Murphy responds that it is a 'wandering to find home'. Neary then evokes the primal maternal image, as well as it's containing function: 'The face [...] or a system of faces, against the big, blooming, buzzing confusion. I think of Miss Dwyer' (4). This is the primal home that both seek, within the containment of the maternal mind; whereas Neary's search is ongoing and displaced to contemporary female figures, Murphy's is directed internally, and is ultimately absorbed into his denial.

3 This imagery is reminiscent of Oliver's experience when he is locked into isolation in *Oliver Twist* (see Chapter 4). There is the ambivalence of a wish for contact, touching ('hugging'), for nurturing ('famished'), and a sense that this can be achieved through connection to absence ('shadow').

4 Alternatively, of course, he is a child, unable to enliven the mother as represented by the little girl. The important point is that it is a *failing* early dyadic relationship.

5 Freud's initial conception (1920, Standard Edition, 18: 3–64) was of an instinct directed towards death and dissolution. Klein found the concept a very powerful one that helped explain the harshness of the early superego, or critical parts of the self. She believed it was operative from birth, and its containment was the most important event of early life. (Klein, 1988a: 248–57)

6 Celia serves a self-reparative function, attempting not only to connect to an absent maternal figure in Murphy, but to nurture (as mother) her *own* sad, infantile-self that is *projected* into him.

7 This passage anticipates Watt's arrival at the house of Knott, where he sits watching dying embers. It also anticipates Endon's sitting in a 'cell' with the judas-window, waiting for another to peer in, as well as Celia's own infantile experience of being imprisoned in her cot. This wavering, pulsating aspect of light, its relation to the maternal, and its effect on the internal universe is revisited in 'The Lost Ones' (see Chapter 5).

8 Apart from the clearly sexual overtones associated with the term 'worming', there is also the sense that it is somehow invasive or deceitful. See section on *Proust* in Chapter 1.

9 There is an element of primary nurturing/theft, as Murphy 'sucks' goodness-as-omniscience from the astrologer.

10 Murphy's wish to retreat to a *controlled* world of randomness can be seen as an autistic withdrawal, reflected in Molloy's obsession with creating a pattern of stone-sucking that will embrace all options. The stone-sucking is also a re-enactment of an early experience of connection at the mother's breast. The decision by the child to accept or reject food is its earliest, and it is instrumental in the nascent development of self and the world. In this view, Murphy's loss of interest in his usual, obsessive ritual is a move towards life, something immediately reversed by the arrival of Miss Dew.

11 The re-enactment with the sheep is highly condensed around a mother-infant emotional rupture. The sheep can be seen as the mother, who cannot be enlivened by a child, who experiences its inability to enliven her as its own failure. Miss Dew (who *doesn't* enliven), can be seen as the infant, with Murphy and the sheep playing a maternal role. This condensation is consistent with the child's feeling of confusion as to its own emotional state, and its role in causing it.

12 Deeper analysis revealed this man's rage at his mother for failing to protect him, and he felt he was not good enough to warrant her love. In keeping himself in a jail/room, he kept that part of himself which was *like* his father, imprisoned. Rooms also function in Beckett to encapsulate the mad or dangerous part of the self that is *felt* to be another person who occasionally invades the self.

13 Miss Clarridge's house is a prototype for later developments in Beckett's drama. There are four dominant characters, a couple (Murphy and Celia) who bicker and are interdependent, a reclusive and despairing other (the old boy), and a vigilant and intrusive other (Miss Clarridge). This structure will be revisited many times in whole (*Godot*, *Endgame*) and in part (*Footfalls*, *Rockaby*), as well as within the internal monologues of later fiction.

14 Asmus (1977) reports that Beckett wanted to emphasize 'the similarity between the daughter and mother: "The daughter only knows the voice of the mother." The strange voice of the daughter comes from the mother'. (339). This would support the contention that the two characters are parts of the same narrative-self, frozen into the earliest stages of human relating, of hearing and being heard, where subjectivity and fiction are born.

15 May's loss of personhood (being mistaken for a thing, i.e. 'a wrap'), is remin-iscent of the chandler's reaction to Murphy's appearance, to Watt's impression on the Nixons (i.e. 'a carpet'), to the Unnamable's loss of physical features, and so forth.

16 In the development of *Watt* there is a similar situation: in an early draft Knott is an abandoned, unheeded child, who is changed, in the final version, into an uninterested, maternal figure. This suggests the intriguing possibility that part of what the narrative-self is struggling to do is to understand the mother's *own* early relations. Here then, May might be fantasizing about her own *mother's* internal world, and Mrs Winter then becomes her *mother's mother*. In *Waiting for Godot*, there is a similar situation – Beckett originally planned for Godot to arrive

as Pozzo, only to displace the absent figure deeper into the play, in the form of the final Godot-figure. Another possibility is that in the fiction May reveals a split in the self into a mad (Mrs Winter) part, and a sane, but deeply repressed part. Finally, in both the play proper and the fiction, there is a clear wish for maternal connection: May's mother stands 'out' of the play to express concern for her child, and in the fiction, the 'reader' is asked to contain the name of the child.

17 We would later discover that the vomiting also reflected her forcing the poisonous thoughts out of her body, and that she experienced her parents as being the poisonous food 'forced down her throat'.

18 Celia sees Murphy from the window while he stands 'as though turned to stone in the middle of a hornpipe' (142).This reflects his dead internal state, and is echoed in *Watt*, where Arsene, upon leaving Knott's house, has a fantasy of turning into a stone pillar. The imagery of the 'frozen hornpipe' recurs in *Waiting for Godot*, where Lucky performs mechanical dances that symbolize his inner deadness, though he no longer does a hornpipe.

19 The *transitional object* is one which allows the infant to experience physical separation from the mother, as it in some sense represents her and her love (i.e. the first teddy bear)

20 In a sense, it is a precursor for the dance between Sam and Watt, which also develops an ambiguity of isolation within contact, and the late piece *Quad*. In the latter play / dance, there is a sense of both separateness and connection as the four figures move with a precision that blurs the distinction between singularity and togetherness. Their movements can suggest both a robotic synchronization that makes them independent, as well as a group functioning as a whole in a closely attuned manner.

21 In effect, Murphy-as-mother shows his *own* mood to Endon, rather than mirroring his friend's emerging infantile-self.

3

This emptied heart:
Watt's unwelcome home

Beckett's second published novel, *Watt*, tells the story of the title character's journey to, stay in, and expulsion from the house of a Mr Knott, to which he has been drawn, or summoned, to act as a servant. After his stay in the house, Watt becomes psychotic, ending up in a sort of asylum. Sam, the narrator, befriends him there, but admits the text may not approximate reality, since he can trust neither Watt's recollection (of his stay with Knott) nor his own recollection (of Watt's telling). Central to the book is the 'unknowability' of Knott, and 'unknowability' permeates the work itself, creating confusion within the reader that reflects the emotional and cognitive state of the main character. *Watt* can be read as an attempted repair of an infantile-self hovering near psychic disintegration (represented by Watt) through reconnection to maternal aspects of Mr Knott, a powerful, early imago variously experienced as withholding, uninterested and sadistic.[1] The novel explores early experience within the Autistic Contiguous and Paranoid Schizoid Positions, and there is a fluidity of imagos. At times, Watt appears predominantly in the maternal role, depleted through endless, unconditional loving of his master, while Knott acts as a devouring, insatiable infant, reflecting the condensed, confused experience of the narrative-self in its relation to an internal mother felt to be unreachable.

Hoefer views Watt's journey to Knott as an epistemological adventure doomed to failure because 'there is no logical formulation to explain Mr Knott' (Hoefer, 1965: 73). She believes Watt's inability to access a reality that underlies mere surface phenomenon causes his ultimate psychological deterioration. This reading suggests the underlying cause of Watt's lack of cognitive, exploratory 'tools' is a primary disconnection from Knott-as-mother, who cannot be *explained rationally* because he cannot be *reached emotionally*. Watt becomes fixed within early positions of human experience that are *before* language and reason. Webb (1970) and Fletcher (1964) also emphasize the theme of the impossibility of all knowledge. Fletcher feels Watt's journey to Knott is primarily religious but, instead of salvation, he finds 'a negative God, the great Nothing of which nothing can be predicated' (Fletcher, 1964: 86). Again, it is Watt's failed *relationship* with Knott-as-mother, the infantile-self's 'personal God', that explains this 'impossibility [...] of all knowledge'. Engagement with the mother's body/mind engenders knowledge, as the security that comes through her containing love reduces the anxiety of psychic disintegration, allowing for an inner 'peace' that makes incorporation of the *whole* world possible. Federman views the novel as 'a narrative experiment which exploits the inadequacy of language, reason, and logic to reveal the failure of fiction as a means of apprehending the reality of the world' (1965: 119). He believes the core of the novel, Watt's journey to, and stay in, Knott's house, becomes a metaphor for the fictional process itself. This notion is central to this reading, which views the novel as a reflection of the underlying narrative-self and its own struggle to maintain an enduring, whole relationship with another (through fantasy), including using the fiction/fantasy *itself* as a container of anxiety. *Watt* is a close study of the experience of early fantasy, the primal fiction that connects the infant to the world that is both mother and self.

Barnard (1970) sees in all of Beckett a powerful expression of the subjective experiences of schizophrenia. His recognition of the core importance of Watt's *relationship* to Knott upon *meaning*, is close to the present study. Meares (1973) also examines the experience of schizophrenia in Watt, particularly the relationship between anxiety and indecision, Watt's tendency to become overwhelmed by stimuli, and the loss of personal boundaries. Levy (1980) notes that some readings of *Watt* tend to see it as an expression of the failure of Logical Positivism, or as an exploration of the implications of the structuralist tenet that reality is linguistic: 'Watt's predicament as a kind of post-structuralist yearning for a place where naive faith in the power of language to explain external phenomenon can once more be satisfied' (Levy, 1980: 28). He quotes Bernal, '"There is nothing as disturbing in modern literature as Watt's nostalgic desire again to seize language and prevent it from failing him"' (Levy, 1980: 28). Levy also points out the importance of Watt's being verified by the other: 'if [he] is not witnessed, or feels ignored by a witness, then he has no assurance of his relation to the outside world' (Levy, 1980: 30), and also feels the narrator attempts to express a subjective experience of nothingness. The present study also recognizes the centrality of authentic language, which depends upon an enduring bond to the mother-as-primal listener, and Levy's recognition of the importance of 'witnessing' for self-development is further elaborated. Finally, there is nothing as disturbing in modern literature as Watt's failure to connect with the mother, and the consequence of this failure to establish the most central, enduring bond of the human condition – a fractured foundation of the child-self.

Hill feels the novel probes the 'precarious effects of a larger network of inconsequence, arbitrary coincidence, and self-defeating discontinuity' (1990: 20), laying more emphasis on the *nature of the relationship* between Watt and Knott as underlying the novel's fragmentation and loss of meaning: 'the figure of Knott has the effect on Watt of demolishing the already fragile structure on his identity as a subject of filiation' (1990: 27). Knott is seen as a 'figure of paternal indifference, engulfment and indeterminacy, apathy, and invisibility' (1990: 27), 'the still core of indifference at the centre of the novel' (1990: 30). Hill also stresses Watt's yearning for fusion with Knott and his anxiety about engulfment, seeing this dichotomy as important to Beckett's work in general. This study develops these points within the concept of the mother–infant matrix, and the fusion/engulfment dichotomy forms a pole of the unwitnessed infant's early schizoid dilemma. Finally, in his study of psychoanalytical 'mythologies' surrounding Beckett, Baker (1998) notes aspects of the novel's 'infant subtext', such as orality and abandonment. He describes some of the birth-imagery in the novel (Baker, 1998: 75), and of the Knott-experience writes: 'On one level it involves leaving the mystical realm [... but also suggests] a weaning-like Fall from oceanic "belonging", and a loss of primordial fusion' (1998: 23). The present study develops and integrates these notions into the overarching thesis concerning the narrative-self's struggle to connect to the mother. It hopes to correct Baker's suggestion that 'the schizoid confusion of *Watt* far exceeds the major myths of psychoanalysis' (1998: 29).

The *nature* of Watt's relationship to Knott is the central organizing principle of the novel; it is a relationship predicated upon *emotional* unavailability, neglect, and disregard. This novel explores the inter-relationship between the child's experience of the mother's love and its ability to understand the world; Watt cannot *know* Knott because Knott-as-mother's inability to love disables the *possibility* of knowledge, of both persons and the world. It is the early knowledge of the mother's body, being lovingly contained within her mind, that would 'bring [Watt the] peace', the freedom from early disintegration anxieties that allows self-integration. The entire text, like a psychoanalytical session or a dream, reveals the predominant themes of abandonment depression, psychosis, yearning for connection and love. The text contains the narrative-self's internal state and re-enacts foundational experiences with early objects. The work is not pathological, but explores aspects of early human experience. Watt's final disintegration is perhaps as eloquent a cry as there can be for an appreciation of the importance of those aspects of human life – connection, respect, love – upon which all else depends.

This chapter looks at early scenes that reflect failed psychic birth: the actual birth of Larry Nixon, and Watt's own arrival into the fiction. Next, there is a detailed reading of Arsene's speech to Watt (as the former prepares to leave Knott's house for the last time) that suggests early anxiety situations; the next section examines Watt's stay in the house, with particular emphasis on the emotional (non-)connection between the two characters, and Watt's reaction to this failure in primary attachment. Finally, there is discussion of various symbols suggesting early maternal failure, of disruptions in nurturing, and of scenes that describe Watt's need for containment by substitute maternal figures.

An unborn self

A central scene in the novel occurs before Watt appears, and embodies an experience at the emotional core of the oeuvre. Mr Hackett is conversing with the Nixons, an elderly couple, and the lady describes the birth of her son, Larry, during a dinner party she was hosting: 'The first mouthful of duck had barely passed [her] lips', when she feels the child move inside her. She continues to 'eat, drink, and make light conversation', while no 'trace of this dollar appear[s] on [her] face'. Labour begins 'with the coffee and liquors', and when the men retire to the billiard-room, she climbs up the stairs 'on [her] hands and knees', in 'anguish' and 'three minutes later [she] was a mother'. The birth is accomplished without assistance (the cord is 'severed' with her teeth), the emotion she describes is 'one of relief, of great relief' and, as the child is separated from her body, there is a feeling of 'riddance' (13–15). This vignette can be a satire of Irish middle-class mores, and certainly one can understand the woman's sense of relief at having independently survived a difficult ordeal. There is a darker side to Larry's birth, however: the father seems almost unaware of his wife's pregnancy, certainly of the labour, and the atmosphere is one of emotional mis-attunement, abandonment, and neglect. The scene is devoid of joy; the mother seems emotionally disconnected from both the experience of birth and from her newborn infant. There is little to suggest the 'oneness' of Winnicott's mother–child dyad, of the attunement so vital to the child's developing sense of self. The entire bonding period is bypassed, the mother returns to her duties as hostess immediately after the birth 'leading the infant by the hand' (15). The text's associative movement continues to reflect a state of abandonment and its genesis in early dyadic ruptures – the passage that soon follows recounts Mr Hackett's fall off a ladder, at the age of one:

> Where was your dear mother? said Tetty.
> She was out somewhere, said Mr Hackett.
> And your Papa? said Tetty.
> Papa was out breaking stones on Prince William's Seat, said Mr Hackett.
> You were all alone, said Tetty.
> There was the goat, I am told, said Mr Hackett. (16)[2]

The associations and imagery remain centred on primary abandon-ment, as an emotional layering of neglect and loneliness develops. The child's only witness, a goat, highlights the yearning for connection, and this image is often repeated within the oeuvre when characters attempt to attach to animals.[3] The decrepit hero of 'The End', for example, survives on cow's milk while resting in self-exile from the world, and the narrator of 'From An Abandoned Work' says:

> Never loved anyone I think, I'd remember. Except in my dreams, and there it was animals, dream animals [...] lovely creatures they were, white mostly [...] it's a pity, a good woman might have been the making of me, I might be sprawling in the sun now sucking my pipe and patting the bottoms of the third and fourth generations [...] No I regret nothing, all I regret is having been born, dying is such a long tiresome business. (158)

A feeling of primary disconnection manifests as an alienation from other persons, as the narrator can only dream of love with fantasy animals. There is a quick dismissal of his poignant, momentary realiza-tion that a loving relationship within a family may have allowed him to prosper. His comment about 'a good woman' touches the notion of the primary maternal object as a foundation of a vital, coherent psychic life: this is reflected in imagery suggestive of early experience (i.e. the 'sucking' of the pipe and the affectionate touching of children). In other words, *within* his fantasy he reveals the absence of a good maternal object, explaining his turn to internal, dream animals for love (as a replacement for a loving internal family). His belief that life is futile is a direct consequence of his difficulty in connecting to good *external* others, something which would require an internal template he is lacking.

The opening sections continue to develop a sense of internal loss and primary disconnection, as Watt is delivered prematurely into the world, without love, experiencing a metaphorical birth by being forced to leave a tram before reaching his destination. Ejected by an angry conductor, he is left standing 'motionless, a solitary figure' (16), a near stillbirth abandoned by the slowly receding lights of a tram that is a womb of (m)otherness. Immediately the underlying feeling-state of the narrative-self (and its objectification in the *subjective* world of Watt) begins to merge, and a dissociative aura develops. Described as an 'it', Watt is 'scarcely to be distinguished from the dim wall behind', and he can be viewed here as an embryonic, genderless self with no discernible human features, awaiting a mother (Knott) who will help to 'create' him. Indeed, Mrs Hackett is unsure of his gender, and Mr Hackett is 'not sure that it was not a parcel, a carpet for example, or a roll of tarpaulin' (16). A mist of 'unknowability' is cast, Mr Hackett '[does] not know when he had been so intrigued' (17) feeling an unusual 'sensation' which he does not think he can 'bear [...] for more than twenty minutes, or half an hour' (17).[4] A sense of psychic dissolution pervades the scene, foreshadowing the stay in Knott's house, and there is an urgency for Hackett to 'know' Watt just as Watt will feel an urgency to 'know' Knott. The boundary between objects and persons dissolves as Mr Nixon says to Hackett: 'When I see him, or think of him, I think of you, and [...] when I see you, or think of you, I think of him' (19). To Hackett's urgent clamouring for information Nixon pleads ignorance, 'nothing is known' (21), despite apparently knowing (in the weak sense) Watt all his life. This inchoate sense of 'knowing' Watt is reflected by Nixon's statement that he does not remember their first meeting 'any more than I remember meeting my father' (23), as we enter a pre-symbolic realm that exists before identity and conscious memory, where the earliest subjectivity is formed. After leaving the group, Watt continues towards his destination via the railroad terminus, and the sense of disconnection from a loving primary object is high-lighted by the song Watt 'hears', which appears in the addenda: 'With all our heart breathe head awhile darkly apart the air exile of ended smile of ending care darkly awhile the exile air' (253). This suggests a primary rupture, the infant's whole world, merged with its mother ('all our heart') lasting only too briefly before separation ('darkly apart') into a world of loveless exile ('of ended smile'), and a schizoid withdrawal that reflects the primal loss ('of ending care'). The result of this loveless, darkened internal exile is Watt's withdrawn passivity, apparent when, after falling over a milkcan, he does not pick up his hat because he does not feel free to do so 'until the porter had finished abusing him' (25). He survives by remaining inoffensive, adopting a submissive demeanour in situations where he stumbles into others' affairs. This is characteristic of many Beckettian figures – Molloy's bumbling with the police, the travails of 'she' in *Not I*, or of O in *Film*, all of whom, like Watt, seem content to circumvent society in the hope of existing in peace on the periphery. Watt's socialization is actually severely disturbed: '[He] had watched people smile and thought he understood how it was done [… but] some little thing was lacking, and people who saw it for the first time, and most people who saw it saw it for the first time, were sometimes in doubt as to what expression exactly was intended. To many it seemed a simple sucking of the teeth' (25). He is unable to articulate one of the earliest gestures, a smile, a biologically wired reaction essential both to early mother and child bonding and to the growth of the child's sense of personhood (Meares, 1993: 66–8). His inability to smile with authenticity suggests an enduring disruption in his ability to be with others in any meaningful way, reflecting the depth of his disconnection from the mother. His tooth-sucking implies a regression to early stages of mother–infant relating – Watt seems to be self-nurturing by sucking at a nipple within his own body, and it also parodies the 'sucking reflex' of the newborn that communicates hunger.

Given this legacy, Watt's journey becomes a search for an emotional connection he has never known. On the train, the aura of reality begins to shift – no longer aware of the other passengers, Watt withdraws into an internal world: '[He] heard nothing of this, because of other voices, singing, crying, stating, murmuring, things unintelligible, in his ear' (29). In concert with this, the narrator presents the first of a number of long ruminative descriptions that appear in the book: 'Now these voices, sometimes they sang only, and sometimes they cried only, and sometimes they stated only, and sometimes they murmured only, and sometimes they sang and cried, and sometimes they sang and stated, and sometimes they sang and murmured [etc.]' (29). These types of passage sometimes run for several pages, providing complete, logical enumerations of the possible arrangements of the qualities of an object or of a situation. In this particular passage, it is the nature of the voices that Watt hears – later examples will be Mr Knott's appearance, the arrangement of his furniture, and the ways five committee members can look at each other in sequence. These passages create within the reader a sense of the closed intrapsychic space central both to Watt's experience and to the text's underlying emotional reality, as words themselves run on obsessively. This experience is often explored in the oeuvre as, for example, in Molloy's description of his 'sucking stones':

> And the first thing I hit upon was that I might do better to transfer the stones four by four, instead of one by one, that is to say, during the sucking, to take the three stones remaining in the right pocket of my greatcoat and replace them by the four in the right pocket of my trousers, and these by the four in the left pocket of my greatcoat, plus the one, as soon as I had finished sucking it, which was in my mouth (64).

These passages have an autistic sense, reflecting the experience of certain patients described by Tustin (1981, 1986, 1990); they prefigure Beckett's continuing exploration of autistic aspects of early experience by using words as 'autistic objects', actual objects used by a child to soothe himself, replacing real interactions with persons. A child may grip a hard toy car, becoming entirely absorbed in this sensation to the exclusion of all external reality, and Tustin suggests these objects soothe by sparing the child the reality of separation from the primary love object. These children, oblivious to the world, have suffered a traumatic, early disruption in their core, primary psychological bond to the mother:

> A sad situation which often seems to be the starting place for autistic withdrawal, is a mother and baby who experience bodily separateness from each other as being torn violently apart and wounded [...] pathological autistic objects seem to staunch the 'bleeding' by blocking the wound. They also seem to plug the gap between the couple so that bodily separateness is not experienced. (Tustin, 1981: 31)

In Beckett's work, birth is often represented as a painful, violent separation, and when viewed metaphorically as premature psychological birth, these images become extremely potent. The heroine of *Not I*, 'out into the world too soon' with 'no love', Hamm relying on his 'old stauncher' as he suffers the realization that Clov-as-mother (or as child) may be gone (i.e. he suffers a 'bleeding' loss of part of himself), and Watt, born from the tram a station too soon, and forced to leave

Knott's house without the emotional sustenance he seeks, all retreat into the autistic world Tustin explores clinically. In this light, Molloy's stones are deeply symbolic objects that, like Watt's tooth-sucking, allow him to reconnect to early experiences of feeding from the mother's body.[5] The autistic object also serves a protective function, creating the illusion of an impenetrable barrier to the external world, and words themselves can be used in this fashion. In an analytical setting, a patient may present a barrage of words, often impenetrable and without pause; words function as *things*, without emotional referent, and block awareness of the separate analyst/mother by shrouding the self in a protective 'second skin' (Bick, 1968, 1986). In *Watt*, Beckett begins to explore this aspect of words, as the long, obsessional passages reflect Watt's own experience, enclosing him in a self-contained world. The effect is shared with the reader: the passages create a sense of claustrophobic encasement, with words literally forming a dense barricade of ink that edges towards a loss of meaning, as the reader becomes frustrated, bored within a closed psychic space. These passages have another important quality, since their *content* reveals the underlying cause of Watt's schizoid withdrawal to be a failure in primary emotional connection. He re-experiences a traumatic situation where Knott is unavailable for repair, and his ruminations both defend against the deep depression engendered by this absence, and reveal it – they can be viewed as attempts to *create* feelings of connection within the self. The core obsessional passages *are* Watt's attempts to know Knott by locating him (203), or by imagining his personal belongings (204) or his appearance (209). Likewise, in the long passage concerning the five committee members at Louit's 'dissertation', who never meet each other's gaze (175–9), the primary importance of recognition is demonstrated. The ruminations about the Lynch family's chances of perfect numerical harmony (101–11) suggest a need for a complete, enduring group of internal objects. Overall, these passages create feelings of non-experience, exhibiting an active destruction of knowledge that protects the self from a persecutory, chaotic mother/world, perhaps reflecting an identification with a mother who herself used such obsessional devices to control the world or her child.

Watt represents the part of the narrative-self that feels itself a pariah on the world's margins: wandering toward Knott, an elderly lady throws a stone at him, and so complete is his divorce from his own body, this violence raises no emotion. Resting under the night sky, he becomes uncomfortable with the moon's shining upon him 'as though

he were not there' (33). The moonlight creates a sense of depersonalization, he is unrecognized, absent, his sense of himself is compressed,
and there is no home in the world – he dislikes both the moon and the
sun, the earth and the sky. The image of the bright, round moon 'face'
connects to early feelings of seeing the mother, of *being seen* by her. The
infant can, from virtually the earliest moments of life, begin to identify
the human visage, and this appears to be hard-wired neurologically.
Watt's disconnection from such primary contact underscores his
isolation from the mother and the world, his dislike of celestial bodies
may be an introjection of his feeling of being unwitnessed and unloved
by heavenly faces. Curling up into the ditch, burying himself, as Molloy
will do, into mother earth, Watt engenders himself, becoming his own
creator, though now enclosed in an autistic world. The deepest human
anxiety mounts, he hallucinates the singing of the long repetitive
number, '*Fifty-one point one/four two eight five seven one/four two eight five
seven one*' (35), strikingly reminiscent of autistic children described by
Tustin, for whom numbers become enclosing, encapsulating objects
that protect them by creating a shell that prevents seepage of the self
into the world. In this way, the autistic number 'enwombs' Watt by
holding him together intrapsychically. The internal voices also sing
verses to him: 'greatgran/ma Ma/grew how/do you/do blooming/
thanks and/you drooping/thanks and/you withered/thanks and/you
for/gotten thanks and/you thanks for/gotten/too greatgran/ma Ma'
(35). Despairing parts of the self view ageing as irrevocably, exclusively
linked to emotional loss (i.e. the Great Mother, old and forgotten) and,
as so often in the oeuvre, the life cycle is compressed and devitalised,
becoming a hopeless decline that ends without meaning: 'grew [...]
blooming [...] withered [...] drooping [...] withered [...] forgotten'. A
second verse that Watt hallucinates demonstrates the despair that
develops from an experience of maternal unavailability, and its effect
on feeding:

> a big fat bun [...]
> for Mr Man and a bun
> for Mrs Man and a bun [...]
> a big fat bun for everyone ...
> till all the buns are done and everyone is gone
> home to oblivion (35)

This 'song' is Watt's core hope for an unimaginable bounty of
feeding for all ('a big fat bun for everyone', i.e. all 'Man'-kind), and for a

happy, 'full'filled internal family living together in loving harmony. This fantasy is catastrophically drained, the source of nutrition is depleted or withheld, and total annihilation results ('everyone is gone'). Watt is unable to maintain an enduring image of a good, loving mother/nutrient-giver; rather, his internal world is dominated by an imago that is withholding, sadistic, or depleted by greedy, sadistic infantile demands, and the final paradoxical line ('home to oblivion') reflects a return to futile entrapment.

On the primitive edge of Knott

Watt's stay with Mr Knott is an attempt at self-reparation, a tragic search for the mother's mind in the hope of creating an enduring, coherent sense of self. Winnicott describes the child's need for 'good-enough' mothering by a caretaker able to attend to its basic needs, allowing for the development of the self – it is the failure to recognize such needs, and the deleterious consequences of such failures on human development, that shall be enacted in the house. Watt's desire to be 'fully born' is suggested by his immediate motivation for leaving the ditch where he lay with the 'voices' prior to his arrival at Knott's: 'The earth [...] he felt it, and smelt it, the bare hard dark stinking earth. And if there were two things that Watt loathed, one was the earth, and the other was the sky. So he crawled out of the ditch' (36).[6] The possibilities of life are compressed, for between earth and sky there is no home for Watt, and no chance for an existence in which he is not suffocated within a neither-/non-space between two bad objects. Thus he begins his quest to be reborn, though he 'never [knows] how he got into Mr Knott's house' (37), the backdoor mysteriously becomes unlocked, as his entry becomes steeped in a sense of contingency. Sitting by the kitchen fire, playing with the ashes, using his hat to give them life, he watches the embers 'greyen, redden, greyen, redden', and while absorbed in this 'innocent little game' (38) the servant whom he is to replace, Arsene, enters the room without his knowledge. A beautifully lyrical passage illuminates Watt's central struggle to master his sense of isolation from the world, something reflected by Arsene's unpredictable (non-)arrival. The passage stresses this mystery, reflecting the Watt's 'fort-da' ash-game,[7] as he controls a myriad of losses by manipulating the embers: his tenuous grasp on the external world, his fragmentary sense of self, his absent internal mother, and the 'light' of reason:

He found it strange to think, of these little changes, of scene, the little gains, the little losses, the thing brought, the thing removed [...] strange to think of all these little things that cluster round the comings, and the stayings, and the goings, that he would know nothing of them, nothing of what they had been, as long as he lived, nothing of when they came, of how they came [...] nothing of when they went, of how they went, and how it was then, compared with before, before they came, before they went. (38)

This description of Watt's interior landscape suggests an isolated-self incapable of maintaining enduring links to its internal objects. The 'comings and goings' are unknowable, and the sense of lost attachment suggests an elusive, internal universe in incomplete contact with the self. The scene foreshadows the desperate sense of lost primary love described in *Embers*::

> Ada: [...] Is this rubbish a help to you Henry? [*Pause.*] I can try and go on a little if you wish. [*Pause.*] No? [*Pause.*] Then I think I'll be getting back.
> Henry: Not yet! You needn't speak. Just listen. Not even. Be with me. [*Pause.*] Ada! [*Pause. Louder.*] Ada! [*Pause.*] Christ! [*Pause.*] Hooves! [*Pause. Louder.*] Hooves! [*Pause.*] Christ! [*Long pause.*]. (103)

Like Watt, Henry's grasp on his internal world (here represented by the hallucinated voice of his dead wife) is tenuous, ever ready to leave without warning, remaining beyond his ability to recall it, fading and glowing like gently dying embers. Henry's only need is for her presence, she need not speak nor even listen, he only desires to be alone in the presence of the mother. Winnicott (1965: 29–36) felt a momentous developmental stage for the emerging-self is the ability to be alone, something made possible by the infant's ability to lose itself in play while in proximity to the mother, who acted in a transitional manner to contain the child as a felt, background presence. Watt's little game with the ashes is, perhaps, a doomed attempt to play in this way. Like the female images in *... but the clouds ...*, *Footfalls*, and so forth, the female visage in *Embers* reflects a primary imago that binds the internal world, but which is only tenuously felt and not enduring. Left alone again, Watt's ember-game ends, they 'would not redden anymore, but remained grey, even in the dimmest light' (39). His fort-da game lost as contact with the external world ebbs, his ability to retain his internal universe becomes tenuous, and he begins to '[masturbate] his snout' (40) like many autistic children who turn to self-stimulation to avert the black hole of nothingness. The servant Arsene returns, aware his days with Knott are over and, in a long, rambling speech, he reveals the nature and impact of the intrapscyhic consequences of his stay in the house.

Arsene begins, as if coming out of a trance, 'Haw! how it all comes back to me, to be sure' (39), and what comes back is a remembrance of his self-state, prior to his Knott-experience, a condensation of schizoid experiences:

> The man arrives! The dark ways all behind, all within, the long dark ways, in his head [...] And all the sounds, meaning nothing. Then at night rest in the quiet house, there are no roads, no streets any more, you can lie down by a window opening on refuge, the little sounds come that demand nothing, ordain nothing, explain nothing [...] and the sky blue again over all the secret places where nobody ever comes [...] sites of a stirring beyond coming and going, of a being so light and free that it is as the being of nothing. (39)

It is possible to view the house as mother's mind, in which the anxious, fragmented infantile-self hopes to be contained; the house *is* Knott *is* the mother, and Watt hopes to rest here (as Murphy did in the 'third zone') to escape the darkness 'all within [...] his head'. Arsene and Watt are lonely, isolated men, fleeing a dark world for refuge, but there is also the intrapsychic world of the infantile-self fleeing deeper into Guntrip's 'lost heart of the self', a place of sanctuary, almost beyond yearning, past the 'comings and goings'. Guntrip saw this as the mind's last desperate retreat, into which it is driven by the despair of being unable to enter into a loving, genuine relationship, and it is this place into which Watt withdraws for reparation, hoping his damaged sense of himself will be recognized and nurtured. In relating such hopes, Arsene speaks of arriving in the house 'after so long, here, and here, and in my hands, and in my eyes, like a face raised, a face offered, all trust and innocence and candour' (40), like the infant seeking the mirroring, self-affirming smile of the mother, he comes to Knott hoping to find an emotional attunement that will allow a move beyond his inner fortress.[8] Knott, and his house, too, offer such sanctuary, the 'fit is perfect' between infant and mother, as a merged sense of loving containment binds the sensual world: 'The sensations, the premonitions of harmony are irrefragable, of imminent harmony, when all outside him will be he, the flowers the flowers that he is among him, the sky the sky that he is above him, the earth trodden the earth treading, and all sound his echo' (40–1). The world loses its terrifying aura, and here, with what Winnicott calls the stable, nurturing 'background mother', Watt has the chance to rest 'without misgiving', to be 'as he is', for the first time since 'in anguish and disgust he relieved his mother of her milk' (41). This captures the ambivalence of early infantile experience – there is 'anguish', the desperate sense that it is the infant who is damaging the mother, draining her, possibly causing the ruptures in early feeding. Alternatively, there is a sense of disgust reflecting, perhaps, an anxiety about dependence on the breast for survival. Now, though, with Knott, there is an opportunity to move back beyond the 'basic fault' to a mental place where one is held psychically by the mother, and where one can begin to feel oneself into the world.[9] One can begin to *be*, feeling disparate sensations coalesce into a coherent self, fragments which are, at first, held together by the mother's containing function – mother and child create each other – Watt will 'witness[es] and [be] witnessed' (42).

Watt's experience with Knott begins with this hope of being at one with a caring, nurturing mother, able to soothe her infant, to merge with it in a mutual witnessing; it will end with the devastation of this hope. Thus, Arsene speaks of the Fall, that 'terrible day' (42) that begins with a sense of calm, primal merger with the world: 'I was in the sun, and the wall was in the sun. I was the sun, need I add, and the wall, and the step, and the yard, and the time of year, and the time of day, to mention only these' (42). Basking in the glow of the background Knott / mother, Arsene experiences a oneness with the external world, as a timeless lack of boundaries pervades his experience. This approximates a primary monadic bliss, beginning *in utero*, a vital part of early experience carried through the life cycle as a sense of internal well-being. Soon, however, a catastrophic change occurs that alters the world for ever. It reflects a premature psychological separation from the mother that is experienced as overly traumatic, overwhelming an infantile-self that is psychically unprepared; if the separation is precipitated by an unempathic or depressed mother, the results can be a depleted sense of self, a depressed or anxious attitude, or even frank psychosis. Arsene sits in the garden, merged with the universe, with the 'background object of primary identification', the Knott / mother, supplying a sense of belonging and security, when the change occurs. He puffs at his pipe in great contentment, like a babe at the breast, his own breast swelling. The boundary between self and mother blurs, there is a feeling of primary rupture, 'let us not linger on my breast' (43), just as the separation begins. Birth images abound – the change lies 'hymeneal still', there is an image of maternal depletion, he says 'bugger these buttons! – as flat and – ow! – as hollow as a tambourine' (42). This imagery is central to an understanding of both Arsene's and Watt's Knott-experience, for there is substantial clinical and experimental evidence that the infant's 'rooting' for the nipple is innate, and is a primary focus of early sensuality (Tustin, 1981: 32). Tustin sees:

> The sensuous connection [of the infant's mouth] with the nipple of the breast [as replacing] the ante-natal umbilical connection with the placenta of the mother [... and that] the constellation of nipple and tongue working rhythmically together with mouth and breast sets the feeling of rootedness in train [...] this basic sense of being rooted sets the scene for the development of a sense of identity, security and self-confidence. Lacking this sense of rootedness, the child's psychic life is dominated by feelings of 'nothingness'. (Tustin, 1981: 32–3)

In one of the central clinical vignettes of her work, Tustin describes a young autistic boy, John, whose terrified sense of dissolution centred around feelings that a 'button' was gone or broken. The 'button' was a clear referent for the mother's nipple and was the boy's 'present day formulation for the previously undifferentiated, unformulated, insuffer-able experience of sensuous loss which had precipitated the autism' (Tustin, 1986: 80). Thus, the button symbol, for both the autistic child and Arsene, comes to represent the entire experiential world of pre-mature, catastrophic separation from the mother, and this is tantamount to a loss of fundamental containment for a fragile sense of self.[10] This loss leads to feelings of fundamental disconnection, attendant feelings of panic and despair, and fears of annihilation and fragmentation. Just as the 'broken button' experience accompanies John's autistic withdrawal into a protective psychic shell, it is at this point in his telling that, for Arsene, 'suddenly somewhere some little thing slipped, some little tiny thing' (43). What slips is Arsene himself, away from the illusory security of the Knott-mother, now feeling alone, separate, and frightened by his smallness in the world:

> There is a great alp of sand, one hundred metres high, between the pines and the ocean, and there in the warm moonless night, when no one is looking, no one listening, in tiny packets of two or three millions the grains slip, all together, a little slip of one or two lines maybe, and then stop, all together, not one missing, and that is all, that is all for that night, and perhaps for ever that is all, for in the morning with the sun a

little wind from the sea may come, and blow them one from another far apart, or a pedestrian scatter them with his foot. (43)

This passage is ripe with imagery of separation and fragmentation – the 'great alp of sand' can symbolize merged experience, both psychically and physically, within the mother/infant dyad. The alp is both the infantile-mind, and a containing, maternal mind, holding together, in unindividuated fashion, the experience of the infant-with-mother. Breast-like in shape, the alp echoes the primary imagery Arsene employs to describe his experience in the garden/mind of Knott. It suggests an experience of, or wish for, holding and containment within the Knott/ mother, but also suggests the tenuous, 'sand-like' nature of that bond. When there is no one to witness, as Knott does not witness, the particles are blown asunder, as the infantile-self is 'untimely ripped' from the maternal mind. Again, the image of the moon suggests an early experience of the mother's face, but in this case it is on a moon*less* night, when the alp-as-infant mind is unseen and unheard, that the disintegration occurs. Arsene's sense of self now fragments, a few particles amidst an overwhelming universe, and these scatter, blown about, much as Murphy ends amidst the sawdust. The sand is a highly condensed metaphor for a self-state both constricted and scattered, both bound by the other and alone, and as prone to fragmentation as sand.[11] These particles of self (memory complexes of feelings and thoughts) are bound together in the child by the mother's containment, something the child eventually internalizes and makes his own. Without this 'glue of the self', the child's self is prone to a Humean nightmare of unconnected sensation, isolated, ever ready to fragment unless held together in a constricted, encasing, and autistic fashion, something often suggested by the oeuvre's imagery of ashcans, bottles, and enclosed rooms. It is this separation that Arsene experiences, the slippage of multitudinous parts of himself that were ill-seen, ill-heard in Knott's mind, parts not processed: 'millions of little things moving all together out of their old place, into a new one nearby [...] I was the only person living to discover them' (43). It is just at this point that Arsene experiences himself in a state of blissful merger with the universe, with the Knott/mother, in a place without boundary, without a sense of demarcation of the self: 'My personal system was so distended [...] the distinction between what was inside it and what was outside it was not at all easy to draw. Everything that happened happened inside it, and at the same time everything that happened happened outside it'

(43). In this state, premature rupture is catastrophic for the developing self, since the child's pre-symbolic mind takes in the world directly, in a manner closer to feeling than thought, Arsene perceives so sensuously that 'the impressions of a man buried alive in Lisbon [...] seem a frigid and artificial construction of the understanding' (43). Arsene demands maternal containment, and the intense vivaciousness of the experience is compared to the terrorized thoughts of a man buried alive, a claustrophobic encasement the later prose and drama will develop. After 'the slip' the world undergoes, like the sun, a 'radical change of appearance' (44). Arsene is frozen in a pre-symbolic, Autistic Contiguous world, with no demarcation between things, no names to bind the sensual world: 'my tobacco-pipe, since I was not eating a banana, ceased so completely from the solace to which I was inured, that I took it out of my mouth to make sure it was not a thermometer, or an epileptic's dental wedge' (44). This oral, 'solace' giving nipple/pipe no longer calms, or nurtures, and this catastrophe is highlighted by the fact that virtual newborns can distinguish between objects within their mouths. Like the pre-representative infantile-mind, Arsene cannot name, nor remember, what he does not see – the pipe in his mouth is *unseen*, and must be lost. He is ripped away from the good breast, the containing mind, and from meaning, something Watt will soon experience himself.

Arsene describes the change as a separation: 'What was changed was existence off the ladder. Do not come down the ladder, Ifor, I haf taken it away' (44), like Ifor, he is left without a connection to another, and now feels his world is changed forever.[12] He experiences this premature separation as an overwhelming, disorganizing loss, 'As when a man, having found at last what he sought, a woman, for example, or a friend, loses it' (44); yet he acknowledges the human need to strive for satiation of instinctual drives such as food and sex:

> It is useless not to seek, not to want, for when you cease to seek you start to find, and when you cease to want, then life begins to ram her fish and chips down your gullet until you puke, and then the puke down your gullet until you puke the puke, and then the puked puke until you begin to like it. To hunger, thirst, lust, every day afresh and every day in vain [...] that's the nearest we'll ever get to felicity. (44)

Experience is generalized from his relationship with Knott, whose only need is for an audience to contain him in his isolation. The all-encompassing intrusiveness of this demand is as an invasion of the self:

food is forced into the body and subsequent attempts to externalize this 'badness' fail, until the only option is compliance, and an acceptance of the bad as part of self. Kohut (1971, 1977) saw the breakdown of nurturing and empathic ties between the mother and child (particularly the mother's ability to allow the child to use her as a mirror) as leading to fixation on more primitive needs, which are breakdown products of unattuned parenting (Siegel, 1996). This passage highlights this from the child's point of view – mirroring needs are forever unmet, since love is unattainable (just as the love of the Knott is unattainable) and Arsene is left forever longing. He describes this absence as 'the presence of what did not exist, that presence without, that presence within, that presence between' (45). This 'presence', the sense of being that is the core of authentic subjective experience, is found within the mother's love, and so the boundaries of the world, 'within, without, between', collapse into a dead, empty despair. Knott is absence incarnate – there is no presence without, and no possibility to take the 'presence within' by incorporating the mother as a valued, calming, and mirroring part of the self.

This absence and premature separation leaves Arsene in hopeless despair: 'Not a word, not a deed, not a thought, not a need, not a grief, not a joy, not a girl, not a boy [...] not a face, no time, no place, that I do not regret, exceedingly' (46). This is, in Bion's terms, negative K, the absence of libido, and Arsene's entire world becomes depleted of meaning, much like the world of the painter friend of Hamm's in *Endgame*, who sees only ash. A similar sentiment is described in a passage dozens of lines long: 'The poor old lousy old earth, my earth and my father's and my mother's and my father's father's and my mother's mother's [...] and fathers' fathers' fathers' and mothers' mothers' mothers'. An excrement' (47). Arsene universalizes despair – everyone's world becomes meaningless, his entire inner world of progenitors, his *internal family*, is left joyless. It is an utter hopelessness, since all persons must share the same 'lousy earth' or internal world, and there is no chance of an alternative reality. This long, ruminative passage both encases and reveals his feeling-state; this denigration of possibility is also a defensive, envious attack on life, since by turning the world into 'an excrement' there can be nothing left for Arsene to desire. The entire life cycle is also devalued: 'The crocuses and the larch turning green every year [...] the pastures with the uneaten sheep's placentas [...] and the children walking in the dead leaves and the larch turning brown [...] and the endless April showers and the crocuses and then the whole bloody business starting all over again. A turd' (47). This imagery reflects Arsene's internal world – depleted of meaning, hope-less, condensed and, like the life represented in *Breath,* there is neither space nor time for joy or rebirth. Worst of all there is no possibility of change: 'And if I could begin it all over again a hundred times, knowing each time a little more than the time before, the result would always be the same' (47). It is an eternal recurrence of Hell, a depleted, regressed self with no contact, nor any *hope* of contact with good or calming internal (or external) objects that could help effect psychic change. It is a feeling of such desperate sorrow that he imagines his 'weary little legs' carrying him away from this 'state or place', '[with] tears blinding [his] eyes', 'longing to be turned into a stone pillar', where perhaps a 'lonely man like [himself]' might come and rest against him' (49). The stone image reflects his dead self-state, and the fantasy that he might provide comfort to another is poignant in its yearning for contact, but his sympathy is withdrawn from the world, since he is in 'no fit state [...] to trouble [his] head' about the difficulties of others' (49). Like a helpless child, he imagines his departure will be catastrophic, and he leaves Knott without 'a hope, a friend, a plan, a prospect' to trudge off into a loveless world until he falls, and 'unable to rise', will be 'taken into custody black with flies' (56). There remains, to the end, a small sense of mercy and hope within the world, as Arsene, an orphan in the world of the living, seems destined for maternal containment within an insti-tutional setting.[13]

Fundamentally, then, Arsene leaves Knott in the Depressive Position, able to experience a sense of loss and mourning. He sees a bleak future, is 'sadder, but not wiser' (56) and has been an Ancient Mariner for Watt, warning his replacement of his lost contact with the world. The tenuous tie to Knott broken, Arsene cannot maintain a sense of calm, self-nurturing, as life itself becomes loss. He tells Watt: 'another night [will] fall and another man come and Watt go, Watt who is now come, for the coming is in the shadow of the going and the going is in the shadow of the coming.' (57), echoing a famous passage by Freud, in *Mourning and Melancholia*. Following the loss of a loved person: 'the free libido was not displaced onto another object; it was withdrawn into the ego [...where] it served to establish an identification of the ego with the abandoned object. Thus the shadow of the object fell upon the ego' (Freud, 1987: 258). Since Knott is absent from the beginning, there is nothing but shadow to bring within, and because the proper work of mourning cannot be done Arsene remains chronically depressed, experiencing life as a fusion between coming, going, and varying forms of separation, with no real point of contact or possibility of loving engagement. There is no sense of human presence, and therefore, in leaving Knott, he is truly alone, since nothing can be taken from the experience. His inner world is condensed into a 'budding withering', a 'coming and being and going in purposelessness' where any feeling of hope is 'dead' (58).

Before leaving Watt in the dawning light, Arsene gives him an idea of the master he is to serve. Knott is an isolated, withdrawn figure about whom it is 'rumoured' that [he] 'would prefer to have no one at all about him' (59). His desire for complete self-sufficiency is thwarted by his infantile nature, in that 'he is obliged to have someone to look after him' (59). Knott's narcissism is extensive, he has but two needs: 'not to need […] and a witness to his not needing' (202). This equation sets up the dynamics at the heart of the novel, and of Watt's suffering, for though Knott needs the other, it is only by default, as a denied admission of failed omnipotence. The other is but a mirror of Knott's illusory self-sufficiency, and any yearning for genuine connection is doomed to fail, since the world acts only as a source of recognition and need fulfilment. Knott and his endless entourage of servants fluctuate between two poles, with Knott as absent, self-fulfilled mother and the servants, 'big bony shabby seedy haggard knockkneed men' or 'little fat shabby seedy juicy or oily bandylegged men' (58) as yearning, love-starved infants, 'eternally turning about [him] in tireless love' (60). Alternately, Knott can be seen as an ever demanding, never grateful infant, about whom hovers an endless parade of very good mother/servants, and it is into this world that Arsene ushers Watt, leaving him as suddenly and quietly as the Ancient Mariner leaves the wedding guest. Watt, like the guest who must face the 'morrow morn', waits for Knott in the slowly dawning 'day without precedent' (64). But whereas the *Rime* yields up a hope for love from an embracing God who 'made and loveth all', Watt is doomed to seek where it cannot be found – from a being that loves only itself.

An imperfect witness

The unfolding non-relationship between Watt and his master is a dramatic representation of early schizoid experience, with the characters forming aspects of a coherent narrative-self. It is an *internal* world, in which the central feeling-state is that of a helpless, hopeless child struggling to maintain an attuned, intimate relationship to its mother. There are several key scenes that reflect this central dynamic organization as Watt, representative of a depleted, fragmenting aspect of self, vainly seeks a nurturing 'background object of primary identification' to contain him. He encounters Knott instead, and exists only as a witness to illusory self-sufficiency, finding that outside of this function he does not exist. A clinical example may set the stage:

> The patient entered analysis complaining of binge-eating, excessive compliance, and the inability to think independently. An unwanted child, she served only two functions for her single mother, to mirror her grandiosity and to care for her when she suffered from her many depressive episodes. The patient's sense of herself was founded on her ability to provide an illusory sense of independence for her mother, something for which she received neither affection nor gratitude. As an adult she vainly attempted to find affection, and allowed herself to be used for the other's gratification and aggrandizement, as she had done earlier for her mother. Ultimately, she experienced an extended period of dissociation, and wandered from city to city in a haze, drifting from one relationship to another with abusive, selfish men. She felt she could be sure of nothing without the input of such men, and could not make decisions, nor have a clear sense of reality without them.

There are many similarities between this woman's experience and Watt's: difficulties in linking thoughts, repressed feelings of rage, abandonment depression and so forth, all linked to an experience of lost contact with a good, nurturing mother. Watt's story is both a re-creation of this internal experience and a revelation of his attempt to repair himself through a failed attempt to discover the mother's love.

Watt's entry into a matrix of early experience within Knott's house / mind begins quietly enough – he has no direct dealings with his master, though he imagines, wrongly, that he would some day. He works ardently at his chores, seeing little of Knott, who himself 'saw nobody, heard from nobody' (69), and indeed, the house is *itself* a sort of autistic shell. Intrusions are rare occurrences – 'fleeting acknowledgments [...] like little splashes on it from the outside world' (69), and the house is a rigid, nearly impenetrable barrier to the world metaphorical of a mind structured on exclusion.[14] This isolation is more abstract and complete in the published version of *Watt*. In the first draft, *Poor Johnny Watt*, Knott is a sixty-year-old man, living alone, abused by two servants, and quickly dismissed by the narrator as never having 'been properly born'. His father, a musician, was a suicide (Coetzee, 1972). By the time the third draft was written Knott's father is no longer mentioned: his past remains speculative, and he has become more abstract in his role as an absent other. Thus, in his initial conception, Knott's person is formed in a relationship with a lost primary object, his dead father, and it is he, not Watt, who has not been born properly. In fact, the story of Larry Nixon's birth is an amplification of the story of the birth of Knott in the first draft (Coetzee, 1972). Within the development of the novel, through the draft stages, there is a blurred sense of an unborn self shifting between Watt and Knott, and this confusion mirrors their relationship in the final version. In *Watt*, both men are damaged, unable to form enduring connections with others, and this underlies the futility of Watt's seeking an identification and love with an object, Knott, who is himself incapable of such a bond. The loss becomes 'intergenerational', in that Knott, product of parental absence and a victim of abuse in the first draft, recreates the unavailability of his own dead father, and apparently absent mother, in his own relationship with Watt – this opens the possibility that within *Watt* the narrative-self is attempting to make sense of its progenitors' *own* internal experiences with primary objects.

It is only by obsessive rumination that Watt feels any connection to Knott: there is no possibility of a genuine evocative memory of the relationship, he must constantly hold Knott in his mind at the risk of losing him altogether. So fragile is this hold that there is no definitive image, but rather a series of speculations as his master, like an elusive electron, is knowable only in his uncertainty. By maintaining an image of him through all-encompassing fantasies, Watt fulfills Knott's own primary need to be witnessed in his not-needing, to be held in the maternal mind:

> What kind of witness was Watt [...]
> A needy witness, an imperfect witness.
> The better to witness, the worse to witness.
> That with his need he might witness its absence.
> That imperfect he might witness it ill.
> That Mr Knott might never cease, but ever almost cease.
> Such appeared to be the arrangement. (203)

Watt, with his own experience of maternal absence, and his need for containment, is the perfect candidate to provide Knott with faulty mirroring (i.e. 'to witness its absence [...] ill' in Knott – the lack of internal connection), though he also attempts to provide, and to receive, love. This allows Knott a tentative connection to Watt, reminiscent of Endon with Murphy, that does not become threatening, but holds both men just shy of total dissolution. Knott exists without experiencing an enduring sense of the world's permanence, '[moving] about the house he did so as one unfamiliar with the premises', and walking 'in the midst of his garden [...] as one unacquainted with its beauties [...] as though they, or he, had been created in the course of the night' (203). This explains Knott's dependence on his servants, including Watt, who act as Winnicott's 'object mother' to provide, with perfect anticipation, for Knott's every physical need. Knott is enmeshed in omnipotent self-sufficiency and not-needing, but cannot tolerate separateness since he needs to be held psychically by the other, to avoid abandonment to psychic death. Watt experiences Knott as elusive, unfixed, and emotionally unknowable – even in his room, where he 'seemed least a stranger', Knott's location is uncertain: 'Here he stood. Here he sat. Here he knelt. Here he lay. Here he moved, to and fro, from the door to the window, from the window to the door; from the window to the door, from the door to the window [etc.]'(204). This passage runs on for several hundred words, creating a hypnotic, derealizing effect in the reader that echoes Watt's experience. It is one of many in the work that creates a primal uncertainty, reflecting underlying loneliness, and disconnection; the style embodies a pervasive isolation, as well as an obsessive need to make contact.[15] The significance of such passages becomes clearer towards the end of Watt's stay with Knott, when are told that he does not experience, consciously, a deep emotional need for his master: 'Watt suffered neither from the presence of Mr Knott, nor from his absence. When he was with him, he was content to be with him, and when he was away from him, he was content to be away from him' (207). After he actually leaves Knott's house, though, he begins to cry, and is surprised by this reaction, not believing such a thing possible, 'if he had not been there himself' (208).[16] However, the next obsessive passage makes clear that any sense of true connection with Knott is an illusion, describing Watt's inability to fix a solid image of Knott's appearance in his mind: 'For one day Mr Knott would be tall, fat, pale and dark, and the next thin, small, flushed and fair, and the next sturdy, middlesized, yellow and ginger [etc.]' (209). This primary, unresolvable distance between Watt and his master provides the novel's emotional force, as Knott never firmly becomes fixed within his servant/child's internal universe. Watt remains enclosed in his autistic shell, unable to bring into himself an enduring, permanent image of

Knott, who refuses to engage his servant with the type of meaningful contact that would make such an internal experience possible. This is reflected in the clinical situation by patients who are unable to maintain a recollection of the analyst's physical appearance, or of the appearance of the office setting, until they feel connected to a safe, maternal aspect in the analyst.

The visit of the Galls, two piano-tuners, whose entry into the Knott-world is seen as a 'fugitive penetration' (70), makes clear the centrality of early dyadic experience in *Watt*. The elder Gall, who is sightless, depends on his son, whose devotion parallels that of Watt to Knott; Watt clearly identifies with the son, and, in fact, seems to admire him. Alas, the piano they come to tune is in tatters, the mice having returned:

> Nine dampers remain, said the younger, and an
> equal number of hammers.
> Not corresponding, I hope, said the elder [...]
> The strings are in flitters, said the younger.
> The elder had nothing to say to this either.
> The piano is doomed, in my opinion, said the younger.
> The piano-tuner also, said the elder.
> The pianist also, said the younger (72).

This incident is important for Watt, and is the beginning of his own 'slip'. In the Galls, Watt sees co-operative contact between a father and son, in contrast to the absence of contact he experiences with Knott.[17] The piano is metaphorical of Watt's inner experience – a communicative tool that relates emotional experience to the world, it has come to grief, lying broken and useless. Watt's own need for authentic communication is thwarted in a house where there is no recognition; his mind, like a broken piano, begins to fragment as he withdraws from the world. The interplay of the Galls has the music-hall cross-talk quality that foreshadows sections of *Waiting for Godot*, and there is some sense of co-operative merger between the Galls that contrasts with Watt's own deep isolation from his primary object. Their dialogue has a catastrophic quality that reflects the hopeless despair Watt is beginning to feel and, in fact, it is communication and relatedness that are now in jeopardy, as Watt sinks inwards into a 'non-correspondence' from others.

The incident with the Galls becomes a model for Watt's experience during his stay with Knott, since it 'continued to unfold, in Watt's head, [... it] gradually lost [...] its sound, its impacts and its rhythm, all meaning, even the most literal [... the incident with the Galls] became a mere example of light commenting bodies, and stillness motion, and silence sound' (72–3). Watt slips into a pre-symbolic realm, where the symbolic tie to the outer world is ruptured, as representations are sent adrift with no verbal organizations to hold them together. He is drowning in a sea of isolated meaninglessness, unable to connect representations to internal emotional meaning: 'The fragility of the outer meaning had a bad effect on Watt, for it caused him to seek for another, for some meaning of what had passed, in the image of how it had passed' (73). Living on the edge of meaning, 'miserably' among face values, he can recall, without any undue significance, 'the time when his dead father appeared to him in a wood [...] or the time when in his surprise at hearing a voice urging him to do away with himself' (74). These traumatic memories are disconnected from emotional significance, and his current trauma evokes *both* his own absent, dead father *and* the sense of primary maternal loss he is now reliving with Knott. The incident with the Galls is a watershed, however, that quickly disintegrates into displacement, so that 'it seemed rather to belong to some story heard long before, an instant in the life of another, ill told, ill heard, and more than half forgotten' (74), and in this is an echo of Winnicott's concept of the breakdown that has *already* occurred, the rupture of the primary mother–infant bond. Watt's sense of himself as a coherent 'I', which can attach mental representations of past events to itself, can 'own' its past, is dissolving as he disconnects from himself, falling apart 'in tatters' like the piano-mind. Watt's experience of dissociation from a triggering event (i.e. the Galls) resembles the speaker's experience in *Not I*; for both a disconnection from a primary object leads to a dissociated, fragmentary experience of life. The Gall experience, screening a darker reality of loss, has itself become 'Not-I', and the incident has a dream-like quality, its significance remaining unconscious, reflective of Watt's own inner experience in both its form (the merged relationship of father/son) and its content (the Galls' diagnosis of primary disconnection in the piano)

Watt does not give up the world of meaning without a fight, since it is not easy for him to let a piece of his own history (of which the incident with the Galls is one example) dissolve into nothingness. The loss of these object representations, tied to his sense of himself as an intelligent, feeling observer, would also mean the loss of the links of meaning that hold the intrapsychic world together. The struggle to elicit meaning from the world of sensation is the stuff of life itself: 'Watt considered, with reason, that he was successful […] when he could evolve, from the meticulous phantoms that beset him, a hypothesis proper to disperse them […] for to explain had always been to exorcize, for Watt' (77–8). Unfortunately for Watt, his efforts to exorcize the spectres of meaningless sensation begin to fail, he finds himself in a state where the world 'resisted formulation in a way no state had ever done' (81). Now the signifiers have been cut loose, and the world is *full* of unnamables:

> Looking at a pot, for example, or thinking of a pot, at one of Mr Knott's pots, of one of Mr Knott's pots, it was in vain that Watt said, Pot, pot […] For it was not a pot, the more he looked, the more he reflected, the more he felt sure of that, that it was not a pot at all. It resembled a pot, it was almost a pot, but it was not a pot of which one could say, Pot, pot, and be comforted. It was in vain that it answered, with unexceptionable adequacy, all the purposes, and performed all the offices, of a pot, it was not a pot. (81)

This derealization couples with an alienation from the world not only of physical objects, but of persons, since he feels sure that the pot remains a pot for everyone *but himself*. This is related to a deep sense of depersonalization, for he begins to decouple from a sense of existing as a living, sentient being, since 'he could no longer affirm [of himself] anything that did not seem as false as if he had affirmed it of a stone' (82).[18] The deepest of human anxieties besets him: psychic annihilation triggered by the loss of one's loving internal objects, and because these anxieties are not contained, he loses the sense of living. Despite his chronic sense of withdrawal, Watt likes to be able to say of himself: 'Watt is a man, all the same, Watt is a man, or, Watt is in the street, with thousands of fellow-creatures within call' (82) and clearly the breakdown of meaning is engendered by Watt's losing contact with persons. He becomes overwhelmed by a sense of abandonment and intense loneliness, feeling 'greatly troubled' by this change, and 'more troubled perhaps than he had ever been by anything' (82). Ogden (1989) describes a similar experience in terms of a collapse from the Depressive Position, in which one can experience an object as whole with ambiguous mixtures of emotion, to the Autistic Contiguous Position, which is pre-verbal and sensation dominated. This results in a tyrannizing imprisonment in a closed system of bodily sensations that precludes the development of potential space. He describes a personal experience akin to Watt's:

After dinner one night [...] it suddenly occurred to me how strange it was that the thing called a napkin was named by the conjunction or the sounds 'nap' and 'kin'. I repeated the two sounds over and over until I began to get the very frightening feeling that these sounds had no connection at all with this thing that I was looking at. I could not get these sounds to naturally 'mean' the thing that they had meant only minutes before. The link was broken, and, to my horror, could not be mended simply by an act of will. I imagined that I could, if I chose to, destroy the power of any and all words to 'mean' something if I thought about them one at a time in this way. At that point, I had the very disturbing feeling that I had discovered a way to drive myself crazy. I imagined all the things in the world could come to feel as disconnected as the napkin had become for me now that it had become disconnected from the word that had formerly named it. Further, I felt that I could become utterly disconnected from the rest of the world because all other people would still share in a 'natural' (i.e. a still meaningful) system of words. (Ogden, 1989: 80)

Ogden, like Watt, realizes the central importance of symbolized thought to the core self, the terrorizing realization that without language all connection to others is lost and, more importantly, without a primary connection to others there can be no authentic language in the first place.[19] Unable to experience himself as human, in spite of recalling images of his mother's teaching him to view himself as such, Watt feels the deadened claustrophobia of a closed psychic world, and he 'might just as well thought of himself as a box, or an urn' (82), like so many other Beckettian characters who lose the sense of potential internal space. Unlike Ogden, this is not merely an experiment for Watt, who cannot maintain a core sense of self because he lacks a strong, stable internal object that could counter his fragmentation in times of stress, since neither the image of his mother, nor any sense of connection to his 'current' mother, Knott, can enliven him. Watt's deep fear of abandonment, and his loneliness, are triggered by the Galls' visit, which retraumatizes him, causing a deep, permanent regression to a pre-symbolic, disorganized experiential world.

Watt's desperate need for a soothing, containing core maternal introject is also demonstrated by his yearning for someone to 'hold' the world for him:

It was principally for these reasons that Watt would have been glad to hear Erskine's voice, wrapping up safe in words the kitchen space, the extraordinary newel-lamp, the stairs that were never the same and of which even the number of steps seemed to vary [...] not that the fact of

Erskine's naming the pot, or of his saying to Watt, My dear fellow [...] would have changed the pot into a pot, or Watt into a man, for Watt [...] but it would have shown that at least for Erskine the pot was a pot, and Watt a man. (83–4)

He needs a mother to 'wrap up safe in words' the world of primary sensation, to help define and outline his experience by establishing a self as subjective, enduring and delineated. There is the feeling that if the world is real for others, if it can be named and made real for them, then his own experience can be amended and brought into a symbolic realm. The entry into the symbolic realm is not sufficient (nor properly possible) without the core connection to an enduring, loving mother whom the infant wants to reach, and Watt's body is indeed in an 'unfamiliar milieu', in that he remains, as an infant at birth, in an unbounded world of sensation, without the mother to contain and bind the chaos.

The possibility that he has lost the world does not entirely create despair or panic in Watt, for whom 'there were times when he felt [...] satisfaction [...] at his being so abandoned by the last rats' (84). The rats, metaphorical inhabitants of his inner world (as they were in Murphy's), tend to be experienced as invasive and disturbing, and there is a regressive pull towards complete schizoid withdrawal: 'It would be lonely, to be sure, at first, and silent, after the gnawing, the scurrying, the little cries' (84). This attraction to the loss of his inner world, at times so appealing, is always overpowered by a need for the mother to drive off the terror of complete psychic annihilation: he often longs to hear Erskine's voice 'speak of the little world of Mr Knott's establishment, with the old words' (84). Watt still strives for connection, a sense of being that can only come with belonging, and for the relatedness that creates subjectivity. There remains, when the world is dissolving into unnamable fragments, the core acknowledgment of the human need to relate, an acknowledgment Watt 'would have appreciated more, if it had come earlier, before his loss of species' (85).

Hungry for love

Watt is subjected to a reversal of the normal 'holding environment' during his stay with Knott, as *he* becomes the mother who attends to *Knott's* physical and psychological needs for nurturing. Knott, for example, is a sort of omnivore – his weekly allotment of seven luncheons and seven dinners is prepared on Saturday nights in one large pot, and consists of a very long list of 'all the good things to eat, and all the good things to drink' (87). This 'mess' must be boiled for four hours and becomes a sort of primal nutrient, transcending the basic 'goodness' of its individual ingredients, '[a] quite [...] new good thing' (87). The preparation of this 'good food', a most precious and fulfilling mother's milk, falls on Watt who has *himself* come to Knott seeking sustenance and security. It is a 'task that taxed Watt's powers, both of mind and body' (88) – tears and perspiration fall from his face and body as he labours over the sacred pot. It is a profound emotional ritual for Watt, one that provides Knott 'the maximum of pleasure compatible with the protection of his health' (88). So deep and destructive is Knott's narcissism that even here he denies Watt the opportunity to experience an emotional closeness – the dining times are constructed such that he is never seen by his servant during the meals. Watt is deprived of the love, resonance, and attunement that might accompany the sharing of meals, and the primary intimacy of the nursing couple is lost, robbed of its emotional intensity by Knott's self-enclosure. Watt's failure to repair this disconnected internal nursing relationship results in fragmentation and depression, and a deeply repressed rage, something he enacts in a reversal after he leaves the house:

> Birds of every kind abounded, and these it was our delight to pursue, with stones and clods of earth. Robins, in particular, thanks to their confidingness, we destroyed in great numbers. And larks' nests, laden with eggs still warm from the mother's breast, we ground into fragments, under our feet, with particular satisfaction. (154)

Primitive rage and envy are at work in Watt, now clearly feeling abandoned and unwitnessed by the mother. Displacing his attacks, which continue, he and Sam sometimes seize 'a plump young rat, resting in our bosom after its repast, we would feed it to its mother, or its father, or its brother, or its sister, or to some less fortunate relative' (156). This is a reversal, as Watt becomes a loving mother to the rats, only to change without warning into the polar opposite, a violent, sadistic mother who initiates a nightmarish, cannibalistic feast, in which families devour themselves. This enactment also suggests his raging jealousy of the other servants, baby rats/birds left behind to continue a fantasized relationship with Knott. Watt exists in a confused, borderline state, where the mother is felt to be as unpredictable as the self, oscillating rapidly between a nurturing, all-embracing love and a violent, sadistic withholding. The case of Mr D. reflects this type of rage; the patient felt a deep, primal disconnection from his mother – she was a monster who withheld food from him. During a Christmas break early in our work, he experienced deep rage at me-as-mother for abandoning him, and he drowned seven of his pets. He stated he felt 'sorry for them' and wanted to put them out of their misery, they must be sad and lonely. Only years later was he able to experience the fury he felt at this time, and realize he was killing *himself* out of despair, murdering his *mother/myself* out of anger.

While with Knott, Watt also learns about a long-departed servant, Mary, one in the long series of workers drawn into service only to be discarded as others come along. The emotional absence that permeates the house has a bad effect on Mary: 'little by little the reason for her presence in that place faded from her mind, as with the dawn the figments of the id, and the duster, whose burden up till now she had so bravely born, fell from her fingers, to the dust, where having at once assumed the colour (grey) of its surroundings it disappeared' (51). Mary responds to the house's emotional vacuum by becoming psychically disorganized – her conscious sense of herself fades along with her sense of purpose, and like her duster she begins to dissolve into the background greyness. Her isolation prompts a regression, a re-emergence of the core caretaking function of feeding, and as Mary deteriorates physically her appearance resembles other Beckettian heroines (e.g. May in *Footfalls* or the heroine of *Rockaby)*, also representatives of the 'lost heart of the self'. Mary is 'propped up in a kind of stupor against one of the walls in which this wretched edifice abounds, her long greasy hair framing in its cowl of scrofulous mats a face where pallor, languor, hunger, acne, recent dirt, immemorial chagrin seemed to dispute the mastery' (54–5). She is in a catatonic state – she has a 'dreaming face', her body acts as an automated feeding machine as her hands flash 'to and fro', like 'piston rods' (55) from a food sack to her mouth, while not a muscle stirs that is not intimately involved in the process of self-nurturing that occupies her every waking hour. That Mary's face still reflects her hunger is not surprising since the food she ingests is a symbolic replacement for the emotional responsiveness and love she really craves. Guntrip (1968) describes such a 'love-hunger' in one of his patients, a woman, who felt compelled to eat whenever her husband came into the house, realizing she was 'hungry for him' and his love but could not show it. She dreamt 'she was eating an enormous meal and just went on endlessly. She is getting as much as she can inside her before it is taken away [...] she has no confidence about being given enough' (Guntrip, 1968: 72). Mary's decompensation, and her attempt to maintain a primary maternal connection by bingeing, are mirrored in the following clinical example:

> Ms A.'s binge eating had its roots in childhood neglect and deprivation. She had terrible difficulty 'thinking' independently and would position herself as a mirror for the other's desire. She experienced my talking to her as nurturing and filling, stating that the content was less important than the calming function my words provided. She used the television as a hypnotic distraction, lying on a couch covered by her favourite duvet, bingeing on sweets, and described how she felt dissociated from her eating as if her body was an automaton, her arms, hands, and mouth working in synchrony to feed her while she focused her attention on television talk shows. Her mother had suffered a post-partum depression, abandoning her to an incapacitated grandmother with the result that Ms A.'s feedings were infrequent and unpredictable. At eight years of age, she was again abandoned to a hospital for a fairly serious illness, and she remembered the depressive anxiety that accompanied her feeling unloved and forgotten. Her only visitors were an elderly aunt and uncle who brought her an endless supply of candy, which she remembered eating ravishingly, not stopping until they were all consumed, feeling calmed by her feeding, but also anxious lest the candy (and the kindly couple) be taken away before she finished filling her empty self. Thus began a lifelong coping mechanism through which she was able to tolerate unbearable feelings of abandonment and loneliness by continually and symbolically repairing her early and severe sense of primary maternal absence.

Like Mary, this patient binges to counter depression, and her dissociative state during her binges is a direct echo of Mary's 'automatic' behaviour, which reflects an attempt to repair a rupture in her internal world. The duvet became a sort of 'second skin' (Bick, 1968) that contains her fragmenting self, while the participants in the television shows people her depleted internal world as a loving, sharing inner family. For Mary, as for Ms A., a ruptured internal nursing relationship leads to somatTised enactments of inner despair; as a despairing, withdrawn part of the infantile-self, she tries to symbolically reconnect to a loving mother in the hope of reparation.

Ships in the night

A number of symbols reflect the primary dislocation between Watt and his master. Once his isolation from Knott becomes fully apparent, Watt tries to develop a relationship by peripheral means. Aware that Knott sometimes rings for Erskine late at night, Watt spends long hours ruminating on the nature of this communication system, its mechanisms, and the reasons for its establishment. His thinking becomes terribly convoluted, obsessional, and paranoid and he decides to examine Erskine's room, but has difficulty with the lock, thinking 'Obscure keys may open simple locks, but simple keys obscure locks never' (124), and one could see Watt as the simple (infantile) key that cannot gain access to the obscure (maternal) lock that is Knott. He cannot fix any value to this thought in his mind, oscillating cruelly between regretting the thought, and finding comfort in its clarity. Unable to form a judgment, having lost the ability to attach emotional foundations to thought, he continues in this paralyzed state, until, by means unknown, he finds himself in Erskine's room, with a broken bell symbolic of a communicative access to Knott for ever beyond his ken. Like a ruptured synapse, the bell no longer functions, and Watt's dream of communicating with Knott, even indirectly, is shattered.

The bell is a central symbol whose significance is formed by the role it plays in linking Knott and his servants. It is reminiscent of a vignette in Kohut's *Analysis of the Self,* which describes a patient intensely enmeshed with his mother, who 'controlled him in a most stringent fashion', his eating times were 'determined by a mechanical timer which [she] used as an extension of her need to control [his] activity' (Kohut, 1971: 81–2). Knott also experiences his servants as extensions of himself, and the entire house is designed to place strict limits on their actions, in order to control them, guaranteeing fulfilment of his needs in a safe, predictable way. Knott, just as the mother in the clinical vignette, reverses the roles of child and mother when it suits his needs, and both discourage individuation of their child/servants. The patient's mother, as Knott has done (with the bell), installs a buzzer in the child's room: 'From then on she would interrupt his attempts at internal separation from her whenever he wanted to be alone; and she would summon him to her, more compellingly (because the mechanical device was experienced as akin to an endopsychic communication) than would have been her voice, or knocking, against which he could have rebelled' (Kohut, 1971: 82). Knott also controls his servants by means of the bell, again blurring the roles of mother and child: the servant/mother is summoned to attend to the helpless Knott/child, but it is Knott who dominates the relationship. There is a distortion of normal maternal attunement, both the child in Kohut's vignette, and the servant, lose their autonomous boundaries. The normal dyadic relationship becomes parasitic in both cases and, as a consequence, Watt really begins to lose his mind, just as Kohut's patient 'felt increasingly that he had no mind of his own' (Kohut, 1971: 83).[20]

Alone in Erskine's room, Watt observes the 'only other object of note' to be a picture on the wall: 'A circle, obviously described by a compass, and broken at its lowest point, occupied the middle foreground, of this picture. Was it receding? Watt had that impression. In the eastern background appeared a point, or dot' (128). He struggles to grasp the painting's meaning, particularly the relationship between the circle and the dot, wondering how long it will be 'before the point and circle [enter] together in the same plane' (129). That they are in a vital, significant search is not in doubt: 'had [they] sighted each other, or were blindly flying thus, harried by some force of merely mechanical mutual attraction, or the playthings of chance. He wondered if they would eventually pause and converse, and perhaps even mingle, or keep steadfast on their ways, like ships in the night' (129).

The painting represents the possibility of communion between two distinct and separate objects, destined to meet, or to go on for ever, silently, in their aloneness. Watt finally settles on the following formulation, the dot now transformed into a 'centre', it was perhaps 'a circle and a centre not its centre in search of its centre and its circle respectively, in boundless space, in endless time' (129). The painting symbolizes the relationship to his Knott/mother: alone and fragmented he seeks a centre to his being, a strong, cohesive sense of self. His internal world is empty, there is a break in his sense of self, just as there is a break in the circle without its centre. Both Watt and the circle are searching for something to enter them, to make them whole, and he yearns for an enduring, internalized mother to hold him together. Conversely, though, the circle is Knott, and in Watt's fantasy it is the mother/circle who is looking to contain something that is both a part of herself, and not a part of herself – her child – and to hold it internally/psychically, as she once held it physically within her own body, allowing it the secure freedom to begin to create a world for itself. Alone and unheld by the mind of a mother who does not witness him, and with no hope of containment, Watt is left adrift like the dot, breaking apart under annihilation anxieties, and continuing a doomed attempt to contain Knott in order to maintain the dyadic bond. He enacts his fantasy of merger with Knott in his reading of the painting, and the desperate hope that somehow, magically, this reading connects to, and will shape, the real intentions of Knott himself. Tustin also speaks of the circle's importance to the withdrawn child: 'I began to realize that the 'shapes' the autistic children were talking about to me were not these objective geometrical shapes which we all share. They were entirely personal shapes which were idiosyncratic to them, and to them alone [...] the circle being an especially comforting one for all of them' (Tustin, 1986: 120). There is something about the circle that binds sensation for the child, protecting it from the terrors of an indigestible world, and Watt dwells on his circle that is *both* Knott *and* Watt, yearning for completeness and loving containment. As he thinks about the centre and the circle in their search for each other 'in [the] boundless space, in [the] endless time' that are the domain of pre-verbal experience, he mourns the reality of his own loss in the house of Knott, and '[his] eyes filled with tears that he could not stem' (129), another example where a realization of the fantasy nature of an attachment to an unreachable internal imago creates a powerful emotional experience.[21]

In Knott's house, all is 'a coming and a going' (132), there is no space for a living presence or genuine relatedness. Watt struggles to maintain the illusion there is some sense to be made of his stay with Knott, thinking that if it *appears* to be arbitrary it is really be a 'pre-established arbitrary' (134). He cannot tolerate the idea that Knott is entirely detached, unconcerned with his servants' worlds: 'For otherwise in Mr Knott's house, and at Mr Knott's door, and on the way to Mr Knott's door, and on the way from Mr Knott's door, there would be a languor, and a fever, the languor of the task done but not ended, the fever of the task ended but not done' (134). This door imagery is reminiscent of 'neither', and the wandering 'to and fro' again suggests the homelessness, a self isolated between inner and outer worlds, itself and (m)other.

To the end, Watt maintains his view of Knott as a sanctuary, a saviour who will hold and heal him: 'Mr Knott was a harbour, Mr Knott was haven, calmly entered, freely ridden, gladly left' (135), imagery reminiscent of Mahler's 'safe anchorage' within its mother's mindful care. This is the heart of Watt's fantasy – being held by Knott would allow him a peace in the world, and in himself, he has not known in a lonely, despairing life in which he has been driven by both 'the storms without' and 'the storms within' (135). In coming to Knott, he hoped to find 'in the need, in the having, in the losing of refuge, calm and freedom and gladness' (135), a wish for primary containment that would allow him to leave this refuge, when he is ready, as a whole, sane person. Later, while thinking 'of all the possible relations between [the various] series' that he has ruminated over in his attempt to 'know'

Knott, Watt's mind drifts to a distant time when he was young, lying 'all alone stone sober in the ditch, wondering if it was the time and the place and the loved one already' (136). He hears the croaking of three frogs, at intervals:

```
Krak!  –     –     –     –     –     –     –
Krek!  –     –     –     –   Krek!    –     –
Krik!  –     –   Krik!   –     –   Krik!    –     (137–8)
```

The pattern continues until all three voices are aligned as in the first instance, and this image is another powerful metaphor of Watt's need for connection with the mother, of his yearning for a sense of being in an intimate harmony. The frogs' voices go out of sequence as they separate, but return 'home' to be as one, as a child wanders from the mother to return to her side in safety, eventually coming home to the 'background mother' *internally* even when alone. There is a 'coming and going' of the voices as they work within a boundary of a lasting, permanent community, a sense of autonomous belonging is created, one that is tolerable and safe. There is a striking similarity between the patterns of these voices and the manner in which Feinsilver contacted a severely withdrawn schizophrenic patient 'J'. After months of 'meaningless', seemingly random monologue, Feinsilver realized there might be inner meaning to what the patient was saying, specifically that the word 'riggin' might refer to a star American football player. He began to mirror the wording of the patient, in an attempt to show him that he was at one with him, and not threatening. Eventually, Feinsilver was able to slowly separate himself from the internal pattern and establish himself as a real other for the patient (Fromm and Smith, 1989). The frogs' song serves a similar function for Watt, in that the voices begin together, separate, and explore their individuality within a community, finally returning to the source and to a unity. It is this very early type of mirroring that the mother provides for the child, bringing him into the community of minds, and it is here that Knott fails Watt.

Aliv not ded not

Watt's inability to engage Knott results in ego-failure (e.g. loss of language, hallucinatory voices), in his defensive strategies (e.g. obsessive ruminations, intellectualization), and in his schizoid relationship with the world. He lives in a dead universe, entrapped by ruminative speculation about a world to which he does not connect emotionally.

Watt is beginning a process of repair when he enters the house, the 'wild dim chatter' he occasionally hears coming from Knott's lips is comforting, and he grows 'exceedingly fond' (209) of it. Living only in the moment, his experience is uncoloured by enduring emotion: 'Not that he was sorry when it ceased, not that he was glad when it came again, no' (209). However, burgeoning emotion begins to link various states of Knott's absence and presence, and Watt edges towards a Depressive Position – there is a both a sense of loss and of joy that emerges in the metaphors surrounding the experience: 'But while it [Knott's voice] sounded he was gladdened, as by the rain on the bamboos, or even rushes, as by the land against the waves, doomed to cease, doomed to come again' (209). The experience of hearing Knott's voice is likened to a variety of soft, natural sounds, images that are evocative of the quiet, gentle murmuring of the mother with baby. There are many similar allusions in the oeuvre: Krapp's gently rolling bliss with the girlfriend/mother among the rushes; Vladimir and Estragon's mistaking 'the wind in the reeds' for Godot (19) and so forth, all reflecting an early experience of recognition and connection to the mother. There is a sense of this in Sartre's conception of the gaze, which became a starting point for Lacan: 'Of course what *most often* manifests a look is the convergence of two ocular globes in my direction. But the look will be given just as well on occasion when there is a rustling of branches, or the sound of a footstep followed by silence, or the slight opening of a shutter' (Sartre, 1958: 257). The images used by Sartre are found in Beckett: 'footfalls' appearing in the short play of the same name, as well as in *Murphy*, suggesting in both an early sense of connection to a mother who recognizes the infant. The opening, closing doors that appear in 'neither' and *Watt* echo the '*shutter*' imagery that reflects the polarity of acceptance through, and exclusion from, love. These sounds are not always ones that elicit a sense of security. In *Waiting for Godot*, the tramps mistake the sound of 'the wind in the reeds' for a terrifying arrival, and later, in fast-paced crosstalk, speak of 'all the dead voices' that rustle like leaves (62), reflecting disconnection from a benevolent primary object. As Acrisus said: 'To him who is in fear everything rustles', in the paranoid state there can be no proper, loving recognition behind the sounds, only emptiness or hostile intent. This is the inherent ambiguity of the Paranoid Schizoid Position, that the same object, or its representation, can elicit both good and bad feelings, depending on the internal state of mind of the infant self.

Watt hovers close to mourning, almost able to experience Knott's absence as a loss. His general indifference to the world begins to melt away as contradictory states of pleasure/displeasure, love/hate, merge into a coherent sense of self-with-other linked by an emotional bonding. Regarding urination: 'He now envisaged its relaxation and eventual rupture, with sadness, and gladness, distinctly perceptible in an alteration of great rapidity for some little time, and dying blurred together away, in due course' (232–3). He is at the edge of the Depressive Position, able to tolerate ambivalence. Unlike Arsene, however, who appears to be entering into a mourning process as he leaves the house, Watt cannot tolerate the confusion and overwhelming emotions that the rupture with the Knott precipitates – he regresses back into a severely autistic position. After leaving the house he travels to a sanitarium of some kind, where he relates his story to the narrator of the novel, Sam, while they walk together on the grounds. In this telling, Watt's need for connection is made manifest, as he makes use of Sam as a containing mother to hold him together in the face of terrorizing anxiety and rage.

While recounting the last part of his stay with Knott, Watt is in a kind of somnambulistic delirium, his voice rapid and low, and he begins to invert his use of language, sentences, words, and letters. From these descriptions of his non-relationship with Knott comes an emotional climax that expresses the schizoid longing for contact with the mother:

> Most of day, part of night, now with Knott. Up till now, oh so seen little, oh so heard little [...] so I moved, in mist, in hush [...] Abandoned my little to find him [...] to love him my little reviled. This body homeless. This mind ignoring. These emptied hands. This empty heart. To him I brought. To the temple. To the teacher. To the source. Of nought. (164–6, modified)

Finally, toward the end of his stay, Watt spends more time with Knott, but this merely physical presence does not provide a deep emotional connection. He has not seen or been seen for so long, moving in a world of 'mist' and 'hush', abandoning his living sense of himself to be near Knott. He comes to the house in a state of deep, dependent humility, with his body made 'homeless' by a premature, incomplete birth, with an impoverished internal world closed off to experience by schizoid withdrawal, and a sense of himself as barren of love. Knott is a 'temple', as the mother's body is a holy place that embodies the world to the infant and, as mother Knott is a 'teacher' who could show Watt how to create the world. Certain critics (e.g. Baldwin, 1978) have highlighted the religious implications of these passages, but they also demonstrate the core emotional dynamic that exists between Knott as a maternal figure and Watt as an emerging infantile-self.

Towards the end of his stay with Knott, a primitive merger-experience develops, but it is a gross distortion of the normal maternal 'concern' that is found in a union held together by love and reverie: 'Go to, cam day lit. Knot not, Watt not. Sprit not, bod not. A ded not, aliv not. Awak not, aslep not. Gay not, sad not. Tim for, lived so' (167, modified). This reads like a 'death in life' nightmare, a disembodied, depersonalized account of 'neither' experience diametrically opposed to the warm, loving experience of a holding oneness that *leads* to experience. Like the dot and circle in Knott's painting, the two of them, Knott and Watt, exist together in isolation, and Watt is truly alone 'in the presence of the mother', without any internal sense of her presence to protect him from the terrors of nothingness. In the final passages, Watt relates to Sam about these times together with Knott, the full impact of neglect becomes apparent: 'Sid by sid, two men. Al day, part of nit. Dum, num, blin. Knot look at wat? No. Wat look at knot? No. Wat talk to knot? No. Knot talk to wat? No. Wat den did us do? Niks, niks, niks. Part of nit, al day. Two men, sid by sid' (168, modified). In addition to demonstrating the breakdown of his core ego functioning, these passages reveal the failure of maternal attunement; Watt does not exist for the mother, and attempts to maintain the threads of a relationship by remaining close to the source of absence. The experience of 'niks, niks, niks' is made somehow less annihilating if he remains close, but there is quite clearly a cry for primary containment through sensual touch, something Watt expresses through the hope that the *'niks'* will envelop him as a *'skin'*.

Watt's relationship with Sam provides a complement to his Knott-experience. On one occasion during their stay together, while walking in the garden behind his residence, Sam comes upon the fence that separates him from the garden belonging to Watt's residence. The isolation of the men wandering alone in their gardens recalls the theme of psychic separation that dominates the work, but in this setting there is passage between the two worlds. Sam spies Watt, now fully regressed, walking towards him, backwards, through brambles and briars: he is bloodied, but oblivious to the pain. As he turns to retrace his steps, Sam gets a look at him: 'suddenly I felt as though I were standing before a great mirror, in which my garden was reflected, and my fence, and I, and the very birds tossing in the wind, so that I looked at my hands, and felt my face, and glossy skull, with an anxiety as real as unfounded' (158).[22]

Sam's experience of this mirroring depersonalization is a natural climax to the work, representing the narrative-self's attempt at reparation, a last desperate grasp to keep Watt a part of a shared world, though, as noted, this is ambivalent. Sam has a deep affection for his friend; he quickly goes to Watt's aid, telling us: 'in my anxiety to come to Watt then I would have launched myself against the barrier, bodily, if necessary' (160). Sam struggles to get to his friend, accepting a position in direct contrast to Knott. He becomes a caring mother who, seeing an infant in distress, experiences an empathic attunement and attends to the pain. The mirroring experience can be viewed as Sam experiencing himself in Watt, sharing a mutuality, or experiencing a projection, so that he is motivated to take action. Once he reaches Watt, he dresses his wounds, cleans him, and grooms him, in a word, heals his body and gives him a sense of human dignity. This contact takes place in between their respective garden/minds, in a sort of intersubjective potential space:

> In Watt's garden, in my garden, we should have been more at our ease. But it never occurred to me to go back into my garden with Watt, or with him to go forward into his. But it never occurred to Watt to go back with me into his garden, or with me to go forward into mine. For my garden was my garden, and Watt's garden was Watt's garden, we had no common garden any more. (164)

There is development within this passage, as both men appear secure to meet within an intersubjective space, despite feeling a greater sense of security within their own containing garden/minds. Sam turns Watt to face him, places Watt's hands on his shoulders, and begins a beautiful, richly metaphorical 'mirror dance':

> Then I took a single pace forward, with my left leg, and he a single pace back, with his right leg [...] And so we paced together between the fences, I forwards, he backwards [...] I turning, and he turning [...] I looking whither we were going, and he looking whence we were coming [...] we paced between the fences, together again after so long [...] To be together again, after so long, who love the sunny wind, the windy sun, in the sun, in the wind, that is perhaps something, perhaps something. (163)

In this mirroring, a ray of loving attunement and hope shines through in a world of despair. Sam's love for Watt is expressed literally in his concern for his friend's physical safety, and metaphorically as a perfectly empathic movement of two selves working together as one. As mother and child, they play together, blurring between the one who leads the dance, and the one who follows, between the mother who teaches life, and the child who learns it. Watt has found a mother to hold him in a selfless containment of his pain and confusion, allowing him to feel himself into the world as part of her body and its movements. It is his sad fate, as a lost part of the narrative-self, that this relationship cannot endure, for Watt is soon transferred from the pavilion never to be seen by Sam again. But of this dancing, this mirroring, that a sad and broken man, never fully born, experiences in the sun and wind, the love of which he shares with a friend, in this reunion, at last, on this 'abode of stones', perhaps we can say: It is something, yes, something![23]

Notes

1 This is not to deny the important paternal aspects of Mr Knott. The focus here is on the earliest aspects of human relating (i.e. where Knott is experienced *functionally* by Watt as a mother). It is also reasonable to look at Knott as a father, (as Hill does (1990: 27, 33)), to which Watt turns for reparation.

2 There is an allusion to the 'joke' related later, during Arsene's speech: 'Do not come down the ladder, Ifor, I haf taken it away' (44) since, for Hackett, there *is* no primary caregiver to watch over him and warn him of this danger. There is also an incoherence in Hackett's description that is typical of individuals with faulty early attachment (e.g. he describes a 'beautiful summer day', in response to the observation that he was left all alone, something which should evoke sadness or anger).

3 The goat reappears in *Waiting for Godot* (where a child cares for Godot's goats). In 'The Expelled', there is a reversal, since the *boy* (who is walking a goat) watches over and cares for the *narrator*. One could view this later narrator as the lonely aspect of the narrative-self that is embodied here in Hackett, and this later scene as a reparative fantasy. Certain patients with a primal disconnection from other persons eventually form deeply meaningful bonds with pets. It is usually a major breakthrough in analysis when the first glimmers of affection or concern for humans manifests itself as tenderness towards animals.

4 This echoes the labour-pains felt by Mrs Nixon, as well as Pozzo's inability to 'bear' or contain Lucky's feelings of depression and anxiety.

5 It is both the *form* of the passage about the stones and its *content* that serves the autistic/self-nurturing function. Molloy's sucking, and its concrete verbal representation, both *protects* him from the awareness of his separateness from the internal mother, as well as *re-creates* a connection to her.

6 In the addendum to *Watt* is written 'never been properly born' followed by 'the foetal soul is full grown' (248), which suggests a completeness of the infantile-self as well as its need for contact to emerge into the world as a whole person.

7 Freud's grandson, in his original 'fort-da' formulation, attempted to master an internal sense of the loss of his mother (who had left the room), by throwing away and pulling back a spool on a string, thus intrapsychically making the disappearing love object return.

8 This 'raising of the face' to the other is reminiscent of the narrator's attempt to connect to the face of a child in 'The Calmative' (see Chapter 1), as well as the visages in the short plays. It is because of a lack of integration within the self that the maternal image cannot be held onto (i.e. ... *but the clouds ...*, *Embers*) or connected to, as in 'The Calmative'.

9 Balint (1968) describes the 'basic fault' as a primary failure in maternal connection. He would later write: '[The analyst must be] felt to be present all the time at the right distance – neither so far that the patient feels lost or abandoned, nor so close that the patient might feel encumbered and unfree – in fact at a distance that corresponds to the patient's actual need' (Balint, 1986). Of course, this 'optimal distancing' applies to the mother as well, and it is in this area that Knott fails Watt, being both too distant, and too invasive (i.e. in his expectations for total nurturing). This sense of optimal distance and placement is a dominant theme in the oeuvre, from Hamm's obsession about his position to the late prose work in which space is mathematically described. In a like fashion, the reader of *Watt* is held at a distance from a depressed/raging feeling-state, by some of the mechanisms described earlier.

10 Arsene's comment about the buttons occurs outside of his narrative about Knott, while he is buttoning up his coat to leave, suggesting an unconscious unwillingness to leave Knott-as-mother, since he fumbles with his clothes in the way a small, anxious child might.

11 The imagery is echoed in *Happy Days*, where Winnie speaks from within an ever encasing/protecting mound of sand, telling a displaced tale that often concerns childhood trauma.

12 The ladder motif will return in 'The Lost Ones', where ladders operate as the means to explore womb-like niches, and to search for ways of connection to a fantasized external world outside of the all encasing cylinder.

13 Jacques (1953) explores this containing aspect of social institutions. In this case it is the narrative-self that places the characters within the institution for protection from abject despair.

14 Watt's dismissal from the house can be seen as his exclusion from the *mind* of the mother, since he is destined to be forgotten. One might view the servants who follow as fantasy examples of other infants who come to take his place inside of the mother's body/mind. This rivalry is revisited in *Waiting for Godot*, where Godot clearly cares for some children.

15 It is interesting that this style may have been in part developed by Beckett's having played numerous solitary word-games while essentially a prisoner in Rousillon. The obsessive need for Watt to fix the location and activities of the Knott/mother is reflected in the reaction of certain patients to breaks in analysis. One patient, for example, was extremely curious to know my *exact* location during the holiday breaks since she felt that it would help her to know

where I was to be staying, and what my daily schedule would be. Without such knowledge she felt I would be lost to her as an internal presence, and it was only by being able to imagine *where I was* and *what I was doing* at any given moment while we were apart that she felt safe and real.

16 This foreshadows the narrator's experience in 'The End', when he leaves an institution after meeting with a Mr Weir, for whom he feels some affection. He states: 'I would gladly have turned back, but I was afraid one of the guards would stop me and tell me I would never see Mr Weir again. That might have added to my sorrow. And anyway I never turned back on such occasions' (81). Both passages emphasize the denial that prevents a full mourning and recognition of loss. This is also reminiscent of the anecdote told by Frieda Fromm-Reichmann, concerning a mute schizophrenic who did not speak not at all during their sessions, but who silently wept after she had left her once the session had ended. It also demonstrates the depth of Watt's dissociation from a loving attachment for the Knott/mother. I have seen this experience clinically innumerable times, as the patient becomes aware of the depth of his or her love for a primary, internal part-object figure from which they are separating as they enter into the Depressive Position. It is a moment of the most dramatic import, as it is in the novel.

17 Baker (1998: 28–30) discusses Oedipal issues surrounding the appearance of the dead father in Watt, and its connection to the relationship of the Galls.

18 This image is reminiscent of Arsene's fantasy of turning into a 'stone pillar', and Lucky's feeling that the world is an 'abode of stones'. It was echoed by a patient who said: 'It is the thought of my parents not having good intentions for me that turns my body into stone'. There are a number of cases in the medical literature of fetuses that have died *in utero* and calcified, without discovery, sometimes for many years. The sense of deadness, *within* the failing containment of the mother, lies at the heart of these fantasies of 'stoniness' within Beckett, and are reflected for example in the story of the birth of Larry Nixon, whose existence was not recognized *in toto*.

19 It is of central importance to recognize that it is *because* of a properly organized pre-verbal experience, built on the foundations of the early mother–infant dyadic relationship, that symbol formation is possible at all. This is *why* Ogden can escape this regression and Watt cannot. It is interesting to notice that in both cases of symbol-loss there is a connection to early orality – Ogden focuses on a napkin after dinner, while Watt focuses on a pot, possibly the very one in which he lovingly prepares his Knott/mother's meals in the vain hope of sharing a nurturing experience.

20 Bells serve similar functions for Hamm in *Endgame*, May's mother in *Footfalls*, Murphy's landlady, and so forth.

21 Trivisonno (1970) also sees the painting as reflecting the relationship of Watt and Knott, in intellectual terms, and Baker (1998) points out the more physical aspect of the circle's birth-breach.

22 This passage suggests the entry of the narrative-self into the fiction it creates, in the guise of the pseudo-narrator, the fictional character 'Sam', whose omni-science is completely flawed, see (Chalker, 1975) and (Ramsay, 1985). Ramsay sees this mirroring passage as a way in which the narrative-self distances itself from the psychic trauma embodied in the character Watt. However, it also

highlights a sense of empathic connection, as the rest of this chapter tries to demonstrate. That Watt is not ultimately 'rescued' in any enduring sense demonstrates the narrative-self's ambivalence in its relationship to the character, an aspect of itself. That the anxiety is as 'real as unfounded' suggests the blurring of the self into the other in a powerful transferential experience. That is, the narrative-self-as-Sam is *both* Watt and *not* Watt, and his loss, as a broken, withdrawn part of the self, is both a relief to Sam and a re-enactment of a maternal failure.

23 There is a great similarity between this scene and the work done between Feinsilver and his patient (see page 124). It is through imitation that the child learns within a loving relationship. Despite Watt's seemingly autistic withdrawal, he responds to Sam's calling out his name (162), and it seems clear that there is a nascent affection still alive in Watt for his friend.

4

A strange situation: self-entrapment in *Waiting for Godot*[1]

Waiting for Godot, a 'tragicomedy' in two acts, was first performed in Paris in 1953, quickly becoming an international success that established Beckett as a major figure in twentieth-century literature. Early commentators viewed the play in existentialist terms to such a degree it became almost synonymous with that movement (Kiesenhofer, 1993). Others have read the play in political or religious terms – Mittenzwei (1969) presents a Marxist perspective, Zeifman (1975) highlights the sense of suffering and its connection to the divinity, and Cohn (1962) sees Beckett as mocking classical Christian traditions. Anders (1965) believes the play is a parable, and most criticism views it as representative of certain abstract features of the human condition, or as a specific allegory. Worton describes a more contemporary view – the central problem of the play is 'what language can and cannot do', and it is 'used to make the reader/spectator [...] wary of the codifications [it] imposes upon us' (Worton, 1994: 68). The present reading examines the play as an exposition of certain feeling-states within an emerging-self, which are *actually* manifested in the character relations, imagery, and so forth. The play reflects the internal world of a self struggling to integrate in face of disintegration anxieties triggered by separation from a loving, primary object. Nealon writes 'in *Waiting for Godot* [...] Vladimir and Estragon are trapped by their modernist nostalgia for legitimation in Godot: they have a totalizing, modernist world view in an infinite, postmodern world' (1988: 526). However, one could suggest the play depicts a nostalgia for something *absolutely* required by the self (of which Vladimir and Estragon are manifestations). This is not any sort of legitimacy, which would imply a false-self compliance, but a secure internal sense of love and recognition. The characters cannot be *literally* nostalgic, since this primary connection is something they have *not* had. The 'infinite, postmodern world' is understandable only as a part of the totality of the human mental universe. It is the province of those positions of the mind that are before the full integration and selfhood of the Depressive Position, but which are concomitant with it in the total psyche.

This brings the experience of the play in line with Anders's comment that 'where the world no longer exists, there can no longer be a possibility of a collision with the world' (Anders, 1965: 145). Godot is the primary maternal object that *is* the world for an emerging-self, without which the self cannot 'collide', or engage, the world in a full, individuated way. The character Godot, who does not literally appear on stage, represents the maternal side of an early dyadic relationship in which the mother is experienced as absent, something that forms the emotional background of the play's represented internal world. The various relationships within the play are dyadic and fluid, with characters assuming various mother/infant roles in condensation; the *types* of couples formed reflect the primary experience of maternal absence and failure of containment.[2] The play reflects a state of being, or rather of *not-being*, with the mother, and the various constellations of characters and their emotional experiences enact this aspect of the narrative-self's experience.[3] The 'codification' and 'impositions' of language within the play are results of this primary rupture between primary containing and expressive aspects of the narrative-self, which struggles to be recognized within an entrapping, unheeding matrix.

The play's appeal can be partly understood because of its elucidation of primary states of human experience. The emerging-self responds to traumatic disconnection from the world/mother with powerful admixtures of rage, despair, and hope, developing powerful imagos to connect these feelings. This chapter looks at a variety of relationships (between the tramps themselves, between Lucky and Pozzo, as well as between the two couples), and explores themes of starvation and primary failure in the nursing bond. In all of this, the dominant relationship that forms the drama's major substratum remains one between an absent, alluring/withholding Godot-as-mother and an ill-seen infantile-self.

A personal god

Lucky's monologue, delivered towards the end of the first act, expresses the emotional heart of the play, and of the oeuvre, by demonstrating the intrapsychic consequences of ruptures in the early mother–infant dyad. Beckett supported this centrality – in the 1975 Schiller Theatre production that he directed, the author opened the rehearsals, some-

what to the surprise of Walter Asmus, the co-director, with the monologue (McMillan and Fehsenheld, 1988: 137). Lucky, having outlived his
usefulness as servant to the self-centered Pozzo, appears destined to be
abandoned at the fair. Pozzo represents the maternal side of a highly
dependent early relationship, and is the provider of Lucky's basic
physical needs. He is the mother with whom the child must engage to
survive, who provides the externality that allows for mutative changes
in the internal landscape. Lucky's long, fragmented speech is an elucidation of his *own* internal state; it begins by describing this 'personal god' /
mother who is 'outside time without extension who from the heights of
divine apathia divine athambia divine aphasia loves us dearly with some
exceptions for reasons unknown' (43). The primary object is experienced
as unknowable, unreachable and uncaring and, even more damaging to
the infantile-self, this 'god' provides a love felt to be *available*, though it
is impossible for the child to connect what it is *doing* or what it *is*, at any
given moment, to the criteria for this love's bestowal.[4] This 'personal
god' / mother loves according to an isolated, internal agenda outside the
child's *potential* experience and so, to survive, the infant must always
remain close, or experience the anxiety manifested in the rest of the
monologue. The mother's arbitrary containment generates the 'calm
which even though intermittent is better than nothing' (43), though
normally it would establish an enduring capacity to 'go on being' by
providing protection from psychic annihilation. I have heard this exact
statement ('it's better than nothing') on innumerable occasions from
patients trying to explain to themselves, and me, their motivation for
remaining locked into unsatisfactory relationships. The terrors of
psychic annihilation that would result from moving away from a
particular person, who represents in the transference a deeply needed
primary object, is unbearable. The loss of the core internal object leads
to an internal void felt to be worse than death. The importance of the
personal god is elaborated in the following selective excerpt:

> that man [...] in spite of the strides of alimentation and defecation is
> seen to waste and pine [...] in spite of physical culture the practice of
> sports [...] of all kinds dying flying sports of all sorts [...] to shrink and
> dwindle in spite of the tennis [...] for reasons unknown [...] and
> considering what is much more grave [...] in the plains in the mountains
> by the seas by the rivers [...] in the great cold the great dark [...] the
> earth abode of stones [...] in the great deeps the great cold [...] the skull
> to shrink and dwindle [...] the tears [...] the labours abandoned left
> unfinished graver still abode of stones. (43–4)

This is as an experience of ruptured early nurturing, for despite the infant's basic physical needs being met ('alimentation and defecation') there is a wasting ('pining') depression born of absence.[5] Absence and abandonment ('dying') taint early socialization, represented by sporting activity, and the self 'shrinks and dwindles' in spite of it all. The infant cannot comprehend the genesis of the rupture in the loving bond to its mother ('for reasons unknown'). This leads to a profound sense of isolation ('in the great cold the great dark') and a feeling of dead, meaningless futility ('the earth [is] an abode of stones [i.e. a dead self and dead others]'). The last desperate images of an unborn self – 'the labours abandoned left unfinished graver still' – triggers an aggressive 'silencing' of Lucky by the others, as his speech strikes a depressive core that cannot be contained, a failed psychic birth (labours abandoned) 'astride of a grave[r]' (90). The abandonment of these labours to complete the infantile-self leaves it in a life 'graver still' than death, which can never be anticipated as a finality. The following clinical material elucidates some of these ideas:

> Mr D. had suffered an early life of abject neglect and, as an adult, spent many years in near complete isolation. He made a ritual of turning off the lights at the start of our sessions, and one day made a slip of the tongue, referring to the sessions as being 'at night', when they actually took place in the early afternoon. Analysis of this led to memory/ fantasies of being locked into a room for hours by a mother who would not heed his cries for contact. I pointed out his re-creation of this internal scene within our space, and how he experienced me in this way, as silent and uncaring. After speaking of his terrible sense of loneliness, he correctly guessed our time was up, saying he was glad to leave as he was about to cry. I said he feared his cries would be unheard, and for the first time in our therapeutic work he sobbed uncontrollably, speaking of the burning tears in the dark room, the sun hidden by blinds, and the annihilation anxiety of being without mother.

This patient's core experience is surely that of Lucky, since both are abandoned, for reasons incomprehensible to them, by a personal god. The patient's last words of that session echo the disorganized terror and imagery of Lucky's speech: 'alone … in the dark … in the dark room … the cold room … tears like fire … wanting her to come … hating her … hating myself for wanting … alone … with only my mind … alone.' This patient learned, independently, about my interest in Beckett, searched out information concerning the author, and told me about a synopsis of *Waiting for Godot* he had discovered. He described his feeling that, at times, I was absent during silences and that, like a Godot-figure, I was uninterested in him. He then described similar feelings experienced with his mother, announced that it was she who was really Godot and that, unlike her, I *had* arrived as a patient, concerned presence in his life.[6]

Pozzo's own 'speech' occurs just prior to Lucky's monologue, and the two are complementary, since the content and delivery of the 'speech' suggests the genesis of Lucky's despair.[7] Pozzo begins by inviting himself to speak ('I can't refuse you'):

> Pozzo: (*who hasn't listened*). Ah, yes! The night […] will you look at the sky, pig! (*Lucky looks at the sky*) […] It is pale and luminous An hour ago […] after having poured forth ever since […] say ten o'clock in the morning […] it begins to lose its effulgence, to grow pale […] paler a little paler until […] pppffff! finished! it comes to rest. But […] behind this veil of gentleness and peace night is charging […] and will burst upon us […] pppffff! like that (*his inspiration leaves him*) just when we least expect it. (*Silence. Gloomily.*) That's how it is on this bitch of an earth. (37–8)

This description suggests life is a slow waning, to the point where one is given to a sense of tranquillity, only to be torn from the world in a sudden, violent rupture. This is imposed from without, by a dark 'night' that makes life futile, since any sense of achievement or 'gentleness' is a ruse – on this 'abode of stones' there can be no enduring meaning or value. Pozzo's speech presents his *own* internal world, one devoid of enduring goodness, predicated on his *own* disconnection from a good internal mother. This is implied by his constant need for encouragement, his avoidance of genuine contact with the tramps, and his greedy, envious devouring of Lucky. This inner experience becomes transmitted intergenerationally between Pozzo/mother to Lucky/child: it is *Pozzo* who is the dark night that comes suddenly upon a tranquil day, invading Lucky's emotional sphere with violence, shattering any 'intermittent calm', deflating any sense of esteem with neglect and abuse. He continually refers to Lucky in the third person, addressing him directly only to command or degrade him, calling him 'pig', 'hog', and 'scum', and with one word orders, 'coat', 'stool', and 'up'. The development of a sense of internal goodness is destroyed in such relationships, a consequence reflected in the following vignette:

> From as early as he could remember, Mr C.'s father treated him with utter disgust, referring to him as a 'pig' in the company of relatives, showing little interest in him, and abusing him physically when he was

unable to follow orders quickly enough. As an adult, Mr C. developed a manic-depressive disorder but, because the periods of mania were a relief from depressive despair, he did not seek treatment for years. He lived in an apartment he described as a 'mess', finding peace in isolation. He unconsciously kept himself a 'pig' by living in a messy environment, and treated himself accordingly, living recklessly, as if his own life did not matter. In therapy, this man slowly tolerated the deepest, most shame-ridden, raging part of himself that lived in constant fear of his father. This depressive core, so much like that of Lucky, was organized around his early relationships. This patient was slowly able to connect his sense of an internal, hostile father to that of the 'dark cloud' that he felt followed him, which sought to dampen any spontaneity or hope-fulness. The dark cloud could become a monstrous, destructive tornado, throwing him into emotional despair and deep depression. The cloud came to be understood as containing fragments of memory and fantasy particles, of which the predominant themes were humiliation and rage centred on his early experience. During periods of calm, when joy emerged within him, the 'cloud' began to re-enter his awareness to dampen the development of his new way of experiencing life.

This sense of darkness, coming so suddenly and with such life-destroying force, seems connected to the darkness so eloquently described by Pozzo, which reflects both his own, and Lucky's, internal experience. The abrupt eradication of the child's sense of safety and goodness is a catastrophic event, and is predicated by the loss of the mother's love. Other patients have described this hopeless despair as a fog or enveloping darkness. The blackness, a despairing depression, becomes an inviolate part of the inner experience of the self-with-other, and the constellation feels unchangeable because of the belief that it is something *about* the self that calls forth the darkness.[8] It is important to remember that the primary maternal object, the source of inner goodness and calm, can be overshadowed by another person, as in the case of Mr C., whose father became the dominant figure in his internal world. Further analysis revealed his sadness and rage towards his mother, whom he felt had left him prey to the father because, he believed, he was unworthy of her love. Ultimately this emerged as the foundation of his feelings of futility and disconnection from a loving world.

In the Schiller production, Pozzo cannot contain Lucky's powerful feelings; he cowers, covering his ears during the monologue. There is a re-enactment of the despair's genesis – during the staccato section in which Lucky enumerates numerous sporting activities ('tennis football running cycling'), Estragon bounces like a child, in obvious delight, for the only time in the play showing a clear indication he is authentically happy. Immediately the enumeration is interrupted ('skating tennis of all kinds *dying* flying sports of all sort', italic mine) and, at the word 'dying', Estragon's joy is killed, his bouncing stops. Lucky's use of this word seems generated by an identification with an envious or depressed primary object, and the effect is to destroy his own vitality, as it destroys Estragon's own brief sense of aliveness. During rehearsals for the 1984 San Quentin production, Beckett supported the notion that Lucky's internal state is partly created by his relationship to Pozzo. The playwright agreed with J. Pat Miller's interpretation that he imitate certain of Pozzo's mannerisms, made during his speech, in his *own* monologue as Lucky, 'to create a visual parallel' (McMillan and Fehsenfeld, 1988: 75). During the Schiller production, Beckett also commented that Lucky tries to 'amuse Pozzo' during the monologue, in order to touch him and be kept on (McMillan and Fehsenfeld, 1988: 39). This reflects an identification with the aggressor – the child becomes *like* the adult in order to please and be loved.[9] Beckett re-created Pozzo's projective identification in his own instructions to the actor playing Lucky, by 'making a threatening gesture with his finger' during his instruction the monologue reveal the fact that man must 'shrink and dwindle' (McMillan and Fehsenfeld, 1988: 139). The author, in effect, plays a threatening 'Pozzo' who might create terror in an actor who wishes to please him by accepting the feelings

A background of absence

In *Waiting for Godot*, there are many examples of a maternal figure's failure to contain early anxieties. For example, Vladimir consistently refuses to hear/contain Estragon's nightmares, leaving his partner prey to internal demons. In the second act, he sings Estragon a lullaby, 'Bye bye bye bye bye bye', words that suggest ambivalence about his care-taking role. Maternal ambivalence is expressed elsewhere in Beckett, in the title of the play *Rockaby,* for example, where the rocking suggests early nurturing by a breastfeeding/lullaby-singing mother, as well as an image of aging decline in a rocking chair. The nursery rhyme 'Rockaby baby on the treetop [...] when the bough breaks the cradle will fall, and down will come baby' was used by Winnicott as an example of *maternal* ambivalence towards the infant, something echoed in Hackett's fall off the ladder in *Watt*. Murphy's rocking (and Celia's) also shares this

ambivalence. In light of this, Godot is cast, at times, as a container of
anxiety, an omnipotent object that allays despair. Early in the play, the
tramps, tired of waiting, toy with the idea of suicide, but are unsure
which of them is heavier, and should be hung first:

> Vladimir: Well? What do we do?
> Estragon: Don't let's do anything. It's safer.
> Vladimir: Let's wait and see what he says.
> Estragon: Who?
> Vladimir: Godot. (17–18)

Godot is an object that will not only contain their suicidal despair,
but process it, advising appropriate action through his function of
thinking. Paradoxically, his very *absence* is the foundation of their despair,
since without him they cannot experience the security that would make
living a viable alternative. This is the foundation of their waiting, and of
their sense of unremitting futility. They need the absent/bad mother to
arrive as a *good* mother, to create the internal vitality that would make
movement *away* from her possible. An aura of uncertainty surrounds
Godot – the tramps are not sure why they are meeting him, what they
have asked him for, or even what he might have replied. Their attitude
towards him is deferential, referring to their imagined justifications for
the continued absence, Estragon rationalizes: 'It's the normal thing'
(19). Soon more terrifying aspects of their abandonment manifest, and a
sense of malevolence creeps into their representation of Godot. After
stating their infantile dependence – 'Where do we come in […] On our
hands and knees'- and the loss of their 'rights' (19), the tramps are
frightened:

> Vladimir: Listen!
>   *They listen, grotesquely rigid.*
> Estragon: I hear nothing.
> Vladimir: Hssst! […] (*They listen, huddled together.*) Nor I.
>   *Sighs of relief. They relax and separate.*
> Estragon: You gave me a fright.
> Vladimir: I thought it was he.
> Estragon: Who?
> Vladimir: Godot.
> Estragon: Pah! The wind in the reeds.
> Vladimir: I could have sworn I heard shouts […] at his horse. (19)[10]

A sense of disorganized terror accompanies their primal abandonment, now experienced as hostile and sadistic. The mother's voice, a

wind in the reeds, is unpredictable and ambiguous, moving along a spectrum from loving concern to sadistic hostility.

The boy who arrives at the end of each act, to announce Godot will not come, is the only direct tie to the external Godot/mother. The boy's existence reinforces not only the sense of abandonment, but of rivalry, as the Godot/mother clearly cares for other children. At the end of the first act, after the child is frightened by the loud uproar Pozzo and Lucky make while departing, Vladimir questions him. The child admits working for Godot, for whom he minds the goats, and that he is not beaten, though his brother (who minds the sheep) is:

> Vladimir: And why doesn't he beat you?
> Boy: I don't know, sir.
> Vladimir: He must be fond of you.
> Boy: I don't know, sir.
> Vladimir: And why doesn't he beat you?
> Boy: I don't know, sir [...]
> Vladimir: You're not unhappy? (*The Boy hesitates*) Do you hear me?
> Boy: Yes, sir.
> Vladimir: Well?
> Boy: I don't know, sir.
> Vladimir: You don't know if you're unhappy or not?
> Boy: No, sir. (51)

Through this interrogation, Vladimir hopes to become closer to Godot, perhaps to understand why the Godot/mother is available to the boy and not to himself. The child demonstrates an inability to 'know' the mother's mind, which appears dominated by splitting (e.g. the beatings of the 'bad' brother). He does not know *why* he is not beaten, nor *if* Godot is fond of him, and cannot even identify whether his *own* internal state is one of happiness, all effects of the non-relationship on the infantile-self. Vladimir comments that he, too, cannot identify his internal state: 'You're as bad as myself' (51). Godot is unpredictable and unknowable, and the need to remain attached to this primary figure shapes the boy (and Vladimir's) internal experience. The boy's inability to formulate a coherent narrative of his relationship to Godot diminishes his sense of autonomous, secure being. The roots of the psychic fragmentation and autobiographical incoherence that exist in the play, exemplified both in Lucky's monologue and the tramps' difficulties with memory and self-coherence, are highlighted in this tenuous relationship between Godot and the child/Vladimir.[11] There is a sense in which Vladimir looks at an aspect of himself in the boy.

Neither is beaten, while the brother/Estragon are, and Vladimir's wish for warmth and comfort beside the Godot/mother manifests in the boy's relationship to Godot. During their second meeting, Vladimir asks the boy to remember 'me', not 'us', as in the first act, suggesting a collapse into an earlier state, in which the relationship with the mother is dyadic, as if Estragon no longer exists.

The play's central psychological concern is a lack of inner security, predicated on a disconnection from the good mother. This prevents the resolution of the Paranoid Schizoid position, leaving the tramps in fear of constant retaliation from the world. Vladimir's desperate comments at the end of each act make this clear – the words reflect a dissociated state, a fear of non-recognition, or a fear that any recognition given will not endure. From Act I:

> Boy: What am I to say to Mr Godot, sir?
> Vladimir: Tell him ... (*he hesitates*) ... tell him you saw us.
>   (*Pause.*) You did see us, didn't you? (52)

Act 2:

> Boy: What am I to tell Mr Godot, sir?
> Vladimir: Tell him ... (*he hesitates*) ... tell him you saw me and that ... (*he hesitates*) ... that you saw me.
>   ([...] *With sudden violence.*) You're sure you saw me, you won't come tomorrow and tell me that you never saw me! (92)

This is 'seeing' in its deepest sense, the mother's recognition of the child as an autonomous being, which allows her to hold the child within her mind, containing and processing its anxiety so it can experience a secure inner state. Vladimir mirrors both a child's primal fears of abandonment, and a paranoid mother's anxiety about losing her child's recognizing love (as Mrs Winter does in *Footfalls*, when she hallucinates the existence of her daughter). These scenes with the Boy suggest early experiences coalescing around a fear that a primary object does not contain an enduring image of the self, and therefore will not return – the fear, in other words, that love is transient (as discussed in *Proust*). In the Schiller production, Beckett altered the action slightly, the boy withdraws in a very calm, detached manner, walking in reverse. The ambience is dream-like, highlighting a sense of the stage as internal space, something further suggested by Beckett's comment that the characters are 'as thin as ghosts', and that the stage design should reflect the fact they are 'all trapped' (McMillan and Fehsenfeld, 1988: 80). The loss of the boy ruptures Vladimir's connection to the mother. There is a suggestion that in the boy he experiences aspects of his *own* past attachment to a maternal figure, and has been looking into an intra-psychic mirror in the child's face. In both acts, the moon traces a slow arc across the sky following the boy's departure, accenting, as in *Watt*, a disconnection from a maternal figure. Vladimir's comment at the end of Act I, that he (i.e. like the moon), is '[p]ale for weariness […] of climbing heaven and gazing on the likes of us' (52) suggests he has re-introjected his *own* feeling that the moon/mother, which has just replaced the boy and the connection to Godot, does not find him worthy of recognition.[12]

Together again, for ever

Anxieties generated by the absence of maternal recognition permeate the inner relational world that the play depicts. When he first sees Estragon at the opening of the play, Vladimir appears not to notice him, before finally commenting 'So there you are again' and 'Together again at last!' (9), beginning a struggle between enmeshment and autonomy that forms the heart of a play filled with aborted separations. An unknown gang has beaten Estragon, while he was apart from Vladimir/mother:[13]

> Vladimir: When I think of it … all these years but for me … where would you be … ? (*Decisively*.) You'd be nothing more than a heap of bones at the present minute, no doubt about it.
> Estragon: And what of it?
> Vladimir: (*gloomily*). It's too much for one man. (9–10)

Estragon's separation from Vladimir links a hostile world to the primary abandonment of a Godot/mother who is either *required* for his protection, or who alternatively *punishes* autonomy. This exchange depicts Vladimir's entrapping invasiveness, designed to keep Estragon close by disabling his sense of autonomy. Vladimir's comment that without him Estragon would be a 'heap of bones' connects to important imagery in Beckett. McMillan and Fehsenfeld (1988) write: 'In the story *Echo's Bones* and his early autobiographical poem sequence, *Echo's Bones and Other Precipitates*, bones represent the symbolic white residue of painful memories of dead loves. In both these works, as in Lucky's speech, bones are finally replaced by white stone which is the final less individual residue of memory as the past recedes' (78). In this sense,

Vladimir's comment reflects his *own* anxiety about losing Estragon, rather than a concern for his friend's welfare. Estragon, if killed, would become a fading residue (of bones) within Vladimir's mind, suggesting the lack of an integrated presence that could remain internally alive. The comment keeps Estragon close and forestalls this loss. The sense that, in its deepest form, loss becomes stone-like reflects an autistically defensive frozen-self, failing to connect with properly introjected, good primary figures. The following clinical material may illuminate the dynamics that can evolve from such a frozen state:

> The patient, a man in his thirties, entered therapy as the most overtly negative person I had ever met. Any glimmer of optimism or positive feeling was quickly dampened in our sessions by a hostile inner voice that mocked his aspirations for living. The patient's mother, an extremely self-centered, anxious woman, needed constant attention to contain her anxieties. The father abandoned the patient as a child by spending more and more time at work. This inflamed the mother, leaving Mr B. to be the saviour and favourite son. To ensure that Mr B. would not abandon her, the mother would praise his activities or plans only if they directly related to her needs. She would disparage any activity or wish that she felt would only benefit the patient, just as she attacked any sign of self-confidence or independent joy, which she was incapable of sharing. As our sessions unfolded, I felt optimism ebbing away. By the end of a session, I often experienced a desperate sense of hopelessness that I would ever help this man and that, at best, we would continue on for ever in a quagmire. The interesting thing was that Mr B. would often perk up towards the end of a session, leaving noticeably happier. Often, he would exit laughing, making some small joke, and thanking me profusely for helping him to feel so much better. He would return for the next session, however, desperately negative once again. Mr B. was using me as a container of painful internal experiences, particularly ones that had been enacted with his mother from an early age. In our sessions, it was *I* who became Mr B. as an infant/child, as *he* became the mother, and his entire strategy was to keep me (as child) from leaving him (as mother). This occurred in two steps: firstly, by pouring out a continual stream of negativity and by expressing a futile attitude towards life, he slowly was able to relieve himself, somewhat, of an internal state of anxiety and despair. He often had diarrhoea before our sessions, and was clearly anxious about seeing me. He sensed the possibility of change, since unlike him I seemed to withstand the torrent of negativity, and carried on with life. This gave him hope, but also made him anxious, since it meant giving up the hold his mother had on him (and their way of being together), and that I might grow fed up

with him and decide to terminate his treatment. We came to understand that the emptying of himself before sessions (the dumping out of
his 'mother's shit') also meant that he would have room for me. In fact,
he later felt I provided a 'good feed' of tolerant listening and genuine
interest in his internal world. Mr B. realized being special in his ability to
contain his mother's anxiety became deeply tied to his sense of himself
as a valuable, viable person, and this was the second stage of the
interaction between us, which again enacted an early, internalized
relationship within himself. For as he left the sessions in a relieved
mood, praising me as the only one who could help him, he attempted to
instill in me a sense I could not leave him, as he would fall into despair
without me, that I was indeed special. This sense of being a special
therapist was linked, however, to my working with *him*. The patient's
mother felt herself disabled and frightened, probably because her
internal world was shaped by the death, at age two, of her father, and
her mother's subsequent depressive unavailability. She projected this
sense of despair and anxiety into her son during stressful situations
when she felt she could not cope. This did two things: 1) it relieved her
anxiety and feeling of helpless abandonment, and 2) it caused him to
experience the world in a way beneficial to her. If the world was an
awful place, he would not leave her. If he was able to calm her (by doing
whatever it was she felt she could not do) *he* felt special, something she
fuelled by elevating him with praise. In his relationship with me, Mr B.
re-enacted this internal world. He had an anticipatory experience that
the world is dominated by this very type of relationship – a world filled
with Pozzos and Luckys, Vladimirs and Estragons, and mothers that
never quite arrive in any real or whole sense.

Vladimir's words, like those of the patient's mother, cut to the heart
of the infantile-self. Without Vladimir/mother, Estragon will be, like
Mr B., a helpless prey to a hostile world. When Estragon responds, in
futile defeat, 'And what of it', to the suggestion that he will die without
Vladimir's decision making and support, his partner shifts his strategy.
He creates guilt within Estragon, pointing out the suffering his
'support' is causing him, suggesting it is all 'too much', and that it is 'too
late' to ever separate. Estragon, in pain, struggling with his boot, now
listens to Vladimir's nostalgic, suicidal fantasies, before finally getting
his partner's attention again:

> Vladimir: Boots must be taken off every day. I'm tired of telling you
>   that. Why don't you listen to me?
> Estragon: (*feebly*) Help me!
> Vladimir: It hurts?

> Estragon: Hurts! He wants to know if it hurts!
> Vladimir: (*angrily*) No one ever suffers but you. I don't count. I'd like to
>   hear what you'd say if you had what I have.
> Estragon: It hurts?
> Vladimir: Hurts! He wants to know if it hurts! (10)

Vladimir continually ignores Estragon's suffering, blames him for the problem, establishes himself as the thinking, more capable partner, and expresses his own sense of burden. Finally, *told* by Estragon, in clear protest, that the pain is *real*, Vladimir deftly reverses roles, becoming a sufferer unheeded by a selfish partner. The tramps' relationship, one of entangled dependency, reflects the intense, contradictory, and ambivalent feelings the infant experiences towards a mother unavailable for containment of anxiety. For example, the second act opens with Vladimir spotting Estragon walking with his 'head bowed':[14]

> Vladimir: You again! [...] Come here till I embrace you.
> Estragon: Don't touch me!
>   *Vladimir holds back, pained.*
> Vladimir: Do you want me to go away? (*Pause.*) Gogo! [...] Did they
>   beat you? (*Pause.*) Gogo! [...] Where did you spend the night?
> Estragon: Don't touch me! Don't question me! Don't speak to me! Stay
>   with me!
> Vladimir: Did I ever leave you?
> Estragon: You let me go. (58)

The relationship is confused, merged. Vladimir's initial aloofness at seeing Estragon also suggests an inability to maintain a coherent image of his friend within his memory, reminiscent of a young child's difficulties with 'object permanence'. Estragon, as abandoned child, displays the type of protest and angry despair that Bowlby (1973, 1980) chronicled in institutionalized infants and children. He refuses the mother's embrace, resists a sensual re-merger, and his reaction to the possibility of separation ('Don't touch me! [...] Stay with me!') reveals the difficulty he has maintaining the mother as a whole object. He is in a borderline state, attempting to maintain contact with Vladimir-as-good-mother, while simultaneously raging at Vladimir-as-a-bad-mother who tolerates his absence, failing to prevent his departure, and leaving him prey to a hostile world. This confused sense of merger continues, as Estragon, having heard his partner sing in his absence, feels hopelessly defeated:

> Vladimir: One isn't master of one's moods. [...] I missed you ... and at
>   the same time I was happy. Isn't that a queer thing?

Estragon: (*shocked*) Happy? [...] And now?
Vladimir: Now?... (*Joyous.*) There you are again ... (*Indifferent.*) There
we are again ... (*Gloomy.*) There I am again. (59)

This demonstrates a blurring of mother/infant roles, and the
enmeshed quality of the relationship, its impact on individuation, and
the emotional consequences. Estragon is depressed and depleted ('it's
over and done with', 59) since he believes it is *because* he was gone that
Vladimir felt the relief signalled by his singing. Such a feeling of pure
badness is common in enmeshed mother/infant dyads, and operates in
a reciprocal fashion. Mr B.'s mother became depressed or anxious when
her son returned home to report he had enjoyed himself. Her feeling
was similar to Estragon's – she imagined Mr B. had *realized* how much
of a killjoy she was, and would soon abandon her. She would then
attack his joy by devaluing whatever activity he had engaged in, or
enumerating the ways she had suffered while he was out having fun.
Just as the tramps' roles fluctuate in no neatly discernible way as
separation anxieties and guilt entwine them, so Mr B. and his mother
would enact the roles of abandoned child and suffering caretaker in
turn. Vladimir expresses this volatility and sense of estrangement ('One
isn't a master of one's moods'), and the ambivalence is clear, if
unsustainable ('I missed you [...] and at the same time I was happy').
The ability to sustain separation and joy together is impossible, because
an unreachable Godot/mother shapes their experience. Vladimir drifts
from a joyous recognition of separateness ('there *you* are'), through an
indifference of mutuality ('there *we* are') and, finally, to a sense of
gloomy solipsism ('there *I* am'). Vladimir adopts the strategy of Mr B.'s
mother, attacking Estragon's sense of autonomy to keep the dyad
together. When Estragon accepts that his partner suffers because of
him, and admits he *also* feels better on his own, Vladimir asks why he
always crawls back home:

Estragon: I don't know.
Vladimir: No, but I do. It's because you don't know how to defend
yourself. I wouldn't have let them beat you [...] I would have
stopped you from doing whatever it was you were doing.
Estragon: I wasn't doing anything.
Vladimir: Then why did they beat you?
Estragon: I don't know.
Vladimir: Ah no, Gogo, the truth is there are things escape you that
don't escape me, you must feel it yourself [...] it's the way of
doing it that counts. (59–60)

By infantilizing Estragon's attachment to him (the 'crawling back'), Vladimir reinforces the behaviour through humiliation. The boy's constant refrain of 'I don't know sir', discussed earlier, is a direct echo of Estragon's own disorganized narrative in this exchange – Estragon is the helpless, child-like partner who causes the needed mother to feel gladdened at his loss. However, when *Estragon* expresses a willingness to separate, Vladimir quickly points out he is *really* a weak, disabled infant who needs a mother for protection. Like Mr B.'s mother, Vladimir projects his *own* anxious dependency into Estragon, as well as a sense of inadequacy – 'the truth is there are things escape you that don't escape me, you must feel it yourself'. He continually tells Estragon that he cannot think for himself, and that the world will attack him for simply *being himself* ('it's [your] *way* of doing it that counts', my italic). Soon, the final effect of such projections becomes clear – Vladimir tells Estragon he must be happy they are back together, even if he is not conscious of this:

> Vladimir: Say you are, even if it's not true.
> Estragon: What am I to say?
> Vladimir: Say, I am happy.
> Estragon: I am happy.
> Vladimir: So am I.
> Estragon: So am I.
> Vladimir: We are happy.
> Estragon: We are happy. (60)

Estragon is confused, feeling it necessary to fulfil Vladimir's need for narcissistic control. Like the boy who stays with Godot, he asks for identification and validation of his own internal emotional state ('Happy about what [...] Would you say so'), although there is a sense of irritation and a realization that resistance is futile. Vladimir leads him into a merged state, in which he becomes an acquisition of his partner's self: 'I am happy [...] We are happy.' He draws his partner into dyadic entanglement, where one's happiness *is* the ability to make the other's wishes come true. The following vignette elucidates aspects of this type of forced-merger experience:

> The patient's father had sexually abused her from an early age. Bringing her fictional work to read to me in her sessions, it became evident a good figure had emerged in it. This figure, variously represented in different stories, protected her (as heroine) from abuse, by listening and believing, as I did (in actuality and transferentially). As the patient

became conscious of this, she decided, for the first time, to begin a diary in which she documented her experience of abuse. She arrived one session to tell me she was making unprecedented progress in her fictional work, now that her father had been forced from it into a more conscious form of writing in the diary. However, an old phobia suddenly had become more intense. I told her she had awakened her father's anger, by beginning to speak *in her own undisguised voice* for the first time (to me, and in the diary). She then described how her father often had spoken to her imploringly, in an infantile manner that demanded a correct response. If she failed to answer correctly, he became more insistent, until she felt such disintegration anxiety she felt compelled to reply as he wished. Throughout the years of abuse, she felt ensnared by his words, in merged union with a more powerful, controlling voice that could destroy her. This came from a father she hated, but whom she also loved, something mirrored in her fiction, where he was disguised. Subsequently, she read me an essay done years earlier, in which she focused on two dyadic exchanges in two plays. In both, one character was able, solely by the clever, manipulative use of words, to entangle, control, or ridicule the other. When she finished her reading she said, 'I cannot believe that I have been writing about my father all my life.'

Her use of fiction to disguise a deeply depressed, raging part of herself resembles Lucky's use of art, both in his metaphorical dance (see below), and in his monologue, to disguise (and reveal) his depressed feeling-state. Just as Lucky fears direct confrontation with Pozzo, and must resort to forms of expressive art, so this patient's writing explored her inner sense of despair and rage. Like Estragon, who must say 'I am happy', this patient felt she had to respond to her father in a way that complied with his demand for omnipotent control. Her dependency on him as a primary object, coupled with a fear of abandonment, would eradicate her sense of self at those moments, just as Estragon loses the boundaries of his self in the exchange quoted above. Later sessions demonstrated the power of the subjugation. The patient felt that continuing to expose and confront her father would cause him to reach from beyond the grave to harm her. There was also the realization that it was a part of herself (the encapsulated experience of her father within) that she feared awakening. Ultimately, it became clear that much of her writing was also directed towards her mother, towards whom she felt terrible rage for having failed to protect her, and failing to understand her suffering. The writing, much of which was given to her mother, was an attempt to repair her sense of a damaged, primary relationship, in which she was ill-seen, and ill-heard.

This patient found that in the telling (indirectly, through her fiction, and directly to me) there was healing. Beckett's short story, 'Enough', explores the theme of entrapment through an incidence of childhood sexual abuse. The story also links reparation with the presence of a good, internal auditor that can witness the trauma-telling, and it touches upon the healing properties of fiction-making. The narrator begins:

> All that goes before forget. Too much at a time is too much. That gives the pen time to note. I don't see it but I hear it there behind me. Such is the silence. When the pen stops I go on. Sometimes it refuses. When it refuses I go on. Too much silence is too much. Or it's my voice too weak at times. The one that comes out of me. So much for the art and craft. (186)

Whatever the narrator is experiencing, it is overly traumatic and causing a dissociation. The opening line ('All that goes before forget') can be read both as a declaration (i.e. 'I forget all that goes before') and as a self-command (i.e. 'Forget all that comes before!') based on the fact that 'too much at one time is too much' for the self to contain. Alternatively, of course, it can be an introjected command by the *abuser* to forget the abuse. These lines also describe the narrator's concern with the auditor/transcriber. The narrator is aware that the pen that turns the experience into words needs 'time to note', and by concentrating solely on the present, the narrator leaves the traumatic memories within the other for containment. The pen, and presumably the auditor, is out of sight, behind the narrator, and this recorder's motives are unclear, falling anywhere along a spectrum from interrogator, artistic creator, or even psychoanalyst. Since the motives are unclear, the opening line can also be a command to the *recorder* to forget the past trauma – the narrator may be insecure having the memory made real within another mind. On many occasions, patients have commented on my note-taking in these ways, their feelings mirroring this ambiguity. There can be a sense I am creating something beautiful and important out of their words and stories, which will help me understand and help them. Occasionally, there can be a paranoid sense that I am an interrogator, recording their stories to expose them to outside agencies, to later turn against them, using their own words as evidence against them. Primarily, the recorder in 'Enough' is an aspect of the self, a part-object, to whom the core self is *able* to speak, telling its story, putting itself into the other, and the words, for containment. Silence is unbearable, since it inaugurates separation from the other, who is vital for the containment of the anxieties implicit in the telling/reliving of the story/memory complex.

Both Mr B. and the female writer experienced overwhelming pressure to conform to the other's thoughts, feeling compelled to take in those thoughts as part of themselves. The narrator says: 'I did all he desired. I desired it too. For him. Whenever he desired something so did I [...] When he didn't desire anything neither did I. In this way I didn't live without desires. If he desired something for me I would have desired it' (186). These lines, a new paragraph, can be seen as the beginning of a new story/memory, or a development of an ongoing exposition. What is told is a blatant exposition of childhood sexual abuse, and of the merger and identification with the aggressor seen in all abuse victims: 'When he told me to lick his penis I hastened to do so. I drew satisfaction from it. We must have had the same satisfactions. The same needs and the same satisfactions' (186–7). The narrator, six years of age when the abuse began, was 'barely emerging from childhood. But it didn't take [...] long to emerge altogether' (187). What *has* emerged from childhood is not an autonomous self, which remains buried, anxious, and frightened, but a compliant, disguised false-self. The child was used as a non-human object, despite any seeming sense of genuine affection on the part of the adult. For example, the couple would walk side by side, holding hands that are gloved:

> He did not like to feel against his skin the skin of another. Mucous membrane is another matter. Yet he sometimes took off his glove. We would cover in this way a hundred yards or so linked by our bare extremities. Seldom more. That was enough for him [...] I would say that odd hands are ill-fitted for intimacy. Mine never felt at home in his. Sometimes they let each other go [...] Whole minutes past before they clasped again. Before his clasped mine again. (187)

This passage condenses the internal experience of early abuse. Firstly, there is the sense it is the child itself that is 'bad' or 'dirty'. The older man refuses, for the most part, to take hold of the child's hand, preventing the intimacy of skin contact so vital to the young mind. The wearing of gloves brings a clinical quality to their relationship, as if the child might contaminate the elder, and perhaps, in non-sexual moments, the contact raises subtle guilt within the elder. The narrator/child feels something wrong – 'Mine never felt at home in his', and 'odd hands are ill-fitted for intimacy' seems to refer to the relationship as well as the age/handedness difference. The child seems compelled to clarify who is the true initiator of contact ('Before *his* clasped *mine* again'). The overwhelming need for intimate, non-sexual contact becomes reason for an ongoing presence that, as the older man ages, blends into a sense of duty that blurs into a sense of love. Like Watt, Murphy, and the tramps in *Godot*, the child yearns for the touch of recognition of his true self: 'When I bowed down to receive his communications I felt on my eye a glint of blue bloodshot apparently affected' (189). The ambiguity is clear and poignant – what the child wants is a *causal* relationship, that its presence and patience would *effect* the elder, but instead receives an undone ('apparent') recognition of false *affect*. Ultimately, the child is dismissed, like Watt, without a clear, delineated reason, realizing, like Lucky, he is not loved 'for reasons unknown'. Like most in such relationships, this child experiences its final abandonment as its 'disgrace' (190). The recollections of abuse continue to intrude into the story, which weaves between present telling and past inner reality:

The ambiguity this story's title reflects the contradictory emotions inherent in its telling. Mr C., sexually and physically abused as a child, once came to a session and after a brief moment where he experienced his rage as directed outwards, instead of at himself, yelled at some internal presence 'Enough!'. When he regained his composure, he explained he had been speaking both to the perpetrator of the actual abuse (as if it were happening at that moment) and as well, he shouted at the internal agency that made him feel as if he were somehow to blame, torturing him by replaying the memories in the present. It was a defiant cry of protest at an internal abuser, and to an internal auditor (and of course a cry to me). Likewise, in the narrator's tale are the roots of the child's feeling of failing the elder, since the latter feels gloved contact is 'enough'. There is hope that the telling will be enough for the auditor/part of the self that records and requires the telling, and that anxious rage will be allowed to pass. Finally, there is a defiant 'no' to the elder, as the narrator separates past from present, asserting separateness from the abusive situation. The loneliness of such relationships is expressed in its description as a timeless, endless wandering, and by the final line 'Enough of my old breasts feeling his old hand' (192), which demonstrates the enduring, entrapped quality the past maintains in the psyche of the abused child. The term 'old breast' can refer both to the *past* situation, and to an actual *present* and *truly* 'old' breast that still feels the old hand as if it were contemporary.

The last farandole

The most fundamental way early mother–infant bonding can be damaged is through ruptures in the primary nurturing situation. This section examines two scenes in which such fundamental disruptions occur. Towards the end of the first act Pozzo suggests that Lucky, 'who taught [him, i.e. Pozzo] all these beautiful things', perform for the entertainment of the two tramps:

> Pozzo: Dance, misery! [...] *Lucky dances* [...]
> Estragon: Is that all?
> Pozzo: Encore!
>   *Lucky executes the same movements, stops.*
> Estragon: Pooh! I'd do as well myself [...]
> Pozzo: He used to dance the farandole [...] the fandango, and even the
>   hornpipe. He capered. For joy. Now that's the best he can do.
>   (40)

Lucky's dance is a grotesque representation of both his self-state and his relationship to Pozzo-as-mother, demonstrating his role as a deeply depressed part of the self. He is called 'misery', an apt title that reflects what Pozzo projects into him through denigration and countless humiliations. Lucky once danced 'for joy', filled with a love of movement and physicality that is every infant's endowment. Now, after years of suffering Pozzo's neglect and abuse, his movements are mechanical, lifeless, suggesting a series of symbolic titles. Estragon sees the dance as 'The Scapegoat's Agony' and Lucky serves the function of a scapegoat, being a repository of Pozzo's negative projections and abusive attacks. Vladimir sees the dance as 'The Hard Stool', which accurately describes, in concrete terms, another aspect of Lucky's sense of badness (equated with feaces), a poisoned, debased self-image that Pozzo forces into him, as well as the complementary imago of the sadistic mother.[15] As infant, Lucky is too weak to re-project the bad feelings into Pozzo. In any case, they would be immediately returned, since Pozzo cannot tolerate the anxiety of accepting he is anything but perfect. The experience of a patient, who came to analysis suffering from narcissistic depression and rage, reflects this aspect of Lucky's dance. He had been physically abused as a child, and as the analysis progressed he described feeling that at his core he was a 'piece of shit', a useless, worthless person who should die. In one session, seething with anger and despair, he felt something horrible inside of him, and that he had to defecate or vomit. He said it was now his abuser who was a 'piece of shit' that he had to expel from his own body, so he might be free of the tormenting.

The final description of the dance comes from Pozzo himself, who calls it, perhaps most appropriately, 'The Net'. Pozzo's intensive projections of his own inadequacy and dependency incapacitate Lucky, and the slave has become embroiled, enmeshed in a net with a mother like that of Ms A. This woman entered therapy because of a bingeing disorder, following a series of relationships with sadistic men who abused her, but upon whom she felt entirely dependent. As an infant, she imagined she would have tried anything to win her mother's affection, believing she would only be loved by making her mother happy. It was the inevitable failure of these attempts that led to her feeling enslaved, since she needed her mother to survive. She could not tolerate growing out of her current dependency on sadistic figures because she felt she was still a helpless child. She feared *both* this dependency and its frustration, which would mean an outpouring of raging sadism that would destroy the very person upon whom she depended. She reported the following dream: *She was dancing before a large audience and genuinely enjoying the freedom and beauty of her movements, as well as the bodily sensations they evoked. Her mother came upon the stage dressed in black, carrying a small infant who was hooked up to a large, frightening machine by a complex array of tubes and lines. The patient attempted to continue her dancing but it slowly became more lifeless and mechanical as she felt obliged to care for the infant, which she finally took from her mother.* The patient's associations led to an appreciation of this dream. She was the *infant*, hopelessly dependent, tied to this sadistic, withholding mother who envied and hated her attempts to feel free, to escape the deadly bond. The *dancer* was the hidden part of her, filled with a sense of freedom and joy, and it was *these* feelings that evoked the appearance of the envious mother upon her internal stage. The dancer's inability to continue the dance demonstrated her dependency on the mother. However, the infant also represented the *mother*, seen as the dependent part of the dyad, and the guilty need to care for this mother-as-helpless-infant caused the dance's cessation. The *machine* was a highly condensed symbol, alternatively her cold, mechanical mother, whose minimal affection was needed to keep the patient alive, but also the dead, mechanical part of the patient herself. In the transference, the patient saw me in varying lights. Firstly, I was the audience appreciating her dance of life, but later I became the machine, a transitional 'mother', who cared for her infantile-self, but whom she was afraid to trust completely while her mother was still onstage. Finally, I would become the 'dancer' herself, trustworthy and loving, coming to help her-as-infant by taking custody of her infantile-self from the deadly mother, though there was a fear I would be destroyed by taking on this burden.

This dream elucidates aspects of Lucky's dance, which also progresses from a joyous exhibition of a living-self to a mechanical set of desperate spasms. The rope that ties Lucky to Pozzo, like the tubes and lines connecting the infant to the machine, is a malignant umbilical that cannot be severed without an alternative source of internal nurturing. Lucky has no opportunity to develop autonomy, remaining entangled in the lines, ropes, and tubes of this broken, early dyad. His dance breaks down into a series of slow, dying expressions of his despairing entanglement. The tramps comment on this:

> Vladimir: A running sore!
> Estragon: It's the rope.
> Vladimir: It's the rubbing.
> Estragon: It's inevitable.
> Vladimir: It's the knot.
> Estragon: It's the chafing. (25)

The rope becomes a grotesque travesty of the nursing bond, torturing and emaciating Lucky. It reflects the destructive connection between Pozzo-as-a-mother who fails to contain and enrich the Lucky/child's internal experience, feeding him poisonous thoughts that undermine vitality and self-worth. The most primary early nurturing experience, the life-giving, physical connection that exists from the moment of conception, distorts into a macabre display of despair, and a plaintiff cry for love.[16]

Lucky, who once 'danced for joy', remains 'tied' to Pozzo in this deadly, enmeshed fashion, having somatized his despairing internal world by becoming essentially mute. Pozzo claims Lucky is still 'trying to impress [me], so I'll keep him' (31), and this is an integral part of the net of despair that Lucky's dance symbolizes. The slave yearns to win Pozzo's love, no longer because he truly hopes to share the inherent joy of life found in the early mother–infant bond, but because all that is left is the faint hope he will be tolerated. Lucky is so profoundly depressed he is unable to accept food from Pozzo, demonstrating an early infantile reaction to the bad breast, which cannot be trusted and is felt to be poisonous (as Pozzo's words are). The most damaging effect is a constant inability to feel secure, as the world/mother is always a poisonous threat, and the following exchange demonstrates the damage inflicted upon Lucky's self-esteem, as it manifests in an apathy towards feeding. Pozzo, having finished eating, has just tossed several chicken bones on the ground, where Estragon 'stares at them greedily', and asks him whether he needs the bones:

> Pozzo: Do I need the bones [...] No, personally, I do not need them any more [...] but [...] in theory bones belong to the carrier. He is therefore the one to ask [...] *Estragon goes towards Lucky, stops before him.*
> Estragon: Mister ... excuse me, Mister ...
> Pozzo: You're being spoken to, pig! Reply! (*To Estragon*) Try him again.
> Estragon: Excuse me, Mister, the bones, you won't be wanting the bones?
> Pozzo: (*in raptures*) Mister! (*Lucky bows his head*) Reply! Do you want them or don't you? (*Silence of Lucky. To Estragon.*) They're yours. (*Estragon [...] begins to gnaw them.*) I don't like it. I've never known him to refuse a bone before. (*He looks anxiously at Lucky.*) Nice business if he fell sick on me! (27)[17]

Lucky's despair is so deep he cannot accept nutrition, but Pozzo reveals his *own* anxiety about losing him, since he cannot survive without the slave, whom he requires as a repository for the bad parts of himself. Pozzo is enmeshed as well as 'enmesher', like the mother-as-infant in Ms A.'s dream of dancing. He maintains narcissistic equilibrium through a grandiose sense of omnipotence, and an omnivorous, devouring attitude reminiscent of Mr Knott:

> Pozzo: The more people I meet the happier I become. From the meanest creature one departs wiser, richer, more conscious of one's blessings [...] even you, who knows, will have added to my store. (29)

Pozzo diminishes dependency by imagining himself as an omnipotent omnivore for whom the world serves only to fulfil his need for goodness. Like a vampire who sucks the life out of the world, but is never fulfilled, he must seek out new victims. He cannot experience an enduring love for those meets, they are simply mirrors of his false autonomy. The following clinical vignette elaborates the psychological significance of the 'chicken-bone' exchange:

> Early in his analysis Mr D. experienced me as hostile, grandiose, and withholding. During one period of our work he spoke about his mother

– he felt she had only left 'the crumbs' for him, referring both to his sense of emotional deprivation and actual periods of unpredictability in early feeding. As an adult, he imbibed large amounts of sweetened drinks, much like he devoured the sweetened water he was given on an irregular basis as an infant, which had calmed him while he spent hours alone in a darkened room. Mr D. once angrily commented that I felt superior to him, only leaving him 'crumbs'. I connected this not only to his recollections of his mother, but to a fantasy he had mentioned several times before, one he connected to a half-forgotten story he had read as a child. In this fantasy, he was a small boy who would go before a large ogre to ask for 'more food' (clearly a reference to *Oliver Twist*) only to be denied, mocked, and attacked. After my interpretation, he felt deeply saddened, saying he always felt he would not receive enough from the world, since it was a big, horrible monster in front of which he would have to beg.[18]

Mr D.'s *Oliver Twist* fantasy suggests a starving-self locked in a desperate struggle with an emotionally absent mother. The child is attacked for wanting life, represented both as actual food and as the mother's nurturing love. Oliver, of course, never knew his mother, who died of hypothermia moments after his birth:

> [T]he pale face of a young female was raised feebly from the pillow; and a faint voice imperfectly articulated the words, 'Let me see the child, and die' [...] the surgeon deposited it [the baby] in her arms. She imprinted her cold and white lips passionately on its forehead, passed her hands over her face [...] and died [...] her blood had been frozen forever. (46)

Oliver's entry into the world actualizes Mr D.'s sense of maternal abandonment. His feelings of physical and emotional starvation begin early (he is referred to in the third person and seen as a nuisance). Both Mr D. and Oliver are separated from the earliest experience with the mother, a loving nurturing close to her warm body. The confrontation with the 'ogre' (that Mr D. remembered from his childhood reading) takes place in the workhouse, where the other boys select Oliver to go forward:

> Oliver [...] was desperate with hunger, and reckless with misery. He rose from the table, and advancing to the master, basin and spoon in hand, said [...] 'Please sir, I want some more.'
>
>   The master was a fat, healthy man; but he turned very pale [...] the boys [were] filled with fear.
>
>   'What!', said the master at length, in a faint voice.

'Please, sir,' replied Oliver, 'I want some more.'
The master aimed a blow at Oliver's head with the ladle, pinioned him in his arms, and shrieked aloud for the beadle. (56)[19]

Here is the central confrontation of the infant's emerging-self, despairing with hunger and loneliness, reaching out for life and connection to a feared but needed maternal object, only to be attacked for its very love. In *Waiting for Godot,* Vladimir's song, which opens Act 2, echoes this exchange:

> A dog came in the kitchen
> And stole a crust of bread.
> Then cook up with a ladle
> And beat him till he was dead.
>
> Then all the dogs came running
> And dug the dog a tomb
> And wrote upon the tombstone
> For the eyes of the dogs to come:
>
> A dog came in the kitchen
> And stole a crust of bread [etc.] (57–8)

This starving, weakened dog/child, like Mr D., Estragon and Oliver, dares to ask for more food, but to be so bold as to ask for (or steal) a few 'crumbs', a few 'bones' or a 'crust' is tantamount to dying, since it will enrage the terrible, all-devouring mother.[20] The never-ending, circular song makes clear the intractable, deeply encrypted nature of this internally 'closed system'; the dog's entombment creates a sense of hopeless foreboding, a warning that to seek to feed (or love) is to die or to kill. The cook's use of the ladle as a weapon rather than as a means of nurturing ironically echoes the master's own attack on Oliver, highlighting the hostility inherent in this particular constellation of self and other.

Oliver's state, following his plea for more food, mirrors even more closely the internal worlds (and real worlds) of Mr D. and Lucky. Placed into solitary confinement, he cries bitterly:

[A]nd when the long dismal night came on, spread his little hands before his eyes to shut out the darkness, and crouching in the corner, tried to sleep [...] drawing himself closer and closer to the wall, as if to feel even its cold hard surface were a protection in the gloom and loneliness which surrounded him. (59)

He is locked away, a 'lost heart of the self', in a dark, frozen chamber reminiscent of Mr D.'s cold, lonely room (both internal and real), and

Lucky's abandonment 'in the great deeps, the great cold' (44). Oliver turns to the wall yearning for touch lest he, like Lucky, be pulled into the terrors of psychic annihilation. Its hard, cold surface, is an echo of his mother's frozen body, and offers the solace of an autistic object. Here is the deepest, most isolated part of the self, surrounded by a withholding, absent mother whose non-recognition is death.

In the fantasy of Mr D., the story of Oliver, and the exchange between Pozzo, Estragon, and Lucky, one sees the terrifying power of the withholding/envious mother, the sense of being overwhelmed and annihilated by her rage/absence, or one's own feelings of anger and depression. Mr D.'s conscious recovery of these memories/fantasies led to deeply depressive feelings once the anxiety and rage were worked through. Lucky has no such opportunity; he represents the most defeated part of the self, and loses all hope of love and nurturing. He refuses to take even the bones, losing the thread of connection to the good mother that Mr D. maintained with the hope of eventual restoration.

A major consequence of this persisting sense of damaged nursing is the continuation of a paranoid relationship with a withholding or envious internal world/mother, which often results in a feeling of chronic, empty futility. For example, early in the second act of *Waiting for Godot*, Estragon is frightened and requires soothing/feeding by Vladimir-as-mother, who seems depleted and has little to offer save for 'bad' food (turnips). At first, Estragon feels outraged, poisoned by the 'bad' food, until 'good' food is found (a carrot), though only one remains that must 'be made to last' (20). At this point, the idea of being 'tied' to Godot is raised, as Vladimir speaks of their having 'got rid of' their 'rights' (19). They are, in fact, children together, desperate for Godot-as-mother to provide food, protection, and a containing recognition. They sense Godot will forever fail to nurture them, and a paranoid submission to a dominant, withholding/sadistic world develops. Twirling the carrot-stub, Estragon says: 'Funny, the more you eat the worse it gets', to which Vladimir replies: 'I get used to the muck as I go along' (21). This poisoned dichotomy frames an internal world of paranoid resignation. Similarly, Mr B. reported that his mother threw sweet potatoes in his face when he refused to eat them as an infant, and stated this was the core of his negative despair. He either complied with the 'shit' the world offered and lost his own desire (got 'used to it'), or he accepted it, as it was, with increasing despair, but maintaining a remnant of self-respect ('the more you eat the worse it gets'). This compression of internal possibility reflects the two poles of the paranoid stance the tramps enact, which is the source of their incapacity to stay, or to leave. Within this quiet, resigned despair lurks the primal fear of forever receiving bad feeds from the world, never connecting with a good primary object/mother through early memories of love at the breast. They comment on this feeling:

> Vladimir: Nothing you can do about it.
> Estragon: No use struggling.
> Vladimir: One is what one is.
> Estragon: No use wriggling.
> Vladimir: The essential doesn't change.
> Estragon: Nothing to be done. (21)

These are the beginnings of a sense that the *self* is bad, that the situation is unchangeable and deserved. This entrapment, within a broken primary nursing experience, leaves little room for hope since it generates an internal world in which life is a slow, entropic slide into starvation and invisibility.

The presumption of despair

In *Waiting for Godot*, the projective matrix of Pozzo, the tyrannical landowner, and his slave, Lucky develops an internal mechanics of enmeshment to the extreme. This dyad is more highly polarized, more directly fuelled by severe anxieties about separation and dependency, and suggests a more desperate, raging part of the narrative-self.

Despite his dismissal of Lucky, Pozzo admits his servant's responsibility for his own knowledge of 'beautiful things', something which infuriates the tramps:

> Vladimir: And now you turn him away? Such an old and faithful
>   servant?
> Estragon: Swine!
>   *Pozzo more and more agitated.*
> Vladimir: After having sucked all the good out of him you chuck him
>   away like a … banana skin. Really…
> Pozzo: […] I can't bear it … any longer … the way he goes on … you've
>   no idea … it's terrible … he must go […] I'm going mad … (*he
>   collapses, his head in his hands*) … I can't bear it … any longer […]
> Vladimir: (*to Lucky*). How dare you! It's abominable! Such a good
>   master! Crucify him like that! After so many years! Really! (33–4)

This exchange illustrates a rapidly reversing self/other matrix suggestive of an infantile-self that experiences a mother as selfishly absent. Pozzo admits his nurturing by a Lucky/mother who taught him so much, and the tramps exhort their disgust by using imagery that evokes an infantile fantasy of 'sucking' Lucky dry. Pozzo then deftly reverses roles, becoming the overburdened, fragmenting victim. He *becomes* Lucky, forcefully introjecting (and speaking) the very words that reflect the *slave's* internal state. The result is confusion – Vladimir and Estragon dissociate, then merely parrot, through merger and introjection, Pozzo's words: 'He can't bear it [...] He's going mad' (34), demonstrating a breakdown of self/other boundaries, as the good/bad imagos become confused. Indeed, Vladimir's opinion reverses – he sees *Lucky* as ungrateful and cruel. This type of confusion causes the child great difficulty in maintaining a strong, secure self, since traumatic behaviour and boundary violations are not experienced as real. The effect is twofold – there is not only the original trauma, but also a more devastating effect, created by the mother's failure to accept the trauma has happened, or to recognize its effect on the child's psyche. The worst scenario places the responsibility for the pain within the child:

> Pozzo: (*sobbing*). He used to be so kind ... so helpful ... and entertaining ... my good angel ...and now ... he's killing me.
> Estragon: (*to Vladimir*). Does he want to replace him?
> Vladimir: What?
> Estragon: Does he want someone to take his place or not? [...]
> Pozzo: (*calmer*). Gentleman [...] Forget all I said [...] you may be sure there wasn't a word of truth in it [...] Do I look like a man that can be made to suffer? (34)

These are the same transferential patterns enacted between Mr B. and myself, as Vladimir and Estragon experience the same confusion the patient did when confronted with a mother who suddenly devalues all of his past efforts because he failed to respond to a current need. *Lucky* becomes all bad, just as Mr B. felt *he* was all bad following his mother's diatribes, or as *I* felt I was a 'bad' therapist unable to 'cure' him. The tramps accept this projection, and turn on Lucky, forgetting that it is Pozzo who is sadistic and self-centered.[21] Pozzo splits Lucky into an all-good and all-bad child, as Mr B.'s mother would split her perception of him when he failed her. 'He used to be so kind ... and now ... he is killing me' – the child introjects these words, which become part of his anticipatory world, so that he is not only bad, but will have no life if he leaves the mother. In fact, Lucky represents the dying part of the self, and Mr B. believed *he* would become a worthless street-person, a logical outcome of moving away from his mother since, having internalized her vision of him as worthless apart from serving her needs, he would be unable to care for himself. This fantasy was also protective, since he could not be further drained if he had nothing more to offer. It is of interest that one of the patient's two brothers developed a severe addictive disorder and for a time was only kept off the street by the mother's insistence that he be taken care of in the family home. At the core of Mr B.'s internal world was a belief that he and his mother were locked into a hopelessly dependent, merged state, in which neither could survive alone. This is reminiscent of Hamm's telling Clov in *Endgame*: 'Gone from me you'd be dead [...] Outside of here is death' (70). Later, Mr B. felt his mother would die if he left, since she could not survive without him, and that *he* would die of the guilt. As a separation progressed, his mother became physically ill, something exacerbated by her inability to cope with losing her son as a container of her anxiety. Despite his mother's actual illness, Mr B. believed there might be hypochondriacal manipulation involved. There is some evidence to suggest that Beckett intended the Pozzo role to be played in such a way that the blindness of the second act would seem feigned. (McMillan and Fehsenfeld, 1988: 63–4). This suggests the possibility that Pozzo unconsciously, or consciously, cannot tolerate Lucky's loss, but even more, cannot tolerate the *admission* of his need for Lucky, and so develops a hysterical or simply feigned blindness.

This sequence reverses the basic situation, where the mother contains the child's anxiety, since Pozzo acts as if *he* were a needy infant deprived of good-enough mothering by *Lucky*. He demonstrates the most devastating interpersonal exchange between mother and child, *the mother's denial of an already established internal reality*, and one she forcibly projects into the child. Pozzo makes *Lucky* a sadistic persecutor who is now no longer 'kind' or 'helpful' by projecting the greedy, sadistic, and anxious parts of himself into his servant, a broken, disabled creature, full of repressed sadness and rage, afraid of strangers. Pozzo then says 'Forget all I said [...] there wasn't a word of truth in it [...] Do I look like a man that can be made to suffer?' – this devastating reversal denies the essence of the projective attack, replacing it with a posture of invulnerable indifference. Mr B.'s mother enacted similar scenes, after tirades in which she accused her son of incompetence or insensitivity because of some perceived failure to anticipate her needs perfectly. On a number of occasions, she would become calm after such a projective attack and say to third party, in front of him: 'B, what B? I have no son called B. I have two good sons X and Y, but no son called B.' Similarly, Lucky is forced, in the first instance, to accept *he* is the persecutor (not the victim) of selfish demands to curb anxiety, despite all evidence to the contrary.

The confusion the tramps experience about Pozzo's *real* intentions for Lucky (i.e. *Does* he want someone to take Lucky's place or not?), reflects this contradictory message. It is this ambivalence, and the fact that Pozzo actually cannot tolerate losing Lucky, that makes sense of his final denial. He creates in Lucky a sadism not Lucky's to own, which further creates a sense of guilty dependency. His words are double edged: they suggest his earlier attacks (e.g. 'He's killing me') were not true, creating the possibility that Pozzo's 'suffering' is also not real, and that Lucky can *still* be a favoured child/servant. Alternatively, by implying that *such as Lucky* could not make *such a man as him* suffer, Pozzo creates an abandonment anxiety that deepens Lucky's helpless dependency. Lucky will feel, on one hand, that he can *presume* love is available (Pozzo/mother is *not* really hurt or angry, I can repair her), but on the other, that he should *despair,* since he will forever be unloved (Pozzo/mother *cannot* be hurt by me, and does not love me, and so I am lost). This strategy establishes the premise that Lucky is either bad, but now forgiven, or invisible and unneeded.[22] The worst outcome is the child's feeling it is actually insane, since the mother creates a powerful emotional experience that is then denied, and in order to maintain a good relationship the child must disavow aspects of its internal reality. The Beckettian fascination with the dictum, allegedly from Augustine (Hobson, 1956), 'Do not despair, one of the thieves was saved. Do not presume, one of the thieves was damned', elucidates these experiences. Lucky should not *despair,* for Pozzo/mother has forgotten his 'badness', and will love him, need him again, and so he (and she) will not die. However, as the despair lifts, the other side of this constellation comes to the fore. Lucky should not *presume* (i.e. accept the love as natural and enduring), for the Pozzo/mother *cannot* be hurt by him (i.e. recognize him as important to her) and he will be abandoned. This emotional entrapment creates a world of endless schizoid despair of alternating hope and anguish.[23] Mr B. would become intensely vitalized by the prospect of helping his disabled mother, or any number of girlfriends, since he felt his core value was as a 'fixer'. However, any satisfaction would soon vanish, as he felt increasingly suspicious he was being used by someone who, sooner or later, would revert to a selfish, manipulative vampire that would drain and discard him.

The genesis of Pozzo's primal anxiety is clearly a fear of non-recognition:

> Pozzo: (*terrifying voice*). I am Pozzo! (*Silence.*) Pozzo! (*Silence.*) Does that name mean nothing to you? (*Silence.*) I say does that name mean nothing to you? (22)

Both Mr B.'s mother and Pozzo fear abandonment through non-recognition. Pozzo, for example, must be coddled when he wants to sit down:

> Pozzo: I'd like very much to sit down, but I don't quite know how to go about it.
> Estragon: Could I be of any help?
> Pozzo: If you asked me perhaps. [...]
> Estragon: Here we go. Be seated, sir, I beg of you.
> Pozzo: No, no. I wouldn't think of it! (*Pause. Aside.*) Ask me again.
> Estragon: Come, come, take a seat, I beseech you, you'll get pneumonia.
> Pozzo: You really think so.
> Estragon: Why it's absolutely certain.
> Pozzo: No doubt you are right. (*He sits down.*) Done it again! (*Pause.*) Thank you dear fellow. (36)

Pozzo, like Mr B.'s mother, does not feel an enduring, internal goodness, and omnipotently controls Estragon into playing a loving mother. He directs this scene with asides and leading questions in order to get an invitation, which masquerades as loving concern. Mr B.'s mother would similarly stage-manage relations with her son. It became his duty not only to fulfil her needs, but to *anticipate* them as well, with the penalty for failure being a withdrawal of love that forced him to become ever more vigilant. This strategy relieves Pozzo's sense of dependency, re-establishing his omnipotence and, by the end of the exchange, there is confusion about who it is that *really* wants Pozzo to sit. He develops this reversal, suggesting he has been pressured to stay ('if *you* insist'), then feigns that he *really* wants to *leave*, immediately consulting his watch after the invitation is extended, saying: 'But I really am to be getting along' (36). Dependency is projected into *Estragon*, who *wants* Pozzo to stay! For an infant, countless repetitions of such forced projections of a mother's primitive dependency needs creates confusion, but also a desperate dependency that really belongs to the mother. Pozzo's real needs are for recognition, and an omnipotently controlled concern – once these are fulfilled he moves on. Mr B. experienced his mother's interest in him as waning as soon as her needs were met, something which formed the basis of his persistent attachment to *constantly* needy figures. Since Pozzo has controlled this entire exchange, there can be no real introjection of a caring mother, since Estragon's words were actually his own.[24]

Pozzo embodies a desperate but defiant need for others to see him as important, his dependence, and anxiety about abandonment are clear. He admits: 'Yes, gentleman, I cannot go for long without the society of my likes [...] even when the likeness is an imperfect one' (24) and that 'I don't like talking in a vacuum' (30). The genesis of his arrogance in early dyadic failure is apparent: Pozzo's fear of abandonment, which would lead to disintegration anxiety, causes him to devalue those he needs most. This envious attack on inner goodness in others leaves them vulnerable, tied to him, as their sense of autonomy is destroyed, leaving a constant need to gain a tyrant's approval that they believe is their only salvation from despair. The most vulnerable object of envy is the child's love of life itself, and Pozzo and Lucky's envious, merged relationship, which does not allow for autonomy, forms the basis of the Beckettian dictum: 'Better not to have been born at all.' Birth is never finished, it leads only to entrapment and anxiety. In the tramps' persistent wait for the good mother, one sees the embodiment of the infant's life force, as it struggles to form a loving connection, to be *well* heard and seen.

Conclusion

Waiting for Godot privileges us with a glimpse into important aspects of early object relations organized around an experience of absent love. An enclosed system of fluid, shifting representations hovers around a limited set of constellations, which all have enmeshment, dependency, and early separation anxiety at their core:

> Pozzo: I must go [...]
> Estragon: Then adieu.
> Pozzo: Adieu.
> Vladimir: Adieu.
> Pozzo: Adieu.
>   *Silence. No one moves.* [...]
> Pozzo: I don't seem to be able ... (*long hesitation*) ... to depart.
> Estragon: Such is life. (47)

This is the 'essential' that 'does not change', an experience of an early infant–mother dyadic failure, leading to frozen, immutable attachments to primal objects. The complexities of the Godot–mother–infant relationship are inexhaustible, and reflect the powerful confusion the infant experiences in the failing primary relationship. The end of each act, when the tramps declare their intention to go, but do not move, is the culmination of this state of affairs. Godot-as-mother is irreconcilable, shifting between an all-giving saviour who will provide food and shelter, and a withdrawn, devouring tyrant who expects service but does not recognize. The nature of this relationship is contradictory: the tramps desire to leave, but stay, as Godot continuously splits into more than one primary object, alternately felt to be sadistic and withholding, yet also felt to be capable of providing basic nurturing. Godot never arrives as a *whole* mother who could offer them a sense of completeness and a chance to live, *both* apart from her *and* with her, as an enduring, loving internal presence.

The power of the play is also related to its transcendence of this static determinism, as it becomes an exploration of human potential and the nature of psychic change. Towards the play's end, Vladimir is alone with Pozzo, who is enraged about questions about time:

> Pozzo: It's abominable! [...] one day we were born, one day we shall die, the same day, the same second, is that not enough for you? (*Calmer*) They give birth astride of the grave, the light gleams an instant, then it's night once more. (89)[25]

Soon after, alone while Estragon sleeps, Vladimir delivers his most reflective words, wondering if he can ever genuinely apprehend any truth in their situation. He then says:

> Vladimir: Astride of a grave and a difficult birth, lingeringly, the gravedigger puts on the forceps. We have time to grow old. The air is full of our cries. (*He listens.*) But habit is a great deadener [...] I can't go on! (*Pause*) What have I said? (90–1).

Vladimir, like Lucky, is infiltrated by Pozzo, echoing his words ('Astride a grave'), but there is momentary insight as he moves feverishly off to the side of the stage. Pozzo's collapse into a dead, condensed world ('one day we are born [...] one day we die [...] the same day.') of paranoid emptiness, devoid of any enduring, early experiences of love, seems for a moment *not* to 'be enough for him'. There is a hint that Vladimir might leave this encasing system for a more evolving relationship with the world, but this collapses, as the Boy arrives as a return of the repressed aspects of the need for primary recognition. The play *is* one of abject hopelessness, the wait is futile, since Godot has *already* arrived, present in the characters' natures and relationships themselves. It is this fact that makes it a play of the greatest hope, for within this realization comes the *possibility* of *change*, to live in a new, more integrated, and, perhaps, better world.[26]

Notes

1 The phrase 'a strange situation' refers to the experimental situation devised to study early attachment between mother and infant. The infant is left alone with a stranger, and patterns of primary attachment are evaluated upon the mother's return (Ainsworth, 1978). The patterns of attachment in *Waiting for Godot*, engendered by the same sort of primary absence, could be understood in terms of the system devised by Attachment Theory.

2 Of course, triangular and even more complex constellations are not excluded. One could, at times, see Godot as an absent paternal figure, to Vladimir/mother and Estragon/child, or the tramps themselves reflecting a parental couple. This chapter examines early child and primary object pairings, upon which more complex constellations are built. In fact, there is an element of infantilism in Godot, who seems tied to the tramps-as-waiters, much like Knott. Asked who Godot represents, Beckett is quoted as saying that had he known he 'would have said so', underlining the character's elusiveness (Schneider, 1967: 38). He also commented that the tramps represent his wife, Suzanne, and himself at the time of writing, suggesting, perhaps, certain primary transferential elements in the play (Bair, 1978: 254). He is said to have asked actors to emphasize 'boredom', highlighting a sense of internal emptiness and disconnection from life. Boredom can also operate as a repressing affect to control feelings of rage and sadness. The tramps attempt to *control* these feelings by finding substitutes, such as the world games, play, and entrapping dyadic roles.

3 Beckett stressed this core aspect of waiting, while famously refusing to speak about 'meanings'. Calderwood (1986) discusses various approaches to the waiting experience in the play. MacGowran quotes Beckett as saying ' [Godot] doesn't mean God at all. The whole play's about waiting' (Toscan, 1973: 16). This was again emphasized in his deletion of 'Wir' from the German title '*Warten auf Godot*' (McMillan and Fehsenfeld, 1988: 60). The complementary of waiting is *not* waiting, or leaving, and this chapter explores this aspect of the experience. Beckett wrote to Alec Reid: 'In *Godot* the audience wonders if Godot will ever come, in *Endgame* it wonders if Clov will ever leave' (quotation in Reid, 1968: 70). A major question is *why* the tramps do *not* leave, beyond notions of duty or pure dependency. One reason is a primary love for a maternal figure.

4 Beckett saw the speech as reflecting the decline of man, and this has been the general critical view (see McMillan and Fehsenfeld, 1988: 67, 74). It is also a deeply felt *personal* experience of a very *specific* early relationship. Lucky expresses the rage and depression the infant feels when disconnected from the

mother, represented by Pozzo (and of course Godot). As aspects of the narrative-self, Lucky and Pozzo are powerful early internal imagos inherent in all human experience.

5 Klein originally defined the emotion the infant experiences upon entering the Depressive Position as 'pining', but the term did not endure. Beckett captured the ambiguities and ambivalence of the Depressive Position when he stated: 'Where we have both light and dark we also have the inexplicable' (Francis, 1965: 259). This is why Godot is beyond understanding, since he is experienced as multiple part-objects (e.g. good/bad).

6 I have collected three other examples of patients who spontaneously brought references to Godot into an analysis. In each case, the references connected to a sense of isolation and disconnection between the patient and the analyst-as-mother. Technical considerations preclude their publication now.

7 McMillan and Fehsenfeld (1988) note the complementary themes and imagery in the two speeches, as both reflect man's decline. A more intimate, and *causal*, connection can explain Lucky's despair as an aspect of *early* human experience that is implicitly universal.

8 Immediately after his speech, Pozzo solicits praise for its dramatic effect, invalidating his connection to its content. This type of denial, and its effect on the infantile-self is discussed in more detail later in this chapter, and the sense of the 'actor' existing only in a role is discussed in Chapter 5.

9 Pozzo may be re-creating the relationship with his *own* mother, by treating himself (represented by Lucky) in the way he experienced his mother's treatment of him. It is also possible that Pozzo may be re-enacting another aspect of early experience with his mother, treating his servant in the way his infantile mind experienced *his* own treatment of his mother (as overly demanding, selfish, and sadistic). If his mother could not contain her anxiety about these intense infantile demands, there would not have been an opportunity for him to develop more sophisticated ways of relating to others.

10 In the Schiller production, Beckett restored, at this point, a brief exchange deleted in the original published English text. Estragon suggests they should leave, and Vladimir gives a reason for their waiting: 'Tonight we will sleep perhaps with him, warm, dry, our stomachs full, in the straw' (quotation from McMillan and Fehsenfeld, 1988: 50). These primal feelings of nurturing, warmth, and safety suggest early experiences with the *good* mother. The removal of these lines creates a more abstract, vague relationship to the Godot figure.

11 Child researchers have found that the ability to present clear and coherent narratives of early experiences correlates to secure early attachment (Holmes, 1993: 111). Beckett commented (Duckworth, 1966: xiv, xivi): 'The source of the dialogue between the boy and Vladimir is to be found [...] in *Eleuthria*.' In this dialogue between a boy and his father, less abstract than the *Godot* exchange, the boy also demonstrates an inability to connect his internal states to words. He seems isolated and does not enjoy the company of others. He denies being happy, but under questioning can describe certain things that make him 'feel good', such as the state of lying in bed just before sleep. In this, he echoes Mr C. (and Estragon) who also felt this state was the only time he was calm, as falling asleep reflects a withdrawal into an early, protected state. The boy admits to his father he is hungry, but has to be commanded to eat. In all of this, there is a

sense of internal confusion and dissociation from his feeling-states, as well as a deference to the father's need. Finally, when the boy asks *his* only question of the father, which relates to an internal state ('Are you still hungry, papa?/No/Why not?/I don't know, Michael') the father demonstrates he himself has difficulty with internal reflection (or in revealing it). This must be felt as an absence by the boy who wishes to know him, and can explain the child's internal state of confusion. It also reflects the attempt by Vladimir to know Godot through the boy, and their shared confusion about their own feelings. (*Eleuthria* quotation from McMillan and Fehsenfeld, 1988: 49).

12 See McMillan and Fehsenfeld (1988: 104–6) for a detailed description of the boy's/moon's movements: 'The exits present a complex of images connecting the conclusion of each act with the themes of completion and incompletion, unity and separation, presented in the approaches [...] the boy's line leads off to an indeterminate unseen point'. This highlights the loss of an unreachable figure, whose absence becomes *present* in the visage of the moon. In this production, the boy appears very somnolent, stressing his role as an internal object retreating to the past, or to a hidden part of the self.

13 One can view this gang as terrorizing part of the self (an early superego organization). See entry under 'Pathological Organizations' in Hinshelwood (1991). Such an organization, built on terror and intimidation, is seen in *What Where*. Hugh Kenner, interviewed for John Reilly's film *Waiting for Beckett*, comments on this aspect of *Waiting for Godot* as a whole, relating it to the author's experiences living in hiding during the War. It also suggests much earlier experience. Within this dyad's complex enmeshments, there remains the possibility that Estragon fantasizes or fakes the attacks to keep *Vladimir* close. The attacks also suggest a displaced violence directed towards a weaker, infantile part of the self (i.e. Estragon is *indirectly* beaten by Vladimir).

14 Hill (1990: 33) points out that Beckett often uses the image of the bowed head to suggest the dead father. Again, it is important to dissect out, *as well*, more primary maternal connections. The constellations could also reflect parental interactions, or even the infantile-self's fantasy of the mother's relationship with her *own* primary objects, something the mother may unconsciously re-create in her dealings with the child.

15 Building on the work of Abraham (1924), Klein (1988a, Chapter 8; 1988b, Chapter 1) described quite explicitly how young children can experience, in phantasy, the equation of faeces with bad, poisonous persons as parts of the self that need to be expelled.

16 In her discussion of Lucky's dance, Zinman (1995) points out its isolation: there are minimal stage directions, it was rarely discussed by Beckett or by actors who performed it, and it is rarely mentioned by critics. I agree, of course, with her assertion that the dance is a 'work of art and as such it is a non-verbal, miniature version of the play itself' (Zinman, 1995: 311). In a sense, the primal importance of the dance has been re-enacted in its non-discussion, as it mirrors a core sense of non-recognition, of rupture in the primal dance of life between mother and infant.

Zinman further elucidates this in her exploration of the origins of the phrase 'to dance in a net' (309–13). Its most primal meaning is 'to proceed under observation while supposing oneself unobserved', and it is cited in *English*

Proverbs: 'Think not you are undetected. You dance in a nett, and you think no body sees you.' This is a highly ambiguous reality that touches both poles of the schizoid condition. On one hand Lucky's dance expresses the pathos of his being unrecognized by a loving other, as he writhes in sadness, and is a pathetic distortion of the notion of being able to play alone in the presence of the mother. But it also *does* express, and in so doing is self-revelatory; Lucky has *not* died, and his net becomes representative of an internal repressor/protector. I have had many patients who experience this sort of 'netting' as *both* protective and entrapping, as both self *and* other.

Zinman connects the dance to the artistic sense of failure, of having not pleased an audience, and I suggest that, as always in Beckett, this is highly ambiguous. Lucky is *both* child and mother, and his dance represents the failure to give, as well as to receive – Estragon's comment 'Is that all?' at the dance's conclusion condenses the failure – Lucky, it will be remembered, was at one time a nurturer for Pozzo.

Finally, Zinman points out that the dances Lucky no longer performs – the jig, the fandango, the hornpipe, and so forth – are historically ones that centered on vitality, fertility, and connection, within a world of joyous community. Given this, she disagrees with Homan's criticism that Lucky's dance is a 'primitive theatre perhaps, before or without words': 'it seems rather to be after words, an art of civilization's collapse rather than an art of primitivism' (311). Again, I suggest the ambiguity and inclusiveness of both positions. Lucky's dance *is* art, a most primal one. It suggests a lacuna at the beginning of experience, before words, a lacuna that makes authentic communication a difficult and frightening proposition; in this suggestion one sees how the dance touches upon the inexpressible, the failure of words seen in the 'incomprehensibility' of his monologue to the others.

17 Estragon's calling Lucky 'mister' is reminiscent of Murphy with Endon. This respect for a deeply regressed part of the self is immediately undermined by Pozzo, a sadistic, tyrannical part of the self that uses intimidation to control.

18 This splitting of the world into a devouring, grandiose monster/weak, hungry minion forms the core of the Paranoid Schizoid Position. These internal roles are alternately identified with – the analyst becomes one or other in comple ment to the patient's self, in the opposite role. Lacan's elucidation Hegel's Master-Slave dynamic looks at similar phenomenon. The French translation of Freud's 'Über Ich' (English 'superego') is 'Sur moi' or 'above me', which more clearly captures the sense of an agency experienced as grandiose, withholding, and mockingly arrogant, in addition to a more benign seat of authority.

19 In David Lean's 1948 film version of *Oliver Twist*, there is a further parallel to *Waiting for Godot*. Before electing Oliver to go forward, the children witness their masters at a lavish feast, reminiscent of Estragon's observation of Pozzo's 'picnic'.

20 In *Waiting for Godot*, the situation is altered, since Lucky represents the abandoned child-self, and Estragon is given the bones. For Estragon, the withholding mother is, of course, displaced onto Godot.

21 The parallel is not exact. The tramps, in a way, are like me, observers of an enactment of early relations (between Pozzo and Lucky), as I was an observer of Mr B. and his mother.

22 In the therapeutic situation, a variation of this is often at work. At the beginning of each new session, Mr B. felt *relieved* I was not damaged by his previous attacks (as he had been by his mother's attacks as a child) and so could survive as a good mother for him. He was also *anxious* because he could *not* damage me, there was the threat that I was not controllable and would abandon him. Lucky, of course, could not contain Pozzo's attacks.

23 Beckett commented that Lucky was 'lucky' by virtue of the fact he had 'given up his expectations' (Duckworth, 1966: lxiii). This touches upon the core argument of this study, since the one thing the infant *has* to expect is 'good enough mothering'. If it gives up this expectation, for whatever reason, it will collapse into a paranoid state, and possibly marasmus and death.

24 I am reminded of the patient who said: 'When I want your opinion, I'll give it to you.'

25 In their last meeting, it is Pozzo who enacts the role of sufferer, as he introjects Vladimir's earlier phrase 'It's abominable', which was used to express disgust at Lucky's ingratitude. This again demonstrates condensation in the play, and the fluidity of roles.

26 In the first draft of the play, Godot arrives in the person of Pozzo, but the confused tramps do not recognize him (Duckworth, 1966: lxii). Godot is not represented by any single *character*, but is the play itself, inextricably bound into identifications and expectations manifested throughout the work, through his absence. When Vladimir asks the boy what Godot does, the answer is 'He does nothing, sir' (91). This is literally correct, since Godot is a powerful internal imago. Once this is recognized, he becomes emotionally impotent, since Vladimir could then live wholly in the present. Godot existence depends on the tramps own feelings of inadequacy. This is what Vladimir is on the verge of realizing when he states: 'What have I said.' As the core part of the self, he is at a moment of great potential for psychic change.

5

The dispeopled kingdom: the hidden self in Beckett's short fiction

Preceding chapters have examined the experience of primal dis-connection in several of Beckett's works. Murphy's failure to recognize emerging, loving feelings, Watt's inability to connect to an enduring, whole internal presence, the disrupted, enmeshed relationships in *Waiting for Godot,* the images of primal maternal absence in *... but the clouds ...*, *Footfalls* and so forth, all reflect a central feeling-state of non-recognition within narrative-self. This chapter focuses on first-person short fiction, exploring primal ruptures within the narrative-self in the direct fiction, as well as in the 'created' tales of the narrator. The first section examines ruptures of the primary nursing bond in the *Nouvelles* ('The Expelled', 'The Calmative', and 'The End') and in the *Texts for Nothing*. The next section examines central feeling-states within the *Nouvelles*; specifically how aspects of primary dis-connection weave themselves through this little trilogy in a manner parallelling the development of the story. The narrator's own 'recollections' of child-hood experience are re-enacted in his own 'current' tale, as this re-working acts as self-containment. The following section examines the *Texts for Nothing*, how the narrator experiences aspects of the self as threatening, invasive, or even hostile. The narrator's struggle to create fiction, and the struggle to be born psychically, are equated as mani-festations of a true self. The core self maintains its viability through hiding, splitting-off aspects of itself into fiction, struggling against powerful internal 'voices' (i.e. early internal objects felt to be alien). This is a version of Guntrip's regressed ego, a self that is not entirely free or viable, residing in a place where it struggles to live, love and create. It relates to Winnicott's 'true self', the authentic core of being that requires the mother to mirror in such a manner that the infant's primary omnipotence is not prematurely ruptured (see Phillips, 1988: 127–37). The primary intention of this chapter is to elucidate the hidden, unfulfilled sense of the narrative-self, *in relation to an absent other* *within*. The dominant experience remains that of a self that speaks without a sense of being heard, of being seen, in any authentic manner. When the primary, maternal auditor within the narrative-self is not simply absent, but malicious or controlling, the infantile, creative part actively hides within its own narratives.

The final section of this chapter acts as an integrative conclusion to this study; it examines the use of projective identification, and the splitting of the narrative-self, in the late story 'The Lost Ones'. This complex story illustrates the central arguments of this study: the struggle for cohesion within the Beckettian self, its fragmentation as a consequence of disruption in primary infant-self–mother connection, the reflection of the rupture in the imagery, associations and use of the text, the use of various defensive strategies, the blurring of self and other that is the hallmark of very early experience and, finally, the coalescence of psychological birth and the origins of fiction-making within the primal relationship.

Time for Yum-Yum

Aspects of early nurturing experience pervade the *Nouvelles*, often infiltrating the flow of a narrative. Occasionally, a fantasy/memory of ruptured early nurturing disrupts a story generated intentionally by the narrator to calm himself; this often occurs when there is a failure of self-soothing. The title of 'The Calmative' suggests not only the vial of sedative given by a stranger to the narrator, but the actual effect of the *telling* of the fantasy/fiction itself. In that story, the narrator tells a story to contain himself, since he is beset by disintegration anxieties predicated on loneliness: 'For I'm too frightened this evening to listen to myself rot, waiting for the great red lapses of the heart, the tearings at the caecal walls, and for the slow killings to finish in my skull, the assaults on the unshakable pillars' (61). There is a defensive sense of sanctuary in the silences between heart beats, like the long lapses of Murphy's mentor Neary; more fundamentally, these lapses suggest a terrifying disconnection that is elaborated in 'The Lost Ones'. In 'The Calmative', the narrator appears as a debilitated, dispossessed old man, wandering alone in the city. He has escaped, for the moment, an internal 'den' of schizoid anxiety, with 'assassins [...] in this bed of terror', but in 'his distant refuge [i.e. an imagined past or a psychic retreat within the self, he is ...] weak, breathless, calm, free' (62). Walking through the world as an invisible, despised alien, he meets a small boy, 'holding a goat by a horn', who looks at him 'without visible fear or revulsion'. The boy, he believes, has come to see him out of curiosity: this Watt-like 'dark hulk [...] abandoned on the quayside' (66). This boy moves the narrator, and he tries contacting the child, but the only sound that comes is a sort of 'rattle [...] due to long silence'.[1] Nonetheless, this boy shows affection for the narrator, and 'without letting go of his goat he moved right up against me and offered me a sweet out of a twist of paper' (66). There is a condensed quality to the exchange – the pre-verbal 'rattle' of communication, so death-like, is heard by the boy-as-auditor, and he provides maternal concern and early nurturing to the narrator-as-infantile-self, reminiscent of narrator-Sam's holding of Watt after the latter has had a psychotic breakdown. In this condensed scene, the narrator also identifies with an aged, dying parental figure, and the boy acts as a caretaker. This reflects a confused, congealed internal experience; the internal mother feels alien, withdrawn, with the boy-as-infantile-self, witnessing, helpful, hopeful he can heal the rupture between them. The infantile-self also resides within the narrator-as-old-man, depressed, unseen, and wishing for a maternal concern projected into the child.

The boy's maternal acceptance seems primary, and it creates a natural, loving attachment essential to the formation of a coherent self. However, it is only through a split-off aspect of *himself* (i.e. the fictional character of the boy, created in his 'tale') that holding becomes possible for the narrator. This is demonstrated later, when, wandering alone, the narrator approaches a man: 'Excuse me your honour, the Shepherds' Gate for the love of God! [...] I drew a few steps ahead, turned, cringed, touched my hat and said, The right time for mercy's sake! *I might as well not have existed. But what about the sweet?*' (71, italics mine). The non-recognition of the world/mother generates invisibility, the narrator sees himself as a pariah, begging for contact on the margins of the world. He moves from asking for an affirmation of his identity (i.e. his correct location, the time), to eventually begging for a 'light', feeling non-recognition tear at his sense of existence. He retrieves a sense of being by connecting to the maternal presence created by the boy's feeding him the sweet in the earlier, primal, nurturing/recognizing moment. Failure in early nursing experiences often form a core around which feelings of depression and abandonment are built, something evident in patients suffering from eating disorders:

Ms E., a woman in her thirties, suffered from a binge eating-disorder. It became clear she would binge to defend against feelings of loneliness and abandonment. Her bingeing allowed her to reconnect to early maternal holding. She remembered being fed honey on a spoon by her mother at age two, to soothe her during a period when she suffered feelings of loss because of the birth of a sister. Exploring her feelings about herself just before a binge often led to fantasies/memories of primary abandonment. For example, on one occasion, a trigger was her feeling, while on a date with a man, that he preferred another woman. Underlying Oedipal feelings (that she could not compete sexually with other women) was a belief that this man, *as mother*, would not want to provide for her. In response to my interpretation that she had mistaken the penis for the breast, she sighed and agreed, stating that her greatest fear was that no man had enough to fulfil her insatiable love hunger. She feared she would end up starving on the street (like Watt's 'family' she would be back 'home to oblivion' in a world without 'buns'). What she enjoyed about bingeing was its aftermath, lying slobbering and groggy, feeling she was again an infant after a feed, sedated with her own 'calmative'. This was a pleasant, calming experience of retreat, since like the narrator, she experienced the world as a hostile place in which she was an outcast.

There was a vague hostility in this woman's bingeing, related to a belief that her mother (like the character who gives the narrator the 'calmative' in the story) could not contain her depression, and would give her the honey to 'calm her down'. Another patient, whose mother had given him a prescribed sedative as a young child because of his insomnia, felt the need as an adult for various alternative forms of self-soothing strategies, such as a low-playing radio, to replace the early medicinal-'calmative' (that *itself* replaced his mother's usual, patient listening to his anxious night-time ruminations). Similar triggers infiltrate the narratives of Beckett's isolated figures, as they attempt to soothe themselves with their word/food stories. For example, a Mr Weir discharges the unwilling narrator of 'The End' from a sort of sanitarium, which served as a calming, maternal container. After leaving the building, he describes his progress through a garden, following a day of rain:

> The earth makes a sound as of sighs and the last drops fall from the emptied cloudless sky. A small boy, stretching out his hands and looking up at the blue sky, asked his mother how such a thing was possible. Fuck off, she said. I suddenly remembered I had not thought of asking Mr Weir for a piece of bread. He would surely have given it to me [...] I would have gladly turned back, but I was afraid one of the guards would

stop me and tell me I would never see Mr Weir again. That might have added to my sorrow. (81)

Awe and wonder fill the narrator's description of the natural world, though there is quiet despair because of the depleted, life-giving rain. The garden acts as a maternal mind, in which there is re-enacted disruption in the connection to a loving mother. The boy's questioning is a natural extension of the early feeding situation, since the child's epistomophilic instinct connects intimately to the mother's nurturing stance. Here, though, the mother demonstrates blunt aggression towards her child and his curiosity, effectively cutting off his connection to her and to the world, things he wishes to take into himself. This is a direct reversal of the situation in 'The Calmative', where the boy-as-mother acts as a soothing, nurturing presence. It is of no surprise that the narrator's first thoughts, following the fantasizing/remembering of this scene, are for food, and for contact with the kindly Weir/mother who would recognize and feed him. A hostile world, filled with a gang of guards, blocks access to this good mother, leaving the narrator wandering resigned and depleted, banished from his containing, maternal home.

In *Texts for Nothing 3*, there is a complex interplay between feelings of early feeding, maternal containment, and an introjected despair that destroys contact with others: 'And to start with stop palpitating, no one's going to kill you, no one's going to love you and no one's going to kill you, perhaps you'll emerge in the high depression of Gobi, you'll feel at home there. I'll wait for you here, no, I'm alone, I alone am, this time it's I must go. I know how I'll do it, I'll be a man' (110). There is hostility in the world, manifested as a fear the world/mother wants the narrator to die. Love is equated with dying, murder, invasive manipulation; this leads to a retreat, where no one will kill, and no one will love. Parts of the self become other, reflecting a common experience of individuals struggling with powerful imagos. One patient, for example, told me she had spent the night in deep remorse, fantasizing about 'blowing her brains out' to placate an inner voice that kept telling her she was 'no good' and 'kidding herself' to think she could maintain good grades in her university courses. The voice/aspect of herself was a condensation, reflecting a father who envied her, as well as a self-regulating aspect that contained, through threats, both her own aggression (i.e. her wish to 'blow *his* brains out') and ambition. There was an admixture of violence and possessive love – the voice also guaranteed she would not individuate, and not go on to graduate school, leaving her depressed mother behind.

The narrator of the 'Text' struggles with similar confused feelings – there is a reversal, as the persecutory voice takes the depression and separation anxiety into itself ('*I* alone am, this time it's *I* must go [italics mine]'), reflecting the actual origins of the feelings within the primal objects. There is an ambiguous, fantasy escape/exile to the 'Gobi', an isolated, barren place, but also a place of safety. Disintegration anxiety, triggered by a disengagement from the mother's self-affirming love, often manifests (in dreams or fantasies) as isolation in oceans or deserts (Kohut, 1971), places that also offer safety from a hostile, retaliatory world. When the narrator does emerge into a fiction, it is as an infant within the loving containment of a maternal figure, a nanny who takes on primary responsibilities, holding and feeding him: 'she'll give me her hand [...] if only it could be like that [...] She'll say to me, Come, doty, it's time for bye-bye. I'll have no responsibility, she'll have all the responsibility [...] Come, ducky, it's time for yum-yum' (110). Soon though, the narrator retreats into narcissistic isolation, cutting himself off from the possibility of primary engagement with this fantasy mother: 'Who taught me all I know, I alone, in the old wanderyears, I deduced it all from nature, with the help of an all-in-one, I know it's not me, but it's too late now, too late to deny it, the knowledge is there, the bits and scraps, flickering on and off [...] in league to fool me' (110).[2] He is unable to maintain contact with a good mother, especially a dependency on her as a conduit to reality and learning. Paranoia infiltrates the core self-experience, there is a blurring of self and other, a primal doubt about the authenticity of self-experience, and aspects of hostility initially attributed to the world now are 'in league' within. The narrator continues his attempt to create a loving otherness, inventing a friend, perhaps pure fantasy, more likely an amalgam of early inter-actions that provided some sense of containing love: 'Quick, quick before I weep. I'll have a crony, [...] We spend our life, it's ours, trying together in the same instant a ray of sunshine and a free bench in some oasis of public verdure, we've been seized by a love of nature [...] Nothing human is foreign to us' (111–12). There is a sense of urgency, before a sinking into despair, as the narrator finds someone to share a joy of the world, assuaging his sense of alienation. The fantasy is reminiscent of Sam's holding of Watt in the sunshine, and the wish to connect within a beautiful garden/mind suggests a hope for primal, internal sanctuary within another. However, the feeling cannot endure.

He sinks into a terrified belief that others will draw him out, where he will be engulfed by them, and prevented from returning to the more predictable sanctuary of regressed hiding-as-death: 'He'd nourish me [...] ram the ghost back down my gullet [...] with his consolations [...] he'd prevent discouragement from sapping my foundations. And I, instead of concentrating on my own horizons, which might have enabled me to throw them under a lorry, would let my mind be taken off them by him' (112).[3] This fear of entrapped absorption into the other's need is at the core of the schizoid dilemma. The primary feeding situation becomes distorted, the narrator believes his mother/friend would ram life 'back down his gullet', keeping him alive simply to assuage his own anxieties. This reverses the early mother–infant relationship; the narrator becomes an enslaved auditor/container. There is an echo of the passage in *Watt*, where Arsene describes his catastrophic 'fall', a rupture in early connection to a containing presence, as a 'reversed metamorphosis' (44). In this state, if one gives up authentic desire (as a prelude to psychological death), 'life begins to ram her fish and chips down your gullet until you puke, and then the puke down your gullet until you puke the puke, and then the puked puke until you begin to like it' (44). Arsene describes a retreat from the world to a place beyond a yearning for contact. However, life becomes a constant lure, though it is a particular vision of life, one developed through powerful feeding imagery. The world (i.e. a *particular* world) forces itself into one's body, and any attempt to expel it is doomed, as the bad food, the puke, returns until it is accepted. This harks back to *Proust*, where love means invasive possession: 'One only loves that which is not possessed, one only loves that in which one possesses the inaccessible' (35). Schizoid retreat becomes the preferred option, since engagement will mean the loss of the self (or the other): 'We are alone. We cannot know and cannot be known. "Man is the creature that cannot come forth from himself, who knows other only in himself, and who, if he asserts the contrary, lies"' (49). The expression of genuine, selfless joy in the world of another, which finds its basis in the sharing of life between mother and infant, becomes false; there is no possibility of an individuated love that allows for the preservation of an untouched internal space. Mr B., whose mother used him to contain her own primitive anxieties, shared this attitude; he believed love meant the loss of personal integrity and privacy. As an adult, he collapsed back into primary scene of engulfment; accepting any goodness from the world, particularly the love of an interested woman, reactivated his core fear she was feeding him poison, and wanted to ensnare him into controlled dependency. A 'reversed metamorphosis' would occur, the woman became what she 'really was', a devouring mother unconcerned with his internal needs. Taking anything into his inner world was dangerous, since it meant dependence on the other's goodness; he would have to trust the other to respect his right to say 'No'. His words in a session reflect this:

> My life is like a board game you play over and over again, one thousand times you lose, then another thousand, and another, just keep losing until you feel like quitting. Then life comes around, and puts a bowl of shit in front of you and says 'Eat it!' and if you don't you die, you just go along with it, or you try again and just comply. Its just life, always putting you down ... there's no point in having any feelings at all ... what's the point, just to get burned again, so just don't feel anything at all, it's safer.

The sense of hope was deeply buried in this man, as any attempt at engagement was felt to be a prelude being used and discarded; he can only be 'loved' if he is accessible and controllable. His words find their echo in Arsene's deterministic despair: 'And if I could begin it all over again a hundred times, knowing each time a little more than the time before, the result would always be the same, and the hundredth life as the first, and the hundred lives as one' (47).

A Krappy feeling

In 'The Expelled', the narrator's experience of being hurled bodily out of his own abode is as an expression of premature psychological birth. There is a clear hostility, the narrator is welcome neither within the house nor within the world outside, and the expulsion represents failing containment by a maternal mind. Like the walker in 'neither', two unloving, unreachable worlds entrap the narrator. Hearing the sound of the door slam comforts him as he falls, since this means 'They were not pursuing me down into the street, with a stick, to beat me' (47). The narrator is ambivalent about his expulsion, the house/mind appears both a sanctuary from a dangerous world, but also a place filled with hostile others. Like Murphy or Watt, he survives through artifice, 'I still knew how to act at this period, when it was absolutely necessary' (49). He imagines peaceful safety only in a boundless isolation, wishing for calm he raises his eyes to the sky 'where you wander freely, as in a desert' (49–50). The narrator describes an odd manner of carrying himself, attributing it to a childhood problem:

> I had the deplorable habit, having pissed in my trousers, or shat there
> [...] of persisting in going on and finishing my day as if nothing had
> happened. The very idea of changing my trousers, or of confiding in my
> mother, who goodness knows asked nothing better than to help me,
> was unbearable, I don't know why, and till bedtime I dragged on with
> the burning and stinking between my little thighs. (50–1).

There is a severe disruption in the narrator's early experience of himself and his relationship to the mother. He remains stubborn, refusing to go to her for help despite obvious, admitted physical suffering. Though he suggests she would like nothing better than to help him, the question remains why he resists this help. One possibility is a debased sense of self that allows toleration of such soiling as inevitable or deserved. One must question how it can be that a mother (or any other caregiver) could fail to notice this horrendous difficulty, and take steps to prevent it by questioning the child. This suggests the mother may not have been entirely available to the child for any number of reasons, or that despite his declaration of her good will, he does not experience her in that way. A patient once felt indescribable anger towards me, something she expressed as a silence. She said she would be able to speak to me if I were somehow different, connecting this to her refusing her mother's food as a young child, saying she might have eaten if her mother were a *different* mother. There is also the possibility that the narrator's soiling is an expression of rage towards the parent, as if to say: 'I belong to you and look how filthy I am.' In any case, the vignette is a statement of his early disconnection and estrangement from a social world. He goes on to say, not surprisingly, 'I became sour and mistrustful, a little before my time, in love with hiding and the prone position' (51). He suggests his own past (of which the above vignette is an example) is full of meaningless, 'juvenile solutions, explaining nothing', and that there is no need 'for caution, we may reason on to our heart's content, the fog won't lift' (51). He attempts to dissociate from early self-experience, yet just at this point he connects directly to one of his 'juvenile solutions', an early, powerful feeling-state. Having barely avoided crushing a child while stumbling down the street, he goes on to say:

> He was wearing a little harness, I remember, with little bells [...] I
> would have crushed him gladly, I loathe children, and it would have

been doing him a service, but I was afraid of reprisals [...] One should reserve, on busy streets, special tracks for these nasty little creatures [...] all their foul little happiness [...] they never lynch children, babies, no matter what they do they are whitewashed in advance. I personally would lynch them with the utmost pleasure, I don't say I'd lend a hand, no, I am not a violent man, but I'd encourage the others and stand them drinks when it was done. (52–3)

This narrator is not alone in Beckett in his distaste for children, a loathing based on a powerful envy for the child's joy in living, 'all their foul little happiness'; this envy connects to his own early life.[4] Whether through stubbornness, rage, or a sense he will not be cared for, that a child would stand, sit, and walk all day covered in its own faeces, suffering both the physical pain and inevitable mocking of other children, can only be explained by a severely damaged sense of self. The narrator reveals an intensely withdrawn, disengaged connection to his own body, and to social life, that echoes Winnicott's description of descent into a false self-state. There is also a sense of proud defiance, nobly defensive, that mirrors Lucky's marginalization as a depreciated part of the underlying narrative-self. The narrator's own rendition of his childhood experience parallels his own role as a *fictive* aspect of a cohesive underlying self, one which is shamed and feels shunned. The envy directed towards the happy children reflects a part of himself that he is no longer (or perhaps never was) in contact with. His raging desire to attack children is an identification with a primary internal object felt to be hostile to the joyful parts of the child's self. This may explain his tolerance of the soiling, since he cannot truly imagine another caring for him, though he tacitly denies this. These passages develop a sense of the world as uninterested or hostile, and the genesis of this feeling early in the narrator's life.

The narrator's hostility becomes more evident as the narrative progresses into 'The Calmative', where he is 'too frightened to [...] listen to [himself] rot' (61). He decides to tell himself a story, to help pass the time and mute his fear. Again, it is a narrative of displacement and ejection, of hiding within a hostile city, within a failed, primary container projected outwards. Finding himself at the foot of a staircase, he begins to climb, 'like one hotly pursued by a homicidal maniac' (68). Panting, straining, he reaches the top where he meets, 'a man revolving in the other direction, with the utmost circumspection. How I'd like to push him, or him to push me, over the edge. He gazed at me wild-eyed for a moment and then, not daring to pass me on the parapet side [...]

went back the way he had come [...] all that remained to me was the vision of two burning eyes starting out of their sockets' (67–8). This reflects the paranoid stance dominating the narrative-self, manifested here in the narrator's *own* fictional associations. Feeling pursued, he climbs fearing for his life, only to find *himself* harbouring both homicidal and suicidal impulses. His projections into the other man allow for a sort of 'twinning'. He stares into his *own* sadistic eyes, alternatively fearing for his life and hoping it will end, but *also* wanting to kill the other (experienced as sadistic and 'homicidal') in himself. His murderous desires are manifestations both of rage (a wish to destroy the other) and a wish to destroy that *part* of him so fuelled by hate. He hints at this, asking: 'Into what nightmare thingness am I fallen?' In this collapse into the depths of the Paranoid Schizoid Position, the world becomes a 'thing' – there are neither persons nor a coherent experiencing 'I', only hostile persecutors, as terror and sadism fill the internal universe. The experience of Ms A. elucidates this experience; this woman feared autonomous existence, since it precipitated a sense of maternal abandonment. She presented this core fantasy/memory: *During long periods of abandonment, she would mimic her mother's hateful stare while looking at herself in the mirror.* She became, alternatively, hated/hating mother, as well as hated/hating child, while the reflection would contain the four complementary roles in a sequential condensation. Likewise, the narrator, for whom the meeting in the tower is a fantasy, appears to have placed a powerful, primary imago outside of himself. The 'man' he confronts, with burning eyes, is another manifestation of internal forces that keep him lying in fear; predatory enemies fill his internal space, whom he struggles to kill or put outside.[5] Yet, he senses this state is *not* absolute, and appears to wish for deliverance. Soon, 'a little girl came into view followed by a man holding her by the hand, both pressed up against the wall. He pushed her into the stairway, disappeared after her, turned and raised towards me a face that made me recoil' (68). Implied violence again centres on a threat of harm to a child, another recurrence of a painful, internal drama, though in this scene a loving parent protects the child (although the threat to her is veiled, vague, and it is not clear from *whom* it comes).

The sense of the self as variously pathetic and ridiculous, or raging and endangered, continues into 'The End'. After leaving a sanitarium to re-enter the world, the narrator finds that '[His] appearance still made people laugh, with that hearty jovial laugh so good for the health' (81).

An enduring self-depreciation follows on from the childhood memory of 'The Expelled', as the narrator sees himself as dirty, laughable, and an object of derision, yet with a vague hope of remaining *usefully* amusing. Such a self-view protects against a hostile world, the self is *already* devalued. This allows a hiding within the internal persecutory world (and from one's own rage), just as the narrator hides within the city in the actuality of his story. He is indeed a pariah: resting near a water trough, he notices a horse that appears to be watching him. Again, there is a sense of suspicious disgust, one echoed later in *Film*. In that piece, some dominant images are of citizens' aghast, revolted looks, as they encounter the character 'O', a withdrawn, devalued part of the self pursued through a depleted inner landscape by an observing, perhaps hostile, part of the self that is felt as other.[6] The narrator of 'The End' is not in complete withdrawal. Resting in the park at night, unnamed persons visit him, looking out for his safety: 'It was a long time since I had longed for anything and the effect on me was horrible' (82). This is ambiguous – the 'horrible effect' can refer to a painful, now conscious, need, a softening of his schizoid shell that allows him to experience contact with others. This echoes Watt's tears (upon leaving Knott's house), which also reveal a need for attachment that is not fully experienced as an enduring part of the self. Alternatively, the very *feeling* of need can be the 'horrible' referent, suggesting a turning away from loving experience.

The episode that follows demonstrates the living heart within the narrator, and within the narrative-self. The narrator, having finally found sanctuary in the basement of a Greek woman, discovers that she too occasionally 'peeped in' (84) to make sure nothing has happened to him, perhaps more out of concern for her own welfare than for his. There is some parallel to the scenes in *Murphy,* in which nurses observe patients in their cells, and this narrator appears to be the beneficiary of an apparently benevolent, but uncertain concern. Again, the symbolism suggests a withdrawn, internal place within the self, where the narrator / self hides, yet is watched, bringing to mind the man / rat metaphor in *Murphy,* with its sense of uneasy dependency. Though this narrator remarks: 'Fortunately I did not need affection' (84), he demonstrates his need for companionship:

> Once I sent for a crocus bulb and planted it in the dark area, in an old pot [...] I left the pot outside, attached to a string I passed through the window [...] I sat down beside the window and pulled on the string to keep the pot in the light and warmth [...] I manured it as best I could and

pissed on it when the weather was dry. It may not have been the right thing for it. It sprouted, but never any flowers, just a wilting stem and a few chlorotic leaves. I would have liked to have a yellow crocus, or a hyacinth, but there, it was not to be. She wanted to take it away, but I told her to leave it. She wanted to buy me another, but I told her I didn't want another. (84–5)

This imagery touches aspects of the narrative-self-state; the narrator has a maternal connection to a dependent, child-like object. He needs the crocus to love and nurture, it forms an important part of his life, though the very name suggests an ambivalence towards living (i.e. *croak*us). He is reminiscent of prisoners who, during long periods of confinement, care for pets with which they develop deeply felt relationships. The narrator makes every effort to keep the plant alive, and there is poignancy in his effort to rig up a contraption through which it can remain in the light and warmth. This is reminiscent of the light in which the narrative-self places Celia, where she sits during her lonely afternoon waits for Murphy, feeling a connection to life. This narrator gives the crocus his own bodily fluids and wastes to survive; though there may be some hidden sadistic intent, it appears to be a genuine attempt to maintain a nurturing connection with another being, that is part of himself. His child-like mourning for the plant highlights this: he refuses to have it taken away or replaced. This connects to a more profound level of symbolization, since the plant represents the self-state of the narrator. The plant *is* the infantile aspect of the narrator's core-self, and in trying to keep it alive he demonstrates his own struggle to remain attached to life since, like the plant, he feels decayed and withering. This scene reflects the relationship of the narrative-self to the narrator, since the latter, like the crocus, is kept alive, though on the margins of a full psychic blooming. Again, this is a double displacement: the crocus reveals the self-state of the narrator (much like May's fiction revealed her own internal sense of disconnection), and the narrator *himself* reflects the internal self-state of the underlying narrative-self (much as May herself does, as a character).[7]

The narrator's experience of himself as unworthy and disgusting soon becomes dominant again; the new owner of the house needs the room to house a pig. Shunned wherever he turns, he shuns an old friend: 'He was delighted to see me, poor man' (88). Staying in a ramshackle cabin, he finds himself unable to rise, and a cow saves him: 'I tried to suck her, without much success. Her udder was covered with dung. I took off my hat and, summoning all my energy, began to milk her into it. The milk fell to the ground and was lost [...] She dragged me across the floor, stopping from time to time only to kick me. I didn't know our cows too could be so inhuman' (90). The feeling of unworthy alienation reaches its height, and in a grotesque parody of an early nurturing situation, the narrator feeds from a dung-covered breast, belonging to an uninterested cow/mother. His comment that the cow is inhuman is a poignant statement of the depths to which his self-esteem has sunk. Now, even among animals, he feels no enduring attachment is possible. A sense of paranoia permeates him: 'I reproached myself with what I had done. I could no longer count on this cow and she would warn the others [...] I might have made a friend of her. She would have come every day, perhaps accompanied by other cows' (90). Having stolen milk from the mother (echoing Murphy's escapades with 'cowjuice'), the narrator fears a retaliatory response. Feeling guilty, he berates himself for his *own* inability to socialize, and concludes with a fantasy family of sorts, a herd of mother-cows, who would feed him. In this scene, there is a regression to a ruptured early sense of nurturing, a starvation/death within the mother. Not surprisingly, following this 'it was all downhill' (90), he ends up living in an abandoned boat that takes on the qualities of a casket. It becomes a last withdrawn haven for the self which, like Murphy's garret, is a symbol of enclosing schizoid space: 'There were times when I wanted to push away the lid and get out of the boat and couldn't, I was so indolent and weak, so content deep down where I was. I felt them hard upon me, the icy, tumultuous streets, the terrifying faces, the noises that slash, pierce, claw, bruise' (98). The self withdraws from a perceived, natural violence in the world, violence intentionally directed *at* it. The imagery suggests assault, even rape ('hard upon me'), and frightening others fill the world, as sounds brutally tear into the self. This violence is reminiscent of Belacqua's experience in 'Dante and the Lobster', Murphy's assault by the sounds of the world, and so forth. In his little hideaway, there is a sense of safety as the narrator enters an almost foetal state, perhaps hoping for a rebirth:

I waited for the desire to shit, or even to piss, lent me wings [i.e. to leave the boat]. I did not want to dirty my nest! And yet it sometimes happened, and even more and more often. Arched and rigid I edged my trousers and turned on my side, just enough to free the hole. To contrive a little kingdom, in the midst of the universal muck, and shit on it, ah that was me all over. The excrements were me too, I know, I know, but all the same. (98)

This passage reveals the narrator's enduring sense of his own badness; he is unable to protect his safe haven from soiling. This place is the last desperate refuge for the self in a universe of shit, which begins to encase and foul him. It is a regression to an early mental space, in which there is a final attempt to be loved, cleansed by a maternal presence within. The poison, the 'shit', now comes from within, as the narrator, now in a dis-connected foetal sac, uncontained by the mother (or by a mother that is 'muck' or poison) is slowly encased, suffocated. This recalls the images of the narrator of 'The Expelled' – there is a return to a state of child-like soiling, predicated by disconnection and rage at the world.[8] There is a core condensation in this scene, central to the oeuvre, harking back to the imagery of the stone eggs, the nest, and the maternal sea. The narrator, as good mother, protects his living self within a 'little nest', resting on the edge of an eternal sea, an over-whelming universe, just as the narrative-self protects the narrator at this point in the telling. There is ambiguity, as the narrator's contrivance and soiling of his 'little kingdom' can stand outside the narrative flow as a meta-commentary, merging with a narrative-self that destroys a pristine inner space for itself and its creation. Self and other, teller and told collapse, as poison infests both the narrator-as-mother and the narrator-as-self. Both the self within the boat/nest, and the self within the story/nest are murdered, drowned, yet paradoxically kept alive in a deadened, stone-like state. The narrator no longer can contain the poison, which represents an underlying self-state of anguished isolation. In the final scenes of the story, he has 'visions' that reconnect him to childhood, as he begins to imagine drifting out upon the water in his small boat. He is re-attached to his early life, and remembers looking out at the sea with his father: 'I would have liked him to draw me close with a gesture of protective love, but his mind was on other things.' (98–9). This final failure of attuned reparation by a loving parent coalesces his fantasy/fiction. It is no surprise he will soon apparently suicide, letting his little boat out to sea, and that he will take the calmative to ease him into an easy death, into a final engulfment by the ocean-mother (le mer/la mère), dreaming of a 'story [he] might have told.' (99), a statement that leaves vague the locus of responsibility for this narrative. The calmative, a concretization of his attempts to self-soothe through fantasy, by speaking to the mother/auditor, is taken back into the self. It allows a peaceful suspension within the engulfment of an unheeding maternal ocean, and the hope of a re-awakening, a rebirth, a re-connection in the next story, one that may be better heard.

Within these stories, read as a whole, a primary sense of disconnection to an early maternal figure is demonstrated by the narrator's self-depreciation, his self-soiling, his need to displace his love into other objects, and in the imagery of feeding and paranoia. They reveal intricate evasions of a disconnected, core self, demonstrate its despair, and its need to go on, both through *re-working* the experience (tales that might be 'better told'), and *in the telling* that is itself life.

The hidden self

The following section explores the narrative-self's avoidance of exposure to internal others, as it hides to protect itself. This need to hide develops from a rupture in the earliest experiences with the primary object, leading to a sense that the self exists in a threatened state. This manifests in complex identifications and counteridentifications with the primary object (i.e. becoming like it, or alternatively, *not* like it). In Beckett's later work, this experience becomes the clear focus of narrative-self, manifesting in highly complex constellations within the text. It is important to recognize the subtle, rapid shifts that occur within the texts, as the narrative-self oscillates between identification with a hostile or withdrawn other, and alternatively experiences itself as under attack *by* a hostile other/world. This is an exposition of experiences that form the foundations of mental life, as the infant struggles with powerful feelings of frustration and rage *at* the world, only to subsequently experience itself as under a hostile retaliatory attack now attributed *to* the world.

The narrative-self can counter overwhelming feelings of primal disconnection, and retaliatory rage, by hiding within its own words. This is a complex, risky endeavour. At times, the self experiences its *own* words as originating *in an identification* with a hostile/withdrawn other, and feels trapped by another actually itself. Fictions are created to protect the self; these fictions elaborate the complex interplay between the core self and early experiences that have engendered feelings of anxiety, disconnection, and thwarted authenticity. The following vignette may elucidate these concepts:

> Ms A. had difficulty maintaining an enduring experience of herself as a coherent person with her own desires. A need to comply shaped her internal experience – self-erasure avoided a devastating withdrawal of love. Her internal world collapsed into a hostile, sadistic mother upon whom she depended as a frightened child that could not think.

Occasionally, she would identify with the hostile mother, becoming quite cutting herself. This echoed her actual mother's own experience, shaped by early loss. Her actual mother was anxious and dependent and, unable to contain these feelings, projected them into Ms A. For example, the mother feared becoming overweight. She would send her daughter chocolates, which Ms A. devoured, feeling poisoned; yet she was unable to refuse her mother's 'attempt' to be kind. She gained the weight that reflected her *mother's* desire to eat, sparing her mother the anguish. This was an actualized projective identification; the mother then attacked Ms A. for being overweight.

The manner through which Ms A. began to deal with these anxieties in her analysis mirrored a dominant strategy in the oeuvre. In short, Ms A. was an innately gifted actress; soon after our work began she decided to continue her theatrical education, something she had abandoned as a teenager since she felt her mother's envy of her talent was over-whelming. Winnicott writes: 'In regard to actors, there are those who can be themselves and who also can act, whereas there are others who can only act, and who are completely at a loss when not in a role, and when not being appreciated or applauded (acknowledged as existing)' (Winnicott, 1965:145). Ms A. used her roles to become a sort of 'transi-tional person' in between these positions, who could contact, and hide, from her mother, by being understood, appreciated, and allowed to emerge as a coherent self. To quote Winnicott again: 'It may even be possible for the child to act a special role, *that of the True Self as it would be if it had had existence*' (Winnicott, 1965: 150). In her theatrical roles, Ms A. achieved this, and in its fictions the narrative-self reveals an authenticity that always fade, much like the 'mother' image in *...but the clouds...* does not 'linger', an auditor-audience that disappears within the self.

Within her theatrical work, Ms A. felt she could safely enact complex exchanges with her mother. For example, in *Agnes of God*, Ms A. chose to play a psychiatrist who works with a young woman who has murdered her own baby. In this way, she explored her identification with me (as a good, containing mother/analyst) and our work around her own rage at her mother, whom she felt was a dependent infant she wanted to kill. She also wanted to kill off the part of *herself* she saw as a hopelessly inadequate infant. The role also helped her try to understand why her mother hated her so much, wanting to 'kill' off her authen-ticity. She could confront her mother, in character, without feeling the overwhelming anxiety she would have felt in real life. She recalled playing a role in *Autumn Sonata* as a teenager, saying the line she always wanted to say to her mother: 'You want the spotlight and you carried me in a cold womb'. She consistently chose roles that allowed her to enact primary experiences with her mother that involved rage, sadness, and loneliness, but most fundamentally *a need to understand her mother, as the mother related to herself.*

Within Ms A.'s use of roles to connect secretly to early feelings with the mother, there appears to be a parallel to aspects of the Beckettian narrative-self. Ms A. felt overwhelming disintegration anxiety when trying to emerge as an enduring, coherent self. Through acting, she engaged powerful, internal imagos and experiences in a manner much like the narrative-self. She clearly described how a sense of being *within* the words of another allowed her to experience feelings that were actually part of her. If the internal mother attacked her for being authentic, she countered by pretending it was only play. The theatre acted as a transitional, containing object in which she felt safe. More accurately, it was the *words* of the playwright that allowed her to hide, to reveal herself in safety, within a fiction that was *felt* as real. In Beckett's fictional work, the narrator often creates its *own* fiction as a means of 'playing' that allows for exploration of complex early feelings of rage, depression, and loneliness, all centred in the earliest mother–infant bond. This occasionally becomes direct, as the narrator of the story, a manifestation of the underlying narrative-self, creates a fiction in which we can see the process that reflects its *own* creation. As in *Footfalls*, the core of experience displaced by the dramatic figure, or the narrator, reflects not only its 'own' unconscious experience, but that of the narrative-self that creates it, a double displacement that explains the *genesis* of those aspects of the fiction. May can 'create' a playful fiction that reveals her own self-state, much as Ms A. could play within the words of the playwright, and in both cases the words are both their own, and *not* their own, at the same time.

The following reading, of sections of *Texts for Nothing*, suggests that an important aspect of the text is its revelation of the struggle of the core, emerging part of the self to disengage from primary identifications with withdrawn, controlling, and even hostile early imagos. The stories concern internal experiences of entrapment and enclosure, generated within the self by aspects of *itself, felt* as other; parts of the self that contain intense feelings of failed primary experience appear to the emerging-self as hostile persecutors trying to bend it into conformity. Another vignette may clarify this:

Ms F. came to a session in great distress, after another horrible night, during which she ruminated endlessly about her 'badness'. The source of this attack on herself became clear: she had received the top mark in a course. Her creative, core self now faced the reality that she was growing in ways that were a great pride for her. The intense, near-psychotic attack on herself was generated by her identification with an early imago, envious of her life, but demanding of perfection. Family dynamics made this understandable – the mother used her daughter to contain her own ambitions, but also subverted her, to keep her at home. In her next session, Ms F. reported she had a fantasy of seeing her mother drowning. Instead of giving in to an urge to jump in and go down with her (she knew she would be dragged down), she found a stick and pulled her mother out. She related how the night before the sadistic attack on herself she had been helping her mother study for a course. When Ms F. grew tired and wanted to return to her own apartment, her mother went into a great panic, half-accusatory, half-pleading, telling her daughter she needed her to stay and help her. Ms F. felt guilty and panicky as she left her mother's house, and I pointed out that she kept her mother close, fulfilling her demands; her mother was now *in* her, in the form of her anxiety. She laughed, saying that, in fact, the more panicky *she* became, the calmer her mother appeared.

This is an introjection of a mother's anxiety. Again, such internal states can occur early in life in ways that do not reflect any major maternal failure. The point, in specific relation to the texts, is the manner in which, within one unified self, there can be divergent parts of the self felt by the core self as hostile or persecutory.

The *Texts for Nothing* present a predominant self-experience – entrapment within an enclosed space, where movement *away* is danger-ous to the self (being opposed by early objects), and *stasis* is encasing. For example, the series opens with 'Suddenly, no, at last, long last, I couldn't any more, I couldn't go on. Someone said, You can't stay here. I couldn't stay there and I couldn't go on' (100). As so often in Beckett, there is a sense of a forced expulsion that quickly becomes undone. It is a wandering away from sanctuary, from a primary internal home, between the doors of 'neither'; there is also a complementary sense of immobility based on fear. Fluctuation occurs throughout the work, between a self seeking to leave, and a self compelled not to leave, between a self seeking attachment, and one expelled. These comple-mentary experiences form the heart of an early schizoid entanglement with a powerful, primary figure:

My rheumatism in any case is no more than a memory, it hurts me no
more than my mother's did, when it hurt her. Eye ravening patient in
the haggard vulture face, perhaps it's carrion time. I'm up there and I'm
down here, under my gaze, foundered, eyes closed, ear cupped against
the sucking peat, we're of one mind, all of one mind, always were, deep
down, we're fond of one another, we're sorry for one another, but there
it is, there's nothing we can do for one another. (102)

This is an overt example of primal identification, and the merged
oneness it engenders. The empathic response of the narrator to his
mother's pain is so intense he cannot distinguish actual rheumatic pain
from fantasy, even after many years, and it recalls Ms F.'s confusion of
her *own* internal calm with *her mother's* anxiety. There is a despairing
futility in the passage, and clear indication of an internal split ('I'm up
there and I'm down here'). The narrator experiences himself divided
along a number of lines (e.g. between past and present, self and other,
and so forth). The imagery suggests a deeper, more primal confusion,
one related to early experiences with the mother. The I/'eye' is
compressed, watching, starving, for food and emotional nurturing.
There is violence suggested in the 'ravening', a 'vulture'-like, patient
wait for 'carrion' (perhaps a repetitive 'carrying-on' of a primal experience of anguished 'carrying on'). There is confusion – does the infant
perceive the mother as devouring, or does the infant experience itself in
this way? The next line elaborates this confusion, the narrator is both
'up there' and 'down here', reflecting the child's experience of the
mother's early physical position, as well as, perhaps, a contemporary
sense of the internal mother's aloofness. The self is ambiguously
observed, by itself and the mother ('under *my* gaze'), but since the eyes
are closed, it is ill-seen – 'foundered', sinking (i.e. foundering) under the
weight of on-rushing anxiety and non-recognition, yearning for a
founding establishment within a *finding* maternal mind. The search for
recognition continues in ambiguity, the ear is 'cupped', straining for
living communication, against a peat/teat that *itself* sucks, reflecting its
dual nature, both dead/decaying, *and* nurturing. The intense attachment of the narrator for his mother is clear, as is a final realization they
are *not* one, and cannot connect in a fundamental way that would allow
change. This echoes Ms F.'s fantasy of the drowning mother, though
for the narrator there is a complete collapse of internal space, as the
boundaries between self and other dissolve completely.

The narrator's enmeshment with a primary object is not always
clear and discernible. Complex manifestations of the core entanglement

with an 'other' often emerge through the narrator's attempts to engage or disengage. Such a futile, frustrated enmeshment with a primary object can lead to hopelessness; that nothing can be done for another generates a joyless future since the self must suffer the same fate. The narrator of *Texts for Nothing 2* suggests this: 'A glow, red, afar, at night, in winter, that's worth having, that must have been worth having. There, it's done, it ends there, I end there. A far memory, far from the last, it's possible, the legs seem to be still working. A pity hope is dead. No. How one hoped above, on and off. With what diversity' (108). A memory complex/fantasy is experienced, at first, as exciting, desirable. Immediately, there is retreat to a less certain state ('that *must* have been worth having'), the narrator no longer feels an autonomy that allows pure engagement with the world, an *authentic* ending. Ambivalence towards life is clear – hope is generated by the fact he is still mobile, but the statement 'hope is dead' undoes this. This hopelessness, too, is reversed ('No'); finally there is an internal entrapment of a self experiencing *itself* as buried, enclosed in a deep internal space, Murphy-like in its withdrawal from the 'diversity' of life. The self becomes complete, needing only to observe, to hide from any newness in the world, with *all* that is *strange* kept *away* from it.

The narrator of *Texts for Nothing 3* expresses this feeling of an enclosed surrounding by dominant, hostile imagos that prevent auth-enticity. He asks: 'Is it possible I'll sprout a head at last, all my very own, in which to brew poisons worthy of me, and legs to kick my heels with, I'd be there at last, it's all I ask, no, I can't ask anything' (113). The wish for a genuine, separate existence ('a head') is immediately thwarted within the self by reference to internal poisons that kill desire, creating the submissiveness implicit in the notion he is unworthy of asking for anything. There is an intricate connection between the experience of authentic selfhood and the feeling of liberated possibility that occurs when moving out from a schizoid retreat into full engagement with the world. This movement is eloquently expressed by the narrator: 'See what's happening here, where there's no one, where nothing happens, get something to happen here, someone to be here, then put an end to it, have silence, get into silence, or another sound, a sound of other voices than those of life and death, of lives and deaths everyone's but mine, get into my story in order to get out of it, no that's meaning-lessness' (112–13). This is closed internal space, without contact to a loving presence; it is an almost perfect description of Murphy's inner world, the house of Knott, or *Godot*, places where nothing happens.

There is a cry from the core self to create, to 'get something to happen', so it can end/die properly, followed by a fantasy of movement into silence, to other sounds, other voices, and to a final escape from the self altogether. There is no possibility of authentic connection, where others can be useful or accommodating; love is devouring. Soon after, the narrator describes a sense of happiness, walking with a caregiver:

> To set out from Duggan's door, on a spring morning of rain and shine, not knowing if you'll ever get to evening, what's wrong with that? It would be so easy. To be bedded in that flesh or in another, in that arm held by a friendly hand, and in that hand, without arms, without hands, and without soul in those trembling souls, through the crowd, the hoops, the toy balloons, what's wrong with that? (113)

There is an initial connection, an actual engagement in life – one does not know what lies ahead, a possibility of authentic death. There is containment within living skin ('flesh'), a loving holding, soon dismembered. The 'walk' takes on a child-like aura, but unlike the narrator of the *Nouvelles*, there is less envy for the happiness of the children. The narrator cannot stay long in this fantasy, he answers his own question with: 'I don't know, I'm here, that's all I know, and that it's still not me […] here nothing will happen here, no one will be here, for many a long day […] and the voices, wherever they come from, have no life of their own' (113). The lonely isolation is profound, made more poignant by a primary disconnection from the joy of an attached childhood. The voices that embody these figures are dead, hollow, much as the voices heard by the tramps in *Godot*. They speak of nothing so much as their own distance from any living heart within the narrative-self. In *Godot*, Vladimir pleads with Estragon to 'say anything at all' (63), when they fall into silence after discussing their own 'dead voices'. This is a plea from the heart of the narrative-self, to be recognized, responded to, by a primary other that remains alive, though buried within its own narcissism.[9]

The sense of disconnection from loving internal objects is profound in the *Texts*, often felt as a failure of identity: 'Where would I go, if I could go, who would I be, if I could be, what would I say, if I had a voice, who says this, saying it is me? Answer simply, someone answer simply. It's the same old stranger as ever, for whom alone accusative I exist, in raw pit of my inexistence, of his, of ours' (114). This sense of non-existence echoes Ms A.'s feelings, as she sought a sense of herself within the words of characters in the fictions of another. Without a primary, powerful other to whom she could subjugate herself she felt alone, an 'accusative' disconnected both from herself as subject, and as an object of another. There was also accusation in another sense, since she felt, as the narrative-self does, guilty for abandoning the other by individuating. This mirrored her internal attachment to a needy, elusive maternal figure, itself filled with a tentative, arbitrary being. The narrator echoes this: 'And when he feels me void of existence it's of *his* he would have me void, and vice versa, mad, mad, he's mad. The truth is he's looking for me to kill me, to have me dead like him, dead like the living' (114, italics mine). This is a powerful statement of an embryonic sense of self within the narrator, experiencing a dominant internal other as he *himself* being dead, something due to the *other's* envious wish to destroy authenticity within him. It reflects the wish of a primary object to project its own lifelessness into the self (i.e. 'it's of his he would have me void', much like Pozzo's sense of starvation is projected into Lucky). This is connected to a sense of madness (i.e. like May's mother, 'Mrs Winter', in the fiction she creates). The use of the term 'vice versa' captures the sense of enmeshment as self-object boundaries break down, since the primary connection of love is replaced by annihilation anxiety, as *life* is confused with *death*.[10] However, the narrator himself harbours murderous wishes towards this primary other. A means of escape is to treat him 'like a vulgar Molly, a common Malone' (115), that is, as disconnected fictions within himself: 'what am I doing, having my figments talk [...] that's the mistake I made, one of the mistakes, to have wanted a story for myself, whereas life alone is enough' (115–16). It is a 'story' that becomes the only means through which the self can engage the world, since authentic living is always threatened from within by envious attack, or by a withdrawal of loving presence. Thus, the narrator's eyes close to look 'inside the head [...] to look for me there, to look for someone there [...] where *to be* is to be guilty. That is why nothing appears, all is silent' (117, italics mine). This feeling of self-loss is coupled with a parallel feeling of aloneness, predicated on the notion that *being* is not allowed. Feelings of true authenticity are discouraged. This feeling is close to that of Ms A., for whom any joy or autonomy was immediately dampened by an implied or actual inner attack. The narrator feels that 'one is frightened to be born, no, one wishes that one were, so as to begin to die' (117). This statement reveals the dichotomous nature of the core experience of self-entrapment – birth implies either a terrifying reprisal from an unnamed source or, alternatively, a movement towards an *already* implied dead-end that makes life itself an unworthy venture. It is a

recurrent catastrophe, escapable only by a new beginning, a true birth
that could lead to an authentic, individuated death that *would* be life.

The fundamental feeling of self-burial, of hiding within an internal
world dominated by hostile others, connects to the sense of being lost:
'Did I try everything, ferret I every hold, secretly, silently, patiently
listening? [...] I'd like to be sure I left no stone unturned before report-
ing me missing and giving up. In every hold, I mean in all those places
where there was a chance of my being, where I once used to lurk,
waiting for the hour to come when I might venture forth, tried and
trusty places, that's all I meant when I said in every hold' (127). The
core, emerging-self experiences itself as lost within a hostile space; it
must hide to remain secure. This is an early maternal space, in which
the self struggles to find itself properly held, in a '*hold*', where it can
begin to trust its containment. This passage reflects images often heard
in analytical work, and touches on fundamental experience. Mr D., for
example, often employed the word 'ferret' to refer to himself, and his
need to enter secretly into the world of others. In this way, he tried to
understand their attitudes towards him, to predict if their motives were
hostile or benevolent. He imagined himself 'weaseling' within his own
internal world as well, hiding among the shadows, trying to look at his
own past in a way that would not disturb or infuriate powerful early
imagos. The above passage brings to mind the 'rat metaphor' in
Murphy, since the self envisions itself as mouse-like, frightened, and
hiding from something living beyond the walls. This depicts an actual
feeling-state, where a retreat to internal, enclosed spaces allows for a
semblance of being within a threatening world. In this light, the phrase
'where there was a chance of my *being*' connects to a sense of haven,
reflected in Arsene's description of Knott's house/mind as a place
where the self can begin 'to *be*'. This sense of being lost is difficult to
maintain because of the emotion it triggers. Soon after this passage, the
narrator comments: 'Ah if there must be speech at least none from the
heart' (128), reflecting another retreat into intellectualization as a defence
against awareness of self-estrangement.

All this brings to mind Winnicott's false self, the need to comply
within a dangerous world where love is conditional upon one's *being* a
certain way. Failure to comply with these internal demands leads to a
sense one is bad or being punished:

> Who says I desire them [i.e. various external conditions], the voice, and
> that I can't desire anything, that looks like a contradiction [...] Me, here,

if they could open, those little words, open and swallow me up, perhaps that is what has happened. If so let them open again and let me out, in a tumult of light that sealed my eyes, and of men, to try and be one again. Or if I'm guilty let me be forgiven and graciously authorized to expiate, coming and going in passing time, every day a little purer, a little deader. The mistake I make is to try and think, such as I am I shouldn't be able, even the way I do. (132– 3)

Genuine desire immediately triggers disconnection from an authentic sense of self, a feeling that *another* controls the internal world, and is trying to create a 'void'. This is experienced as an internal contradiction (reflecting the schizoid dilemma); the split is felt consciously, and the self's *own* use of words becomes an autistic barrier to genuine feeling. The engulfing, devouring of the self by words is consistent with inauthentic living, since a need to protect oneself within language suffocates genuine emotional experience. There is a poignant plea from the narrator to be allowed to live, to *be* in the light, among the living. This is immediately followed by the onset of fear, guilt and a further plea to be allowed to enter into a world filled with living time, where one can *actually* die (though there is also the recurrent, invasive sense of futility in the phrase 'a little deader'). The comment that the only mistake is to try and think reflects the inner domination of powerfully felt others, and the last lines carry a militaristic tone (not unlike *What Where* or *Godot*), where the self's only option becomes compliance. A sense that one does not actually exist develops, in a way, the safest position:

Whom have I offended so grievously, to be punished in this inexplicable way, all is inexplicable, space and time […] It's not me, it can't be me. But am I in pain, whether it's me or not, frankly now, is there pain? Now is here and here there is no frankness, all I say will be false and to begin with not said by me, here I'm a mere ventriloquist's dummy, I feel nothing, say nothing, he holds me in his arms and moves my lips with a string, with a fish-hook, no, no need of lips, all is dark, there is no one. (133)

The presence of a powerful, insatiable other is explicit, and the dissociation from the body (and equally from one's feelings) is presented in a manner worked through again in *Not I*. In fact, these brief passages seem a sketch for the later piece, with a speaking voice, in a pain not *felt* as pain, talking into a felt void in which space and time collapse, a pre-verbal and motherless domain. The alternative to such compliance, originating because of harsh early objects, is a retreat into nothingness reminiscent of Murphy's final zone. Such feelings engender hopelessness:

> Give up, but it's all given up, it's nothing new, I'm nothing new. Ah so there was something once, I had something once. It may be thought there was, so long as it's known there was not, never anything, but giving up. But let us suppose there was not, that is to say let us suppose there was, something once, in a head, in a heart, in a hand, before all opened, emptied, shut again, and froze. (141)

Here is the genesis of hopelessness. There is an echo of Murphy's world, where there is 'nothing new', along with a feeling there was *once* something that *did* bring a feeling of living joy (i.e. before the catastrophe of primary rupture). There is an almost organic quality reminiscent of the crocus and its aborted blooming, as the self opens to the world only to experience a catastrophic draining and a subsequent retreat into a frozen self-state. The self *may* possess the thought it once had something, as long as it manifestly *knows* this is false; this engenders the hiding that allows a semblance of being. Ms F. enacted such a dynamic in her university studies, often suffering endless torments before exams or the submission date for essays. She struggled to convince herself (and me) that she was stupid, and could never successfully create. Once, she brought me an essay, just before its submission. Though the essay was excellent, and was rewarded with a top mark, she had attempted to undo this by literally un-writing it; she had used an old printer, and the type was faded, ghostlike. In this way, she *had* something, but could counter internal accusations by claiming: 'there was not, never anything, but giving up.'

Fantasy projections into others become the way the narrator engages the world, finding contact through fictional otherness:

> It's a winter night, where I was, where I'm going, remembered, imagined, no matter, believing in me, believing it's me, no, no need, so long as the others are there, where, in the world of the others [...] and the power to move, now and then, no need either, so long as the others move, the true others [...] wake again, long enough for things to change here, for something to change, to make possible a deeper birth, a deeper death, or resurrection in and out of this murmur of memory and dream [...] he sees his body [...] this impossible body, it's me in him remembering. (149)

Here is a self hidden from its own authenticity ('remembered, imagined, no matter'), hovering on the edge of total withdrawal. It is through fantasy, an imagination *not* dead, that the core self can 'go on', with 'the power to move' in the 'true others'. The passage reveals the wish for authentic birth, but also deep confusion, as the self feels itself part of *another's* projections, and like Ms A., must struggle to remain 'resurrected' in each new tale. In these powerful early identifications and counteridentifications with invasive, internal objects, the core self struggles to maintain its autonomy. Through hiding, playing, creating its own fictions, the narrative-self screams out: 'They? No, I!'

The dispeopled kingdom

This final section, acting as a concluding synthesis for this study, examines the late story, 'The Lost Ones', in which many of the concepts discussed in earlier sections manifest in a highly complex, condensed form. In short, this piece consists of a narrator that has a highly ambivalent relationship to an aspect of *itself*, presented as a cylinder and a race of beings that live within it. The story depicts an entirely *internal* world, in which the narrator represents the core self, and in which the cylinder contains the split-off parts of an internal world / family. The relationship is condensed and fluid, with constantly shifting self / other boundaries, engendered by the earliest experiences of failing contact with the mother. The story exists at the primal edge of creation, of fictionality, born at the earliest moments of connection to the (m)other / auditor within the narrative-self. As such, it becomes an experience about the *possibility* of life, and about the primal fictions that both require life, and allow it. The cylinder becomes a text – a primal tablet that is the mother's containing mind, into which the narrator attempts to write his first tale, touching her mental space with his presence, and being held within hers.

The narrator of 'The Lost Ones' describes the existence of a cylinder within which lives a race of beings. These beings cluster into categories; the cylinder appears to be self-contained, the existence of anything beyond it appears doubtful. This work has presented a number of difficulties for interpreters, and some of these may be resolved by working with the assumption that the text presents an *entirely* internal world. From this point of view, the narrator speaks from a position of authority concerning its own internal experience, and the text is a *record* of that experience. The most fundamental aspect of the self's experience, the aspect developed through the narrative, is a *particular type of very early experience with a primary object*. For reasons not entirely made clear (though there are hints in the text) there seems to have been an early disruption in the relationship of the self to its primary object. The self experiences rage and despair, and these feelings generate the creation of the cylinder. In essence, the cylinder and its contents can be viewed as parts of the narrator which, for reasons developed below, must be split off. The cylinder is an encapsulated area of experience under the control of the self, *to a degree*; however, there are equally aspects of the cylinder, and of the experience of the beings within, which are unconscious aspects of the narrator.

Hill (1990) points out that the work is often viewed as a cosmological allegory; Finney, for example, feels it can be understood as a 'model in miniature of man's condition' (Finney, 1972: 12). Hill also believes the presence of discursive markers ('maybe') and expressions of doubt in the text suggest that if it is an allegory, it is one of its own fabrication, a view shared by Brienza (1977: 148–68). The present reading suggests that the narrator *both* has control over the story-as-self experience but, at the same time, is *also* dissociated from aspects of it. This fluctuates depending on the nature of the projective stance at any given time. This is perhaps closer to Levy's reading: '"The Lost Ones" concerns the limitations of narration far more than the torment of bodies in a cylinder. The story becomes a symbol or means of representing the movement of the narrator behind the story, and only by remembering this will we discover what necessity drives "The Lost Ones"' (Levy, 1980: 98). This reading also sees the narrator moving behind the story, though part of the 'created' story (i.e. the world of the cylinder) is *also* the narrator and his internal world. The necessity that drives the entire piece is desire for connection and the response to failures of connection (i.e. rage, despair and hope). By understanding the role of projective identification within the piece, there is a possible resolution to a difficulty mentioned by Hill (1990: 155), concerning the contradictory omni-potence of the narrator, who seems to alternate between total authority and a less than divine status. The world of 'The Lost Ones', in reflecting the total world of the narrator, is within his 'divine' control. Alter-natively, since aspects of it are 'lost' to him via projective identification, he seems arbitrary, vulnerable to a sense of otherness within the narration. In the final analysis, it is, in fact, a 'cosmological' piece. However, it is a cosmology of two (primary object and self) that merge, reverse, and separate, as the self struggles to touch and be touched, to see and be seen, to hear and be heard. It is a primal tale, the creation of a self, through a textual cylinder in which the self places itself in an attempt to be understood, and loved.[11]

Projective identification is the dominant mechanism at work in the piece. Aspects of the narrator's self are experienced (for reasons that will be developed) as severely anxiety-provoking, to such a degree that they must be placed outside the self and kept within an other. In Klein's view, the first 'other' was, of course, the mother, the primary object of the infant's experience. Following this concept means the cylinder is the body/mind of the mother, as experienced within the internal world of narrator/infantile-self. The entire 'story' of the 'lost ones' is a record of a fantasy attempt to project aspects of the self back into the mother for containment. The other of the text is both the cylinder (experienced as another place, outside the self), and the beings within the cylinder, who are further split into various roles that reflect more specific aspects of the self-experience. Thus, the universe of the text exists along several planes – it is unitary (the narrator alone), a duality (the narrator/cylinder), and a multiplicity (the narrator/beings). It is essential to recognize that all of these planes co-exist at the same time, and that this is possible because the universe represented by the text is predominantly within the Paranoid Schizoid Position. Within an internal world predominantly in this position, boundaries of self/other are fluid. This enables the self to protect its fragile integrity by projecting thoughts, emotions, and other aspects of itself into the other, where they can be processed and contained, to be returned to the self in a less anxiety-provoking manifestation. In this story, the narrator projects complex emotional states into the form of the persons inhabiting the cylinder, their emotional states, their primary desire to make contact, their ambivalence between hope and despair, and into the nature of the cylinder itself. There are also discernible aspects of this projected experience in shape of the narrative itself. This reflects the highly ambivalent relationship between the narrator and the shifting matrix of emotion contained within the world of the cylinder, which is, again, part of his own internal universe.

The story relates the central, predominant theme of Beckett's oeuvre, the struggle of a unified, coherent self to maintain its integrity under the sway of powerful internal anxieties, and its persistent attempts to deflect such anxiety by connection to a primary maternal figure. It is a hallmark of the Paranoid Schizoid Position (which underlies all subsequent human mental experience) that the mother is experienced in a contradictory fashion (with the corresponding self-experience); this is clear in 'The Lost Ones'. The name, the 'lost ones', is ambiguous – the term can refer to the *beings* within the cylinder (they are lost parts of the narrative-self), it can refer to the beings who are sought by the 'searchers' among the population of the cylinder, presumably for a sense of connection and wholeness, or it can refer to the beings as 'lost' in a hopeless, futile sense.[12]

Within the text, several predominant constellations exist. Firstly, the narrator, feeling severe anxiety because of failed maternal containment, is depressed and despairing; this is dealt with by projecting these feelings into the beings within the cylinder, some of whom ('the vanquished') are marasmic with despair and hopelessness. Alternatively though, the narrator can keep a sense of hope alive by projecting it into those beings within the cylinder that are searchers. There is a group that wanders in search of something/someone they feel is lost. Another spends time in the outer zone of the cylinder waiting to climb, and climbing, ladders leading up to niches on the walls, where they rest in solitude. Some believe a way out of the encased world exists. The relationship of the narrator to these beings fluctuates: on the one hand, there appears to be a raging, sadistic component (the narrator has the beings engage in violent acts when they feel frustrated), and he continually frustrates them in a world where attainment (of a way out, of finding a lost one) appears hopeless. In this sense, there is an identification with a primal, sadistic mother who is experienced by the infant, during inevitable failures in nurturing, as tyrannical and destructive. Thus, the beings within the cylinder become infantile-selves under attack and under the control of a dominant mother, or alternatively, a world/mother under the omnipotent control of a raging infant. There are equally moments of hope within the cylinder: the tenacity of the beings to search and to play suggests containment. It is a dead universe, and they are the 'last ones', but within the cylinder there is *some* sense of protection from the void.

A 'flattened cylinder fifty metres round and sixteen high for sake of harmony' (202) entraps the beings. Unwritten codes regulate movement and, among other things, access to the ladders. Temperature and a persistent yellow, sulphuric light modulate along a rhythmic continuum within the cylinder. The cylinder itself is a concrete symbol, reflecting both the internal world of the beings, and of the narrative-self, entrapped and closed off to spontaneous feelings of joy. What the beings appear to be searching for is a primal recognition that would allow separation from their despairing, hopeless state: 'Press and gloom make recognition difficult. Man and wife are strangers two paces apart to mention only this most intimate of bonds. Let them move on till they are close enough to touch and then without pausing on their way exchange a look. If they recognize each other it does not appear. Whatever it is they are searching for it is not that' (213).

The piece is condensed, ambiguous – the relation of the narrator to the encapsulated world fluctuates like the temperature and light within the cylinder. On one hand, the narrator's self-state is itself depressed and withdrawn – the tone of the work is mechanical, lifeless, reading like an engineering treatise: 'Omnipresence of a dim yellow light shaken by a vertiginous tremolo between contiguous extremes. Temperature agitated by a like oscillation but thirty or forty times slower in virtue of which it falls from a maximum of twenty-five degrees approximately to a minimum of approximately five whence a regular variation of five degrees per second' (205–6). The description of these lost people and their travails is equally muted and cold, as if they were themselves automatons: 'Consequences of this climate for the skin. It shrivels. The bodies brush together with a rustle of dry leaves. The mucous membrane itself is affected. A kiss makes an indescribable sound. Those with stomach still to copulate strive in vain. But they will not give in' (202). There is a suggestion these bodies are purely internal, since the sounds they make resemble 'the rustle of dry leaves', an echo of the tramps' dialogue in *Waiting for Godot,* where the invisible voices are also likened to the rustling of leaves, and to *Watt* where Knott's voice resembles a wind in the bamboos. Here the primary organ of touch, the skin, is dried and damaged. The original modality of communication between the self and the world, Freud's 'body-ego' is dried, sucked of life, and the sounds of internal procreation become macabre, as the internal, parental couple is damaged and depleted.

It is therefore no surprise that the narrator has difficulty linking thoughts in a spontaneous, living way: the text, a record of creation, reads like an abstract or an outline for a movie script. To overcome a loss of inertia the narrator appears to ask himself a question: '[What are] the consequences of this climate for the skin?' (202), before proceeding to imagine/remember the answer in the moment; this pattern occurs many times in the story. Such difficulties in linking thoughts reflect the ambivalent relationship between the narrator and the beings. In so far as they are lost, despairing parts of the self that are projected, without a primary contact to the narrator, the break in linking and the mechanical nature of the prose acts as a dissociative defence against despair – the self is *not* like the beings, they are *merely* an exercise in fiction. On the other hand, to the degree that the narrator experiences the beings as *others* who are being sadistically punished, the blocking of associative flow is a result of intense rage, suggesting a fear of retaliation by the others, who are envied for living. This reflects a primary identification, within the narrator, with an envious, sadistic, or absent primary object that he recreates in his relationship with the split-off beings. The following clinical example may elucidate this:

> Mr D. was a deeply withdrawn man, for whom a feeling of 'succeeding' in analysis (which meant impressing or pleasing me with his thoughts) was of paramount importance. He felt that comments I made one day, regarding his propensity to try to engage me in dialogue, were deeply hurtful. He arrived at the following session to explicitly 'produce' interesting material. He proceeded, in a manner eerily similar to the narrative style of 'The Lost Ones', to develop a long, complex fantasy that included his mother, various other family members, and me. There was the same 'exposed' quality to the process, as he openly tried out an idea before proceeding with the fantasy. For example, he would say, 'She is sitting on a rock. What kind of rock? A large rock by the water, no, it is by the side of a mountain.' There was also a sense of entrapment, not only in the rigidity of the fantasy, but in its content; the tale continually circled around rage towards the characters, as well as a feeling of sadness. This man used this fantasy to dissociate from his own feelings of rage and despair; I had deeply offended and abandoned him, by mis-hearing his attempts to connect with me in earlier sessions. The characters in the fantasy became internal 'others' he manipulated to regain a sense of control over his fragmented inner world.

From this perspective, the narrator becomes a raging, envious primary object that seeks to extinguish and humiliate any effort of the beings directed towards enjoyment in life. The cylinder becomes a part of the mind where life itself is tortured and destroyed. This is reminiscent of that part of Mr D.'s mind that would, as a child, entrap animals in boxes to gain a measure of sadistic control over them, and counterbalance feelings of impotent rage. These boxes functioned, in this sense, as the cylinder. The beings are a condensed, complex symbol, representing both the living, loving parts of the self, which the narrator, identified with the sadistic/absent mother who destroys the world (or who is destroyed), attacks by placing in a cylindrical hell. They *also* represent the depressed parts of the self (and possibly the mother) that the narrator wants to lose. There is an echo of Watt's ambivalent treatment of the rats, which he simultaneously nurtures and murders, in a complex enactment reflecting his experience of abandonment.

The beings in the cylinder appear driven by a need to connect with a primary source of love, and the intrapsychic world of the narrator (as revealed in the fantasy) fluctuates between *saving* the beings (as living parts of himself or fantasies/memories of living, loving others) and *destroying* them (thus destroying the bad mother). Hope in such a world is complex and ambivalent. The narrator informs us:

> From time immemorial rumour has it [...] there exists a way out [...] One school swears by a secret passage branching from one of the tunnels and leading [...] to nature's sanctuaries [...] The other dreams of a trapdoor hidden in the hub of the ceiling giving access to a flue at the end of which the sun and other stars would still be shining [...] of these two persuasions the former is declining in favour of the latter [...] This shift has logic on its side [...] whereas the partisans of the trapdoor are spared this demon [i.e. hope] by the fact the hub of the ceiling is out of reach. (206–7)

The denizens of the cylinder maintain an ambivalent, primary hope in the possibility of life. Like the being in 'neither', who walks 'as between two lit refuges whose doors once neared gently close, once turned away from gently part again', they shuffle between two theories of escape from a dying world. A door of hope alternates with one of resigned despair, between a sense of undeniable entropy and entrapment, and a chance to change and move outwards into uncertainty. The beings embody both an indefatigable, noble lust for life, as well as a demeaned, futile magical belief in salvation. These poles are in constant flux within the story, much as the temperature and lighting are in a subtle, modulated transition between cold/dark and heat/light. Ambivalence lives within the narrator as well – hope is initially presented as ridiculous, which is then qualified: 'So much for a first aperçu of this credence [...] its fatuous little light will be assuredly the last to leave them always assuming they are darkward bound' (207). Again, there is an admixture of emotion – hateful, murderous feelings are directed towards the lost ones, exemplified by a mocking, cynical depiction of their dream for escape ('fatuous'), but there is an immediate negation of this stance ('assuming'), darkness may not be their final outcome. The mocking quality is reminiscent of the ending of *Waiting for Godot*:

> Vladimir: Was I sleeping, while the others suffered? Am I sleeping now? [...] At me too someone is looking, of me too someone is saying, he is sleeping, he knows nothing, let him sleep on. (91)

Vladimir, himself ensnared within the schizoid dilemma, waits hopelessly/hopefully for an absent source of internal integration. Like the mythical trapdoors or tunnels of 'The Lost Ones', Godot represents a gateway to life, an escape from the barren internal stage upon which the tramps wait for ever. There is a similar ambiguity about whether there is a malicious consciousness behind the perpetuation of this apparent delusion. The 'someone' who watches him 'sleep' in ignorant, hopeful bliss could be malevolently enjoying his anxious suffering; Vladimir himself here reflects a kindly quality, since he has been watching over Estragon's sleep with maternal concern.

This paranoid space is the world of the narrative-self. There is an uncertain connection to another, which listens, contains, and can be trusted to hear the actuality of the self. Guntrip (1975) describes this sense of ruptured primal connection in his reflections on his analysis with two of the major thinkers in psychoanalytical history, Fairbairn and Winnicott. He explains how all his life he struggled to come to terms with early childhood experiences of his mother's emotional coldness. This culminated when he witnessed his younger brother lying dead in her lap when he was about three years of age. He had complete amnesia for this experience, but its impact was seen in a lifelong, recurrent exhaustive form of depression that occurred whenever he was separated from close fraternal friends, and in lifelong images of tombs, buried men, and death that filled his dream world. One dream in particular motivated his seeking analytical help from Fairbairn: 'I was working downstairs at my desk and suddenly an invisible band of ectoplasm tying me to a dying invalid upstairs, was pulling me steadily out of the room. I knew I would be absorbed into her. I fought and suddenly the band snapped and I knew I was free' (Guntrip, 1975: 150). It is this 'band of ectoplasm' that pulls Molloy forward on his journey, that draws Murphy to Endon, that keeps May pacing in quiet antici-pation of her mother's need for pain-killers, and that 'ties' Vladimir and Estragon to Godot. It is a tie of a dying hope, but a hope nonetheless, of an engaged, living relationship with a mother experienced as absent. Guntrip's journey to inner peace began during his long analysis with Fairbairn. He began to understand his tie to an absent internal mother, but he always felt there was more, an experience of an 'earlier mother who failed to relate at all' (Guntrip, 1975: 152). He felt he must reach this Knott-Mother before he could live, and he eventually began work with Winnicott.

At one point in his analysis with Winnicott, he mentioned that people often commented on his ceaseless activity and energy, and then said he did not like silent gaps in the sessions. Winnicott responded: 'Your problem is that that illness of collapse was never resolved. You had to keep yourself alive in spite of it. You can't take your ongoing being for granted. You have to work hard to keep yourself in existence. You're afraid to stop acting, talking, or keeping awake. You feel you might die in a gap' (Guntrip 1975: 153). This is the gap into which the narrative-self continually fears it might fall, alternately engulfed into the mind of a dominant other for whom it does not exist, or into a void where others do not exist at all. More fundamentally, there is the feeling that it cannot exist without being held, heard, seen within the mother's mind, within the container into which it has projected itself as a primal text. After Winnicott's death, Guntrip had a series of dreams, each moving him back in the narrative of his life. One night, he dreamt he was about three, and looking anxiously for his mother; he hoped she would notice him and his brother, but she was staring off into space, silent and ignoring. The next night he had the following dream:

> I was standing with another man, the double of myself, both reaching out to get a dead object. Suddenly the other man collapsed in a heap. Immediately the dream changed to a lighted room, where I saw [my brother] again. I knew it was him, sitting, on the lap of a woman who had no face, arms or breasts. She was merely a lap to sit on, not a person. [My brother] looked deeply depressed, with the corners of his mouth turned down, and I was trying to make him smile. (Guntrip, 1975: 154)

Guntrip tries to awaken his own infantile-self (in his attempt to make the child smile), just as the narrator of 'The Expelled' tries to contact the child in the shop. It is subtly ironic that the double reaches for a dead object, only to crumble into a heap. The meaning of 'object' is significantly ambiguous here, referring both to an inanimate thing and to 'person'. The double's collapse is symbolic of an emptied, devitalized aspect of Guntrip's self, experiencing itself as alone and adrift (just as many of the characters in Beckett experience this state as central to their subjectivity). The next dream-element is his mother with his dead brother/self in her lap. This is a not-mother, providing no emotional nurturing for the self, filling her child with deadness instead. She is faceless, armless, breastless, and unknowable. She manifests in Beckett as the ever absent, ever promising Godot, as the deadly indifferent Knott, in the cold, unseeing eyes of Endon, and as Krapp's 'love' in the punt. This is the frozen heart of loneliness is itself paradoxical. It is this place that Guntrip and the narrative-self must both avoid (to be able to live, if inauthentically) and revisit (to feel the hope of reunion, the chance for change with the internal mother that will allow authentic life). In this place, the core feeling of the narrative-self is born: 'I can't go on' (without the security of the love of a good internal mother), 'I will go on' (to escape this frozen, dead world). It is of note that Guntrip does not comment on any feelings of jealousy for his young brother, or rage at the mother, in his analysis of the dream. For him, the explorations provided some solace, some movement; for the narrative-self, the exploration is ongoing and inescapable. The narrative-self itself becomes the mother, abandoning hopeless characters in worlds devoid of genuine love and attachment. This is the heart of the womb-tomb, where birth and death are one, and there is no space in between for a self to emerge. However, perhaps there is, for why else would the narrative-self speak at all? For in this space, with the (not-)mother, there is no real other. It is a place before any genuine contact, so there remains a hope for contact; this is why the narrative-self is so intent on starting over, on getting a new start *before* this place of the basic fault, a start with a *living* (and loving) other. It is in restarting that hope lies, since there is no final escape from a closed world. Again, a dead mother could be mourned, taken into the self; a mother who is there, but unseeing, faceless, unhearing, keeps the self alive and searching for connection. As in *Ohio Impromptu*, all manifestations of the narrative-self come to the same end, with no finality. In that short piece, there is again a dominant theme of primary disconnection from a maternal, containing figure, as Reader tells a tale of 'a last attempt to obtain relief [by moving] from where they had been so long together to a single room' (285). Hoping to escape the pain of mourning (or celebrating) this separation, this 'birth', the subject of the tale attempts to erase all sense of internal presence by going 'out to [...] back to where nothing ever shared' (285–86), reverberating between an unfelt mother and an unfelt self, holding himself together through long, repetitive pacing in a place before an actual, living mutuality. Listener, who hears the tale, controls its flow, much like Knott controlled the servants with the bell. This highlights the sense that the tale is a depiction of an internal enactment, with separation at its core: 'Could he not now turn back? Acknowledge the error and return to where they were once so long alone together. Alone together so much shared. No. What he had done alone could not be undone. Nothing he had ever done alone could ever be undone'

(286). There is a condensed confusion reminiscent of Watt's walks with Knott; a precarious sense of existence that is constricted, shared on the edge of mutuality, but then pulled back to protect an isolated self from a failure of containment. Childhood 'terrors of the night' stifle attempts at individuation, and like the figure in … *but the clouds* … the subject of the tale struggles to survive these torments alone, until the dawn. The tale contains within itself its own genesis – a man arrives one night, sent by the 'dear one', and begins to read to the subject of the story, until finally this 'reader' is instructed by the 'dear one' that there is not need to 'go to him again'. There is a sense in which this 'tale within a play' suggests early connections to a calming mother, a connection that becomes suddenly disrupted, aborted. There is a complex blurring of self and other, as the 'subject' of the tale can be viewed as the Reader of the play, retelling the events that led to this state of affairs. The central point is the sense of entrapment within the self, and more funda-mentally, the attempt to reach a primal, internal other/auditor, to be understood, contained. Reader, an infantile part of the narrative-self, relates a primal text, in the hope its processing by Listener will allow for its amendment, and a subsequent amendment in their relationship. If both Listener and Reader are parts of the same underlying self, then Listener's control of Reader's telling mirrors the tale within it. The telling becomes the method of entrapment in both instances, an enmeshment with a primary object. This piece mirrors the dream of Guntrip in its intensity, and one can view Reader's telling as somehow nurturing to the Listener ('words are food'), with Reader reversed into a parental role, calming Listener with the tale, and with his subjugated telling. The tale, locked into repeated, aborted, false rebirths, kills authentic experience, destroys creativity in the infantile, exploring part of the narrative-self that Reader represents. The tale-within-the-play, sent by the 'dear one', operates like the bell in Kohut's vignette, it is a displaced reminder of the existence of the 'dear one', whom the listener of the story can neither escape, nor connect to. The tale-within-the-play is the prototype of the relationship of Reader and Listener; Listener becomes an internal, controlling 'dear one' that robs Reader of his primal tale, never contains it, or allows it to just to be. Just as the tale sent by 'dear one' requires a controlled hearing, the telling of the tale by Reader is a forced, controlled telling. Reader becomes the subject of the tale, an infantile-self entrapped within readings-as-primal-texts that reflect each other and the enclosing relational space. In the end, the play depicts a closed-off section of the self, in which multiple aspects of infantile separation are played out, as Reader and Listener sit for ever in the neither-world, with only words for hope, as the story becomes their only other:

> So the sad tale a last time told they sat on as though turned to stone. Through a single window dawn shed no light. From the street no sound of reawakening. Or was it that buried in who knows what thoughts they paid no heed? To light of day. To sound of reawakening. What thoughts who knows. Thoughts, no, not thoughts. Profounds of mind. Buried in who knows what profounds of mind. Of mindlessness. Whither no light can reach. No sound. So sat on as though turned to stone. The sad tale a last time told. (287–8)

This is the narrative-self's own dream of the absent, primal auditor. No light from the world, and only two becoming one, minds ebbing into mindlessness. Heeding only each other, frozen hearts as stone, with no chance of rebirth. It is a place of paradox, where the self is lost into a frozen other, but where this frozenness protects the self from a frightening world, as eggs/stones/stories hide in an internal nest-space, safe from a devouring, projected sea. Until … the next tale. For although within the text of this piece there is no hope of psychic rebirth, inter-textually the narrative-self moves on, hoping for attachment through speech with whatever listener, whatever auditor, there may be, hoping for another who can contain the loneliness, the need for a love that will allow for change.

There are images in 'The Lost Ones' of this disconnection from the primal mother, which can help explain the relationship between the narrator and the parts of itself within the cylinder. The beings are aspects of the narrator's own search for connection and, as well, punished others from whom the narator feels unattached and raging. Thus we are told:

> Bodies of either sex and all ages from old age to infancy. Sucklings who having no longer to suck huddle at gaze in the lap or sprawled on the ground in precocious postures. Others a little more advanced crawl searching among the legs. Picturesque detail a woman with white hair still young to judge by her thighs leaning against the wall with eyes closed in abandonment and mechanically clasping to her breast a mite who strains away in an effort to turn its head and look behind. But such tiny ones are comparatively few. None looks within himself where none can be. Eyes cast down or closed signify abandonment and are confined to the vanquished. (211)

The centrality of primary disconnection is explicit; some of the 'suck-lings' gaze in trance-like states. Others 'sprawl', withdrawn, depressed, their precociousness echoing the birth of Larry Nixon in *Watt,* as both are robbed of early maternal attunement. There is the poignant image – infants crawling, already beginning a hopeless search for connection, among a forest of legs belonging to nameless strangers who do not see them in any real way. The young woman appears old, withdrawn, feeding her baby mechanically, mirroring her own sense of abandon-ment. Her nurturing complements the starved, repetitive bingeing of Mary in *Watt,* and the mother of Guntrip's dream, echoing the repeti-tive tale sent by the 'dear one' that becomes the child's primal, internal text. Her child is disconnected, straining away, looking, pleading with the world for recognition, as the narrator moves on to discuss the adult 'vanquished' (in whom the life force has ebbed). The statement 'None looks within himself where none can be' is importantly ambiguous – the double negative suggesting both despair (there can be no self within – no subject-'none' lives within, since there is no mother-as-object-'none' within), and hope (the infants, as subject-'none', do not look within, but search outwardly for possible reparation). In either case, the incompleteness of the self rests on a ruptured maternal connection, the infants are internally unwitnessed. Immediately, there is a description of the effect of primal abandonment on the vanquished:

> Eyes cast down or closed signify abandonment and are confined to the vanquished [...] They may stray unseeing through the throng indistin-guishable to the eye of flesh from the still unrelenting [...] They may crawl blindly in the tunnels in search of nothing. But normally abandonment freezes them both in space and in their pose [...] It is this makes it possible to tell them from the sedentary devouring with their eyes in heads dead still each body as it passes by. (211)

Alone in internally dead worlds, the vanquished are the most deeply despairing parts of the narrative-self, their dead eyes signalling their abandonment by the *narrator* as a primary object. They are the proto-Endons, Knotts, and 'she's, wandering so far away from life as to be searching for the nothing that is annihilation, but that is also a descriptor for the mother's absence *as* presence. There remains a sense of primal hunger for attachment ('devouring'), related to sight and recognition, and the description of their internal world as an actual 'frozen' *place* brings it in line with the schizoid experience of entrapped enclosure found throughout the oeuvre. The intensity of the searchers, and its relation to primary connection, is reflected by the comment that 'the sedentary call for no special remark since only the ladders can *wean* them from their fixity' (219, italics mine).

Through its containment of aspects of the narrator's self, the cylinder behaves as an encompassing mind; it serves as a primal textual container (in both senses), holding primary experience within it, both as a physical place, and as a space where words become things. The denizens experience total dependence on this space; it becomes, in accordance with the state of the narrator, a place that enacts a slow, entropic dance towards a hopeless death, or a sphere that protects from the nothingness outside. The following passage reveals an aspect of this:

> What impresses in this gloom is the sensation of yellow it imparts [...] it throbs with constant unchanging beat and fast but not so fast that the pulse is no longer felt. And finally [...] there comes a momentary lull. The effect of those brief and rare respites is unspeakably dramatic to put it mildly. Those who never know a moment's rest stand rooted to the spot often in extravagant postures and the stillness heightened tenfold of the sedentary and vanquished makes that which is normally theirs seem risible in comparison [...] But a brief ten seconds at most and the throbbing is resumed and all is as before. Those interrupted in their coming and going start coming and going again and the motionless relax. (213–14)

The sudden silence is catastrophic, understandable within the symbolic field of the passage. The containment of the cylinder is the only tie to existence for its inhabitants; the sound that emanates within is a spectral connection to another being, when this sound ceases, it signals a fundamental change in their relationship. In other words, this sound imparts actual agency into their world, suggesting the existence of someone *other*. The imagery employed (the 'throbbing' of a 'constant unchanging beat' of a 'pulse') places this external presence within a human context, this experience is essentially an *intra*-uterine one. The beings *feel* this sound the way the foetus connects to the mother through her heartbeat, the dominant experience of otherly presence during life in the womb.[13] The cessation of this sound, signalling the death or withdrawal of the source of life, understandably triggers a reaction that shakes even the most vanquished to their psychic foundations – the loss of the mother is synonymous with an apocalypse of the self. This metaphorical construction touches the core thesis of this study – the internal experience of the mother is the fundamental shaping force of the world, and its loss is felt as annihilation.

This experience of silence elucidates the tension within the oeuvre between the need for ongoing sounds/speech and a desire for silence. When felt as an invasive or controlling (reflecting a particular sort of early experience with the primary object), there is a wish for silence, experienced as a sense of autonomous identity, or, at the extreme, as a final suicidal escape. Alternatively, words are soothing, functioning as containing objects that enwomb the self; this touches Guntrip's feeling of disconnection from Winnicott, during silences in their therapeutic work. His analysis proved fruitful, he began to tolerate silences that had once terrorized him. During one such silence, he lay on the couch, and felt relief when he heard Winnicott move in his chair behind him. Winnicott said: 'You began to feel afraid that I'd abandoned you. You feel silence is abandonment. The gap is not you forgetting mother, but mother forgetting you, and now you've relived it with me' (Guntrip, 1975: 150). Guntrip is here a Beckettian hero, waiting in vain for genuine engagement with the mother, in terror of the abandonment that means annihilation. Being unheld in the mother's mind is death to the infantile-self in Guntrip, and to the narrative-self. This would be the inevitable consequence of a self like the one described in *Proust*, which exists in a fragmented, desperate tie to an eternally changing other. Guntrip experiences Winnicott as a containing, maternal presence, and in the spaces and silences there is disconnection, because he has not properly internalized the other's remembering. These are the 'great red lapses of the heart' (61) that terrorize the narrator of 'The Calmative', reflecting the fear that another beat will not come, within the self-as-body, much earlier within the intra-uterine otherness of the maternal mind. Without this primary presence to protect the unshakable pillars of his being (a presence which *is* the most primary of those pillars), this narrator, a manifestation of the narrative-self, faces a psychic annihilation worse than death. It is this possibility that makes a birth away from Knott, Endon, and Godot impossible, forcing a wandering in schizoid space, since birth is into an incomplete, fragmented, unremembered death.

An appreciation of the primal connection to the mother makes sense of the conclusion of the 'The Lost Ones'. In the last paragraph, the narrator says: 'So on infinitely until towards the unthinkable end *if this notion is maintained* a last body of all by feeble fits and starts is searching still. There is nothing at first sight to distinguish him from the others dead still where they stand or sit *in abandonment beyond recall*' (222, italics mine). The slow, entropic march towards total annihilation is ambiguous, an end that is 'unthinkable' because no self exists that can think it. The narrator qualifies the inevitability of this end by stating 'if this notion is maintained', that is, maintained *by itself*. This suggests a possibility for hope, for internal change, and though it cannot be guaranteed, it is felt to be within the narrator's control, to some degree. This last 'body' is, in fact, the body/self of the narrator, now confronting the world within the cylinder, within the mother's mind; this body represents the last, most regressed part of the self, searching within the primal object for life and connection. The others are now 'dead', though this is again ambiguous; are they merely 'dead *still*' (i.e. motionless) or '*still* dead (i.e. no change in their deceased status)? The title of Beckett's last published work, *Stirrings Still*, echoes this ambiguity, suggesting a deep ambivalence between a hope for final silence of death, and a hopeful hiding.[14] The 'abandonment beyond recall' helps explain the most defeated parts of the self. This primary abandonment by an early object, (i.e. Winnicott's breakdown that has *already* occurred, but is forgotten) is now part of the self, though not consciously retrievable, something close to Guntrip experience of primal loss as an abandonment beyond his conscious recall. In 'The Lost Ones', the 'last of all if a man' slowly rises to open 'his burnt eyes' (223, an echo of Murphy's attack on the unrecognizing eyes), searching the world for a last time. This world is an omnipotent reflection, and projection, of the narrative-self; this 'aged vanquished of the third zone has none about him now but *others in his image* motionless and bowed' (223, italics mine). The final moments of the story point again reflect an internal, primal disconnection:

> The mite still in the white-haired woman's clasp is no more than a shadow in her lap. Seen from the front the red head sunk [...] There her opens then his eyes this last of all if a man and some time later threads his way to that first among the vanquished so often taken for a guide. On his knees he parts the heavy hair and raises the unresisting head. Once devoured the face thus laid bare the eyes at a touch of the thumbs open without demur. In those calm wastes he lets his wander till they are the first to close and the head relinquished falls back into its place. (223)

The image of the infant in the mother's arms recalls Guntrip's dream, his own sense of early disconnection, as well as his rage. The child appears as a shade, and with the mother becomes the innershadow/ outershadow of 'neither'; it is unrecognized, no longer in existence, a complement to the fading maternal imagos of ... *but the clouds ...*, *Ohio*

Impromptu, Watt, and so forth. The narrator/'last one' desperately attempts to connect to this primary, internal mother, within his mind, within hers; she is 'the guide', a 'first one' needed to lead the child into life, the 'last one' struggles, 'devouring' her face with the love hunger of an infant. This forms the other side of the constellation, the 'devouring' reflects the infant's primal, raging need to take in, reflected in Guntrip's faceless mother, and in a patient's dream of a breast-less mother. In an image reminiscent of many scenes in the oeuvre (e.g. Krapp in the punt; Murphy with Endon, Vladimir's pleas to be seen, and so forth), the narrator enters the mother through her eyes. There is ambiguity in this image: the 'calm wastes' can suggest an inner relief within a woman who has escaped, in a Murphy-like fantasy, from a world of terror and hell. However, the image can also re-enact a primal connection, between the aged woman as mother and this 'last one' that represents the creator of this dying world. This is the junction of hope and despair, of sadness and rage, of a wish for hiding and rebirth, and a wish for destruction. There is a sense that this woman, this final 'mother', is destroyed, killed and removed, and that the 'last one' is finally free of desire for a connection to her. Equally though, this can be a re-enactment of a truly primal scene, one that *engenders* the narrator's creation of the cylinder as a means to separate from this experience. The final line of the piece echoes this ambiguity: 'So much roughly speaking for the last state of the cylinder and of this little people of searchers one first of whom if a man in some unthinkable past for the first time bowed his head if this notion is maintained' (223). We are left with a final uncertainty ('roughly speaking') despite the often mathematically precise nature of the story. It suggests that this 'last one' may become a 'first one' and that a circular return is beginning again ('for the first time bowed his head'). The past is 'unthinkable' because an unintegrated self cannot remember an 'unthinkable' trauma that has not been processed, made 'thinkable', by a maternal mind; it is this failure that *is* the primal trauma. Perhaps this describes the genesis of the story – if one recognizes the narrator in the guise of this last one, this final statement reflects the origins of the story. It becomes a description of the narrator's *own* state, which engenders the fiction as a projective attempt at surviving annihilation anxiety by projecting rage, and hope, into the text of a maternal cylinder. It is another attempt at creativity, at establishing a psychic/textual skin with another, an attempt that *must* occur even if it is to be within the enclosed, circular space of the same story, begun yet again, for the first time.

Notes

1 This unintelligible voice, reflecting a deeply withdrawn, inhuman aspect of the self is revisited in *Not I*. It also echoes the deeply withdrawn part of the narrative-self heard through Lucky. The narrator's relation to the boy recalls that of Vladimir to the Boy in *Waiting for Godot*, in a reversal – it is the *boy* who arrives, unlike Godot, to feed and nurture the narrator/infantile-self. This boy tends goats as the *Godot* boy's brother does, and there is a sense that the narrator, like Vladimir, connects to an earlier aspect of himself by meeting the child. In *Endgame*, Hamm takes in a starving child.

2 The maternal relation depicted by the words 'taught me all I know' is echoed in *Waiting for Godot*, where Pozzo claims that it is Lucky who taught him all these beautiful things.

3 There is an allusion to the death of the child in *All That Fall*, where presumably 'discouragement' *does* sap [Mr Rooney's] foundations, if he, in fact, does throw the child under the wheels of the train. Thus, the 'horizons' (infantile-aspects of the self) are destroyed.

4 A child is probably murdered in *All That Fall*, where there is a blurring between sadness at the loss of a child (by Mrs Rooney), and rage by her husband. In the early story, 'A Case in A Thousand', the theme of actual childhood death is already taken up, and there is a hint of something amiss between Dr Nye and the mother of the dying child, who once was his own 'mother' (i.e. nanny).

5 These 'burning eyes' contrast with the lifeless eyes encountered elsewhere, where deadened parts of the self are projected (i.e. Endon, Krapp's lover, the 'mother' in 'The Lost Ones').

6 Buster Keaton, who starred as O, commented that he felt the work demon-strated one could hide from a lot, but never from oneself. The climax of *Film*, where O finally faces his observer, can be viewed as a possibility for psychic change: the pursuing other is finally recognized as *part of the self*. This echoes Vladimir's near realization that Godot is *already* present *within* him.

7 This plant will make its reappearance as the tree in *Waiting for Godot*, which also hovers between life, leaves and hope, and permanent withering and death.

8 There is, of course, a sense that what the narrator would like to expel is this internal sense of badness (like Lucky's hard stool). In a way, the narrative-self does just this, as it projects these feelings into the story.

9 The small child is unable to contain a whole sense of the parent's presence, its endurance in time. One night, while I lay next to one of my small daughters as she fell asleep, I did not respond to one of her questions, hoping she was just about to nod off. She started up, panicked, saying 'Daddy, talk! Say *something*!', reflecting Vladimir's sense of primal abandonment from Godot's presence, and his need for Estragon to speak so that he can feel real, in being *heard/alive* within his partner's mind.

10 This recalls Murphy, who sought this 'void' in Endon, failing to realize it was driven by his own internal identification with a failing internal object, and that Endon was coming to life.

11 In a sense, the cylinder operates as Endon's chessboard, a primal game, a *communication* of contact and withdrawal. The reader, perhaps, plays the role of Murphy.

12 Baker (1998) discusses the primacy of the 'wellhead gaze' within the story, as well as the loss of the internal good object and the centrality of the female figure.
13 I have witnessed this sense of connection to heart sounds from the other side, as a mother is often overwhelmed when hearing the sound of her foetus's heartbeat for the first time on the monitor.
14 Are the stirrings (of the mind/the body) now *still*, quiet, finally gone? Alternatively, is there a sense in which there are *still* stirrings, and a possibility for change and rebirth? Alternatively, of course, and more ominously, this could also suggest the possibility of more suffering.

Epilogue

Like Beckett, psychoanalysts tend to be better with beginnings than with endings. That said, I still believe this study is primarily about love. But how to finish? Perhaps a dream would be best, a dream that came to me after I completed the first draft of this book. *I was walking in a city that I immediately knew to be Paris, along a narrow avenue lined with small trees. At an intersection, waiting to cross, was Beckett, and I approached him, inviting him to a small café for a pint of beer. He agreed, was very gracious, very quiet. We sat in a small booth at the back, and Beckett excused himself for a moment; I thought he must be in need of the washroom. While he was gone, I ordered a pint for each of us and a filet of sole for lunch. Beckett returned, and noticing the food, became horribly outraged. He could see the shock and hurt on my face during his ranting, and quickly became sympathetically calm, excusing himself, he had to leave. We both stood, to shake hands, and he gave me a small piece of paper. It was criss-crossed many times in pencil, a dense, impenetrable series of lines; but as he left I held it to the light, and could make out, at a certain angle, one word, faint, nearly imperceptible – 'network'.*

On the surface, there is anxiety about presenting something to Beckett – would my food / study be rejected? However, I have had a rich associative experience with the dream. From my personal life, it suggests not only my relationship with my father (as Beckett), but also its intersection with his relationship with *his* mother. As an infant, he suffered early and traumatic separations from her, which manifested later in life as anxieties about hunger, and the suitability of foods. These associations touch upon the heart of this study, and it is in the final sequence of the dream, the presentation of the note, that I feel the most confidence.

The note was highly condensed, the cross-hatching of its surface lines made it almost impenetrable to the eye. These lines, these primal shapes that are the basis of the written text, resembled the intricate branching of a nest, as well as the collagen patterns of the skin. I feel it was indeed an attempt at communication, but one that is ambivalent and undone. Within this almost impenetrable ne(s)twork was an ambiguous message – 'network'. This could express an entrapment, but also a cry for contact, for human connection, one locked itself within an ambiguous 'ne(s)t' of primal lines. In my attempt to hear, to understand, I became a primal auditor, turning this text in the light, finding a message that unwrites itself, a wish for hearing that places itself in a protective/imprisoning nest of marks. It is in the act of listening, of struggling to connect, that we *become*. In this, the dream message of the note also becomes an oracular injunction, to 'network' with others in an ongoing dance of life. Reader and writer become twinned, coupled themselves, contained and containing, meeting and separating within the unity of a textual, maternal space, going on alone, yet not alone. This seems to me to be Beckett's primal message to himself, to us – within the nest of his texts, meant to protect a nascent self, there is ultimately the sharing that is life.

References

Works by Samuel Beckett

Proust (New York, Grove Press, 1957)
Murphy (New York, Grove Press, 1970)
Watt (New York, Grove Press, 1981)
Waiting for Godot (London, Faber and Faber, 1977)
Molloy, The Unnamable, in *The Beckett Trilogy* (London, Picador, 1976)
Endgame (New York, Grove Press, 1958)
How It Is (New York, Grove Press, 1964)

SHORT FICTION

'The Expelled'; 'The Calmative'; 'The End'; 'Fizzles 5'; *Texts for Nothing*;
'From An Abandoned Work'; 'The Image'; 'Enough'; 'The Lost Ones';
'neither'; 'Heard in the Dark 2'; 'Stirrings Still' in *Samuel Beckett: The
Complete Short Prose*, ed. by S. E. Gontarski (New York, Grove Press,
1995)

SHORT PLAYS

*Embers; Film; Not I; Footfalls; ... but the clouds ...; A Piece of Monologue; Eh Joe;
Ohio Impromptu;* in *The Collected Shorter Plays of Samuel Beckett* (New
York, Grove Press, 1984)
Breath, Play, Rockaby, What Where, Krapp's Last Tape

References cited

Abraham, Karl (1924), 'A Short Study of the Development of the Libido', in
Selected Papers on Psycho-Analysis, London, Hogarth.
Adler, Gerald (1985), *Borderline Psychopathology and its Treatment*, New York,
Jason Aronson.
Ainsworth, Mary (1978), *Patterns of Attachment: Assessed in the Strange Situa-
tion and At Home*, New Jersey, Erlbaum.

Anders, Guenther (1965), 'Being Without Time: On Beckett's Play Waiting for Godot', in *Samuel Beckett: A Collection of Critical Essays*, ed. Martin Esslin, New Jersey, Prentice: 140–51.

Anderson, Linda (1986), 'At the Threshold of the Self: Women and Autobiography', in *Women's Writing: A Challenge to Theory*, ed. Moira Monteith, Brighton, Harvester Press.

Anzieu, Didier (1993), 'Beckett, Self-Analysis and Creativity', trans. Pierre Johannet, in *Self-Analysis: Critical Inquiries, Personal Visions*, ed. James Barron London, The Analytic Press.

Asmus, Walter (1977), 'Rehearsal Notes for the German Premiere of Samuel Beckett's *That Time* and *Footfalls*', in *On Beckett: Essays and Criticism*, ed. S. E. Gontarski, New York, Grove Press, 1986, 335–49.

Bacal, Howard A. and Newman, Kenneth M. (1990), *Theories of Object Relations: Bridges to Self Psychology*, New York, Columbia University Press.

Bair, Deirdre (1978), *Samuel Beckett*, New York, Fontana.

Baker, Phil (1998), *Samuel Beckett and the Mythologies of Psychoanalysis*, New York, Palgrave.

Baldwin, Helen (1978), *Samuel Beckett's Real Silence*, University Park, The Pennsylvania State University Press.

Balint, Michael (1968), *The Basic Fault*, London, Tavistock.

—— (1986), 'The Unobtrusive Analyst', in *The British School of Psycho-analysis*, ed. G. Kohon, London, Free Associations.

Barnard, G. C. (1970), *Samuel Beckett: A New Approach*, London, Dent.

Bick, Esther (1968), 'The Experience of the Skin in Early Object Relations', *International Journal of Psycho-Analysis*, 49: 484–6.

—— (1986), 'Further Considerations of the Function of the Skin in Early Object Relations', *British Journal of Psychotherapy*, 2: 292–9.

Bion, Wilfred (1956), 'Development of Schizophrenic Thought', *International Journal of Psycho-Analysis*, 37: 344–6, republished in *Second Thoughts*: 36–42.

—— (1962), *Learning from Experience*, London, Heinemann.

—— (1963), *Elements of Psycho-Analysis*, London, Heinemann.

—— (1967), *Second Thoughts*, London, Heinemann.

Bowlby, John (1973), *Attachment and Loss: Separation: Anxiety and Anger*, New York, Basic Books.

—— (1980), *Attachment and Loss, Loss: Sadness and Depression*, New York, Basic Books.

Brienza, Susan (1977), 'The Lost Ones: The Reader as Searcher', *Journal of Modern Literature*, 6, 1: 148–68.

Brink, Andrew (1982), 'Samuel Beckett's *Endgame* and the Schizoid Ego', *Sphinx* 14: 87–100.

Calderwood, James (1986), 'Ways of Waiting in *Waiting for Godot*', *Modern Drama*, 29: 363–75.

Chalker, John (1975), 'The Satiric Shape of *Watt*', in *Beckett the Shape Changer*, ed. K. Worth, London, Routledge.

Coetzee, John (1972), 'The Manuscript revisions of Beckett's *Watt*', *Journal of Modern Literature* 2: 472–80.

Cohn, Ruby (1962), *Samuel Beckett: The Comic Gamut*, New Jersey, Rutgers University Press.

Davis, Madeline and Wallbridge, David (1981), *Boundary and Space: An Introduction to the work of D. W. Winnicott*, London: Karnac.

Dickens, Charles (1985), *Oliver Twist*, London, Penguin.

Duckworth, Colin (1966), *En attendant Godot*, London, Harrap.

Federman, Raymond (1965), *Journey to Chaos: Samuel Beckett's Early Fiction*, Berkeley, University of California.

Finney, Brian (1972), *Since How It Is*, London, Covent Garden Press.

Fletcher, John (1964), *The Novels of Samuel Beckett*, London, Chatto and Windus.

Francis, R. (1965), 'Beckett's Metaphysical Tragicomedy', *Modern Drama*, December.

Freud, Sigmund (1987), *Mourning and Melancholia*, Harmondsworth, Penguin.

Fromm, Gerard and Smith, Bruce (1989) (eds), *The Facilitating Environment: Clinical Applications of Winnicott's Theory*, Madison, International Universities Press.

Gidal, Peter (1986), *Understanding Beckett: A Study of Monologue and Gesture in the Works of Samuel Beckett*, New York, Palgrave.

Gontarski, S. E. (1995) (ed.) *Samuel Beckett: The Complete Short Prose*, New York, Grove Press.

Graver, Lawrence and Federman, Raymond (1979), *Samuel Beckett: The Critical Heritage*, London, Routledge.

Gray, Ronald (1957), '*Waiting for Godot*: A Christian Interpretation', *The Listener*, 24 January.

Green, Julian (1950), *If I Were You*, trans. J. H. F. McEwen, London.

Greenberg, Jay and Mitchell, Stephen (1983), *Object Relations in Psychoanalytic Theory*, Cambridge, Harvard University Press.

Grotstein, James (1985), *Splitting and Projective Identification*, New Jersey, Aronson.

Guntrip, Harry (1968), *Schizoid Phenomena, Object Relations, and the Self*, London, Hogarth.

—— (1975), 'My Experience of Analysis with Fairbairn and Winnicott', *International Review of Psycho-Analysis*, 2: 145–58.

Hardy, Thomas (1994), *A Selection of His Finest Poems*, ed. Samuel Hynes, Oxford, Oxford University Press.

Hoefer, Jacqueline (1959), 'Watt', *Perspective*, 11: 166–82, reprinted in Martin Esslin (1965) (ed.), *Samuel Beckett, A Collection of Critical Essays*, New Jersey, Prentice-Hall, 62–76.

Holmes, Jeremy (1993), *John Bowlby & Attachment Theory*, London, Routledge.

Hill, Leslie (1990), *Beckett's Fiction: In Different Words*, Cambridge, Cambridge University Press.

Hinshelwood, R. D. (1991), *A Dictionary of Kleinian Thought*, London, Free Associations.

Hobson, Harold (1956), 'Samuel Beckett, Dramatist of the Year', *International Theatre Annual* (1) 153–5.

Jacques, Elliot (1953), 'On the Dynamics of Social Structure', *Human Relations*, 6: 3–23, republished as 'Social Systems as a Defense Against Persecutory and Depressive Anxiety', in Melanie Klein, Paula Heimann and Roger Money-Kyrle (1955), eds, *New Dimensions in Psycho-Analysis*, London, Tavistock.

Jones, Ernest (1927), 'The Early Development of Female Sexuality', *International Journal of Psycho-Analysis*, 39: 459–72.

Keller, John, R. (1998), "An Imperfect Witness: Primary Dyadic Failure in Samuel Beckett's *Watt*', *Journal of Melanie Klein and Object Relations*, 16(3): 589–608.

—— (1999), "Labours Left Unfinished: The Entrapment of the Self and Beckett's *Waiting for Godot*', *Journal of Melanie Klein and Object Relations*, 17(1): 95–117.

—— (1999), 'Lucky's Bones: A Sense of Starvation in *Watt, Waiting for Godot* and *Oliver Twist*', *Psyart*, www.clas.ufl.edu/ipsa/journal/articles/psyart1999/keller01.htm

Kennedy, Sighle (1971), *Murphy's Bed*, Lewisberg, Bucknell University Press.

Kenner, Hugh (1961), *Samuel Beckett: A Critical Study*, Berkeley, University of California Press.

Kiesenhofer, Tony (1993), 'Reading Against the Grain: Samuel Beckett's *Waiting for Godot*', *Orbis Litterarum*, 48: 358–69.

Klein, Melanie (1988a), *Love, Guilt, and Reparation*, London, Virago.

—— (1988b), *Envy and Gratitude*, London, Virago.

Kohut, Heinz (1971), *The Analysis of the Self*, New York, International Universities Press.

—— (1977), *The Restoration of the Self*, Connecticut, International Universities Press.

Knowlson, James and Pilling, John (1979), *Frescoes of the Skull: The Later Prose and Drama of Samuel Beckett*, London, Calder.

Langs, Robert (1978), *The Listening Process*, New York, Jason Aronson.

Laplanche J. and Pontalis J. B. (1988), *The Language of Psychoanalysis*, London, Karnac.

Levy, Eric (1980), *Beckett and The Voice of the Species*, Dublin, Gill and MacMillan.

McMillan, Dougald and Fehsenfeld, Marsha (1988), *Beckett in the Theatre*, London, John Calder.

Meares, Russell (1973), 'Beckett, Sarraute, and the Perceptual Experience of Schizophrenia', *Psychiatry*, 36: 61–9.

—— (1993), *The Metaphor of Play*, New Jersey, Jason Aronson.

—— (1986), 'On the Ownership of Thought: An Approach to the Origins of Separation Anxiety', *Psychiatry*, 21: 545–59.

Meltzer, Donald (1975), 'Adhesive Identification', *Contemporary Psycho-Analysis* 11: 289–310.

Mintz, Samuel (1959), 'Beckett's *Murphy*: a "Cartesian" Novel', *Perspective*, 11 Autumn: 156–65.

Mitrani, Judith (1994), 'Unintegration, Adhesive Identification, and the Psychic Skin: Variations on Some Themes by Esther Bick', *Journal of Melanie Klein and Objecy Relations*, 11(2): 65–88.

Mittenzwei, Werner (1969), *Gestaltung und Gestalten im modernen Drama*, Berlin, Aufbau.

Moore, Burness E. and Fine, Bernard D. (1990), *Psychoanalytic Terms & Concepts*, New Haven, Yale University Press.

—— (1995) (eds), *Psycho-Analysis: The Major Concepts*, New Haven, Yale University Press.

Morot-Sir, Edouard (1976), 'Samuel Beckett and Cartesian Emblems', in *Samuel Beckett: The Art of Rhetoric*, ed. Edouard Morot-Sir, Chapel Hill, North Carolina Studies in Romance Languages and Literature.

Morrison, Kristin (1982), 'The Rip Word in *A Piece of Monologue*', *Modern Drama*, 25: 349–54.

—— (1983), *Canters and Chronicles: The Use of Narrative in the Plays of Samuel Beckett and Harold Pinter*, Chicago, University of Chicago Press.

Nealon, Jeffrrey (1988), 'Samuel Beckett and the Postmodern: Language Games, Play, and *Waiting for Godot*', *Modern Drama*, 31: 520–8.

Ogden, Thomas (1989), *The Primitive Edge of Experience*, London, Aronson.

—— (1993), *Projective Identification and Psychotherapeutic Technique*, New Jersey, Aronson.

Perlow, Meir (1995), *Understanding Mental Objects*, London, Routledge.

Phillips, Adam (1988), *Winnicott*, London, Fontana.

Ramsay, Nicola, (1985), '*Watt* and the Mirror Image', *Journal of Beckett Studies*, 10: 21–36.

Reid, Alex (1968), *All I Could Manage, More Than I Could: An Approach to the Plays of Samuel Beckett*, New York, Grove Press.

Robinson, Michael (1969), *The Long Sonata of the Dead*, London, Rupert Hart-Davis.

Rosenfeld, Herbert (1952), 'Notes on the Analysis of the Superego Conflict in an Acute Catatonic Schizophrenic', *International Journal of Psycho-Analysis*, 33: 111–31.

Rycroft, Charles (1988), *A Critical Dictionary of Psychoanalysis*, London, Penguin.

Sandler, J. (1987) (ed.), *Projection, Identification, Projective Identification*, Madison, International Universities Press.

Sartre, J. P. (1958), *Being and Nothingness*, London, Methuen.

Schmideberg, Melitta (1934), 'The Play Analysis of a Three-Year-Old Girl', *International Journal of Psycho-Analysis*, 66: 245–64.

Schneider, Alan, (1967), 'Waiting for Beckett, A Personal Chronicle', in *Beckett at Sixty*, London, Calder and Boyars.

Segal, Hanna (1981), 'A Psycho-Analytic Approach to the Treatment of Schizophrenia', in *The Work of Hanna Segal*, New York: Jason Aronson: 131–6.

Siegel, Allen (1996), *Heinz Kohut and The Psychology of the Self*, London, Routledge.

Simon, Bennett (1988), *Tragic Drama and the Family: Psychoanalytic Studies from Aeschylus to Beckett*, New Haven, Yale University Press.

Stephen, Karin, (1941), 'Aggression in Early Childhood', *British Journal of Medical Psychology*, 18: 178–90.

Stern, Daniel (1985), *The Interpersonal World of the Infant*, New York, Basic Books.

Summers, Frank (1994), *Object Relations Theories and Psychopathology*, New Jersey, The Analytic Press.

Toscan, Richard (1973), 'MacGowran on Beckett', interview in *Theatre Quarterly*, July.

Trivisonno Anna (1970), 'Meaning and Function of the Quest in Beckett's *Watt*', *Critique*, 12(2): 28–38.

Tustin, Francis (1980), 'Autistic Objects', *International Revue of Psycho-Analysis*, 7: 27–39.

—— (1981), *Autistic States in Children*, London, Routledge.

—— (1986), *Autistic Barriers in Neurotic Patients*, London, Karnac.

—— (1990), *The Protective Shell in Children and Adults*, London, Karnac.

Winnicott, Donald (1965), *The Maturational Processes and the Facilitating Environment*, London, Hogarth.

—— (1971), *Playing and Reality*, New York, Basic Books.

—— (1973), 'Fear of Breakdown', International Review of Psycho-Analysis, 1.

Webb, Eugene (1970), *Samuel Beckett: A Study of his Novels*, London, Peter Owen.

Worton, Michel (1994), '*Waiting for Godot* and *Endgame*: Theatre as Text', in *The Cambridge Companion to Beckett*, ed. John Pilling, Cambridge University Press, 67–87.

Zeifman, Hersh (1975), 'Religious Imagery in the plays of Samuel Beckett', in *Samuel Beckett: A Collection of Criticism*, ed. Ruby Cohn, New York, McGraw-Hill, 85–94.

Zinman, Toby (1995), 'Lucky's Dance in *Waiting for Godot*', Modern Drama 38: 308–23.

Index

The index lists Beckett's works cited and discussed in the text and includes references to independent occurrences of character names.

Beckett Trilogy, The 30
Breath 20
... but the clouds ... 19–20, 70, 71, 101, 172, 208, 213

'Calmative, The' 52, 172, 173–4, 176, 181–2, 212

Disjecta 13

Eh Joe 74
Embers 101
'End, The' 10, 94, 172, 175–6, 182–7
Endgame 30, 32, 35, 58, 77, 97, 162
'Enough' 149–52
'Expelled, The' 172, 179–81, 186, 206

Film 96, 183
'Fizzle 5' 16
Footfalls 27, 33, 36, 45, 69–73, 101, 119, 142, 172
'From An Abandoned Work' 12–13, 94–5

'Heard in the Dark 2' 36
How It Is 30, 35, 58

'Image, The' 36

Krapp's Last Tape 28, 78, 125, 206, 214

'Lost Ones, The' 30, 173, 198–204, 209–14

Molloy 69, 70, 74, 96, 97, 98, 205
Murphy 10, 15, 17, 21, 22, 23, 25, 28, 30, 49–69, 70, 73–4, 75–87, 105, 112, 125, 139–40, 152, 172, 173, 179, 183, 184, 185, 192, 195, 197, 205, 206, 210, 214

'neither' 26, 30–2, 70, 123, 125, 179, 190, 204, 213
Not I 11, 24, 30, 96, 97, 197
Nouvelles 15, 32, 33, 172, 193
    see also 'Calmative, The'; 'End, The'; 'Expelled, The'

Ohio Impromptu 207–9

Piece of Monologue, A 44–5
Play 59
Proust 37–44, 45–7, 142

Rockaby 69, 119, 139

Texts for Nothing 30, 172, 176–8, 189, 190–1, 192–8

Unnamable, The 32, 59

Waiting for Godot 17, 21, 23, 26, 27,
    30, 32, 35, 50, 58, 66, 69, 78,
    113, 125, 133–7, 138–49, 152,
    153–4, 155–6, 158–61, 162,
    163, 164–7, 172, 193, 194,
    196, 202, 204–5, 206, 214

Watt 10, 16, 17, 21, 23, 26, 31, 32,
    36, 66, 77, 78, 90–4, 95–119,
    120–9, 139, 152, 172, 177,
    178, 179, 202, 203, 205, 206,
    207, 208, 210, 214
What Where 197